BARBALIEN™
RED PLANET

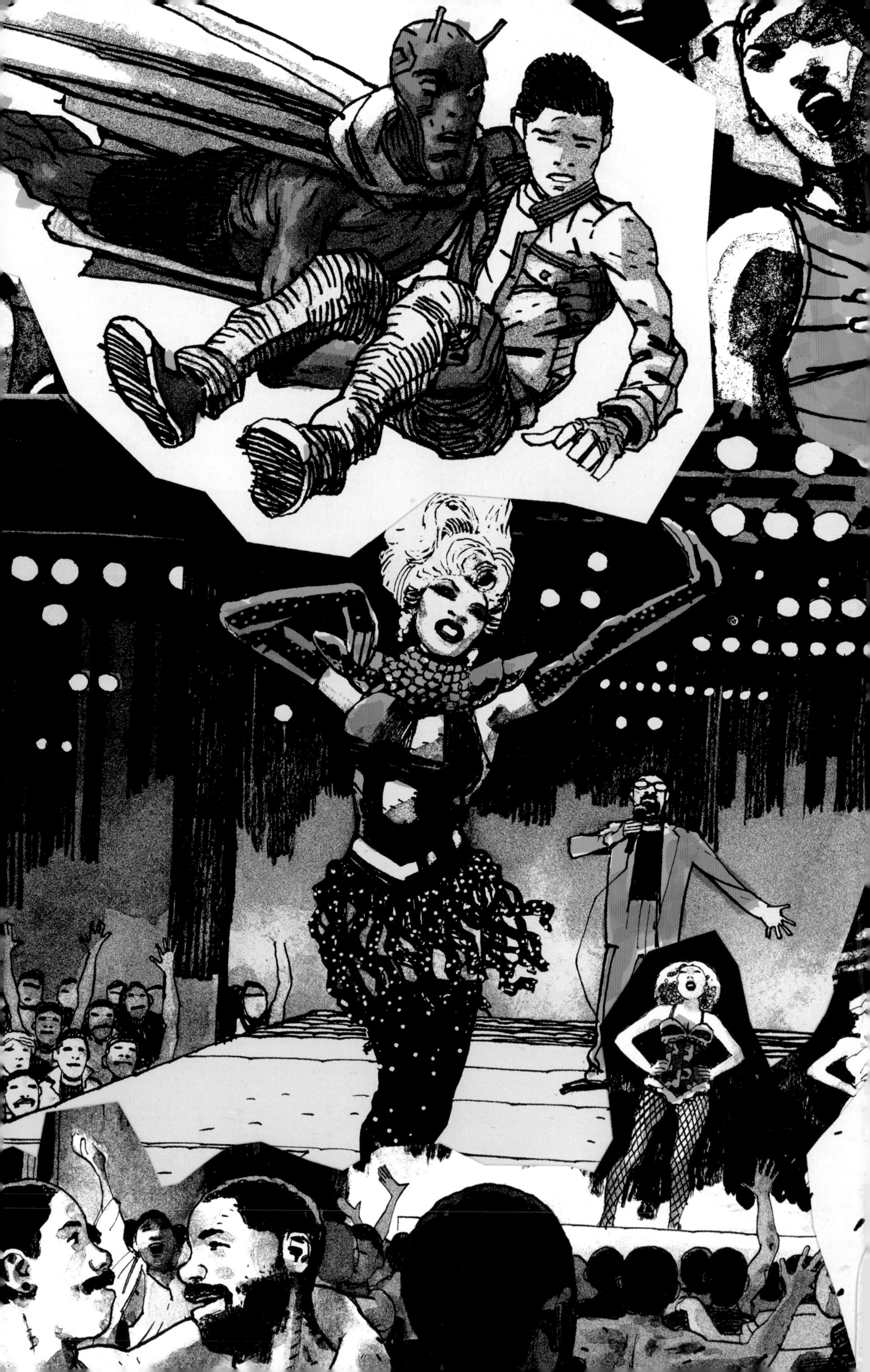

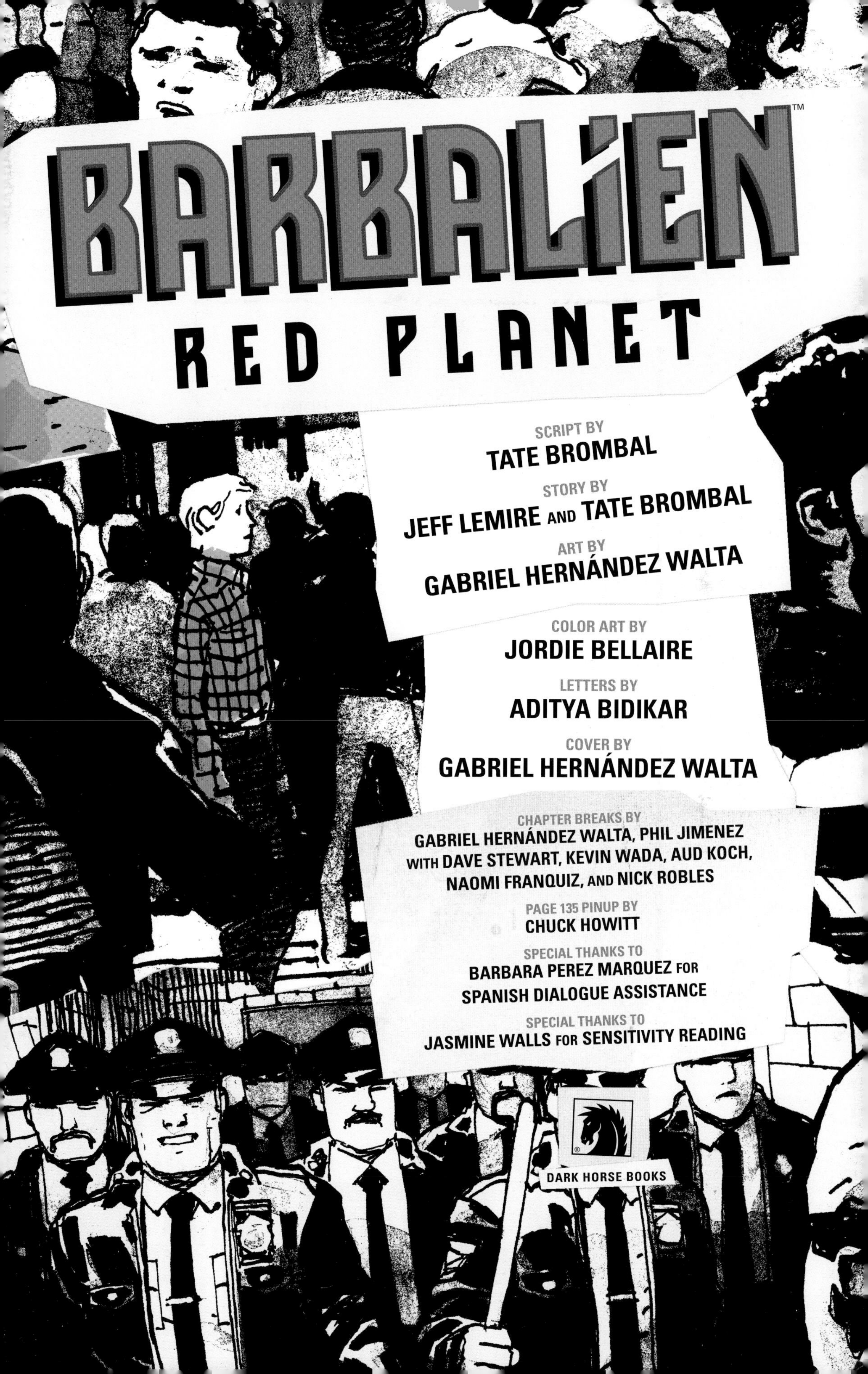

BARBALIEN™

RED PLANET

SCRIPT BY
TATE BROMBAL

STORY BY
JEFF LEMIRE AND TATE BROMBAL

ART BY
GABRIEL HERNÁNDEZ WALTA

COLOR ART BY
JORDIE BELLAIRE

LETTERS BY
ADITYA BIDIKAR

COVER BY
GABRIEL HERNÁNDEZ WALTA

CHAPTER BREAKS BY
GABRIEL HERNÁNDEZ WALTA, PHIL JIMENEZ WITH DAVE STEWART, KEVIN WADA, AUD KOCH, NAOMI FRANQUIZ, AND NICK ROBLES

PAGE 135 PINUP BY
CHUCK HOWITT

SPECIAL THANKS TO
BARBARA PEREZ MARQUEZ FOR SPANISH DIALOGUE ASSISTANCE

SPECIAL THANKS TO
JASMINE WALLS FOR SENSITIVITY READING

DARK HORSE BOOKS

PRESIDENT & PUBLISHER
MIKE RICHARDSON

EDITOR
DANIEL CHABON

ASSISTANT EDITOR
CHUCK HOWITT

DESIGNER
ETHAN KIMBERLING

DIGITAL ART TECHNICIAN
JOSIE CHRISTENSEN

BARBALIEN: RED PLANET

Collects issues #1–#5 of the Dark Horse Comics series *Barbalien: Red Planet*.

DarkHorse.com

To find a comics shop in your area, visit comicshoplocator.com

First edition: March 2021
Ebook ISBN 978-1-50671-581-0
Trade paperback ISBN 978-1-50671-580-3

10 9 8 7 6 5 4 3 2 1
Printed in China

Neil Hankerson, Executive Vice President • Tom Weddle, Chief Financial Officer • Randy Stradley, Vice President of Publishing • Nick McWhorter, Chief Business Development Officer • Dale LaFountain, Chief Information Officer • Matt Parkinson, Vice President of Marketing • Vanessa Todd-Holmes, Vice President of Production and Scheduling • Mark Bernardi, Vice President of Book Trade and Digital Sales • Ken Lizzi, General Counsel Dave Marshall, Editor in Chief • Davey Estrada, Editorial Director • Chris Warner, Senior Books Editor • Cary Grazzini, Director of Specialty Projects Lia Ribacchi, Art Director • Matt Dryer, Director of Digital Art and Prepress Michael Gombos, Senior Director of Licensed Publications • Kari Yadro, Director of Custom Programs • Kari Torson, Director of International Licensing • Sean Brice, Director of Trade Sales

Library of Congress Cataloging-in-Publication Data

Names: Lemire, Jeff, writer. | Brombal, Tate, writer. | Hernandez, Gabriel (Hernandez Walta), artist. | Bellaire, Jordie, colourist. | Bidikar, Aditya, letterer.
Title: Barbalien : red planet / Jeff Lemire, Tate Brombal, Gabriel Hernandez Walta, Jordie Bellaire, Aditya Bidikar.
Description: First edition. | Milwaukie, OR : Dark Horse Books, 2021. | "From the world of Black Hammer"--Cover. | Summary: "Mark Markz has found his place on Earth as both a decorated police officer and as the beloved superhero, Barbalien. But in the midst of the AIDS crisis, hatred from all sides makes balancing these identities seem impossible-especially when a Martian enemy from the past hunts him down to take him back, dead or alive"-- Provided by publisher.
Identifiers: LCCN 2020045069 (print) | LCCN 2020045070 (ebook) | ISBN 9781506715803 (trade paperback) | ISBN 9781506715810 (ebook)
Subjects: LCSH: Comic books, strips, etc.
Classification: LCC PN6728.B276 L46 2021 (print) | LCC PN6728.B276 (ebook) | DDC 741.5/973--dc23
LC record available at https://lccn.loc.gov/2020045069
LC ebook record available at https://lccn.loc.gov/2020045070

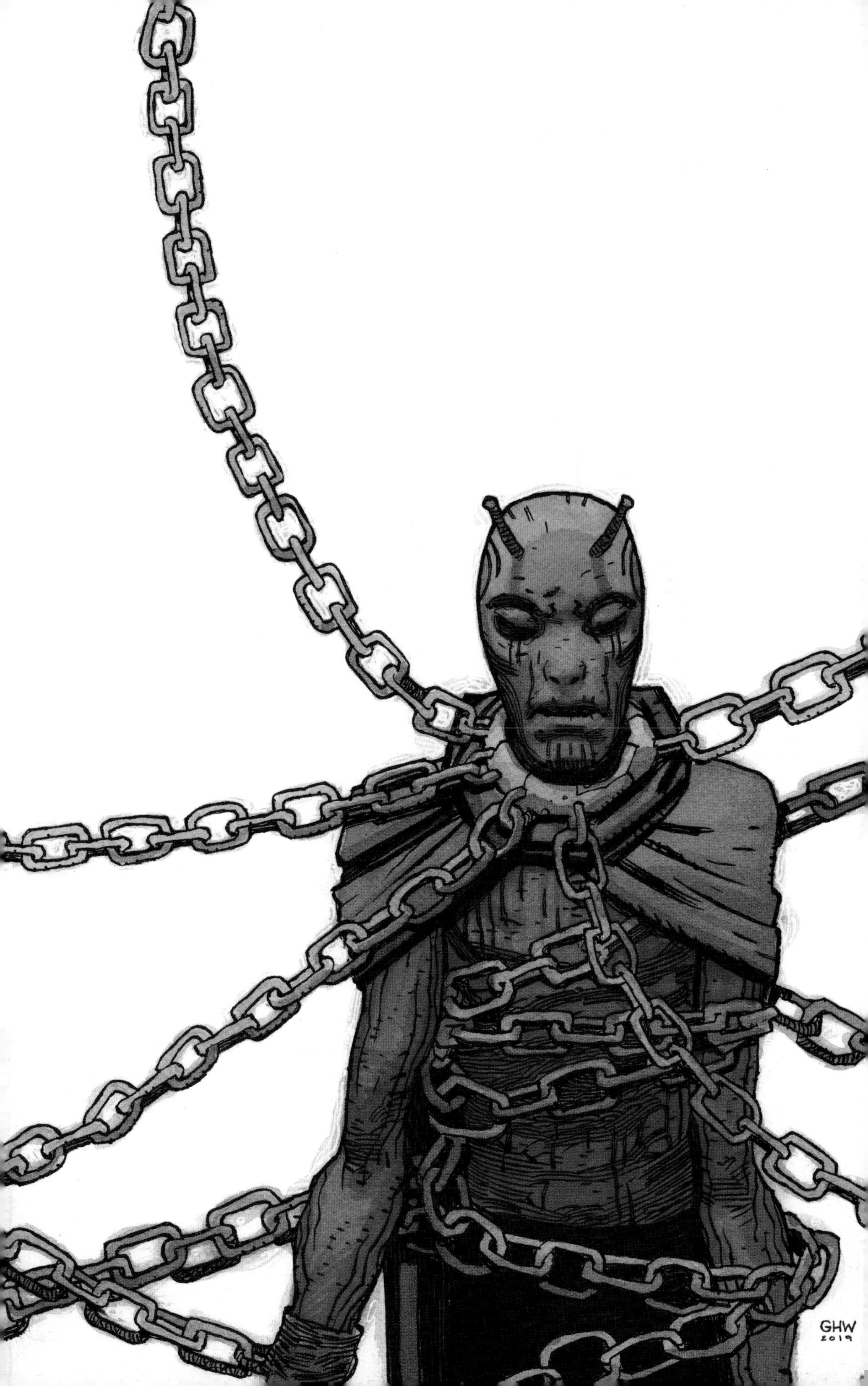
GHW
2019

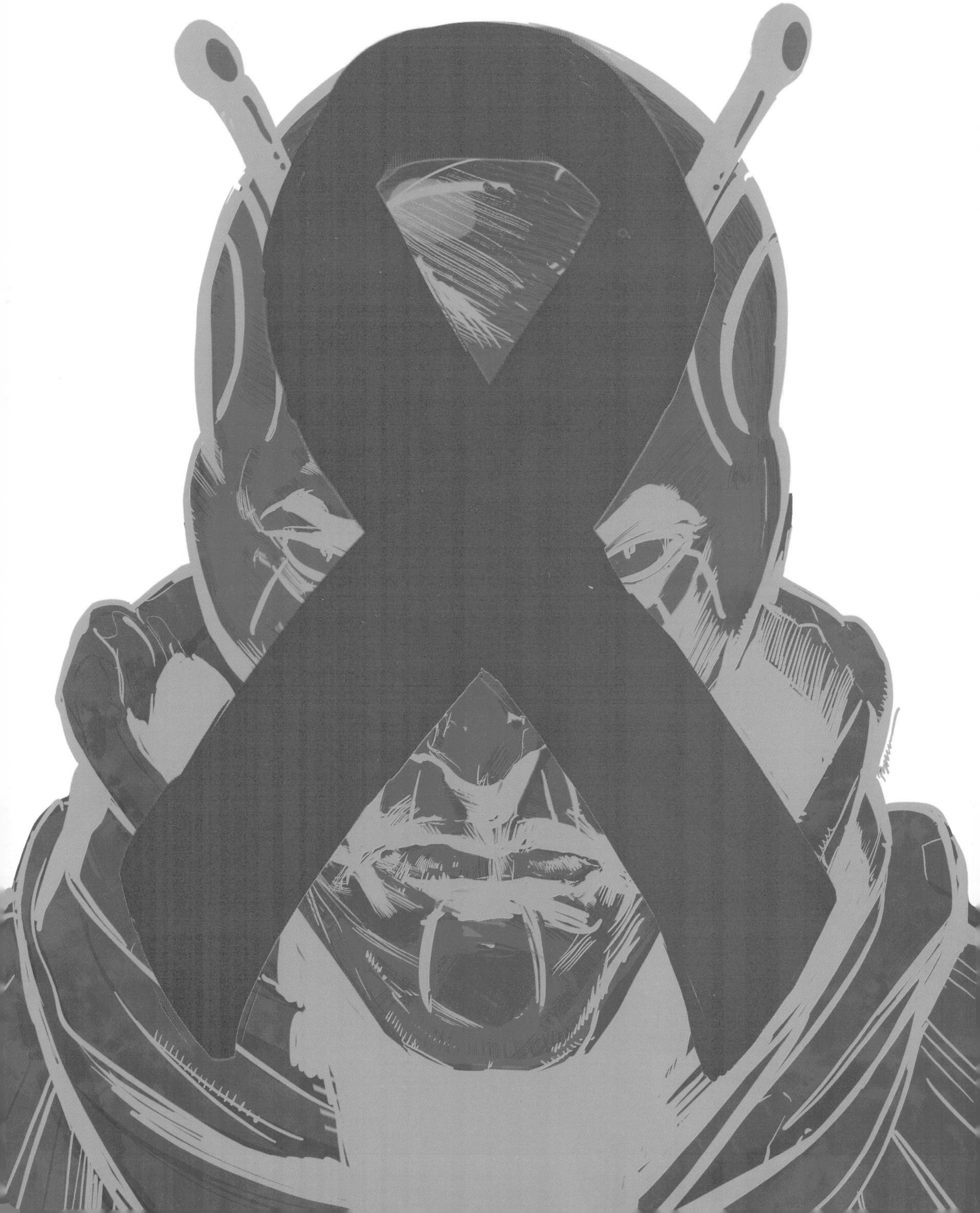

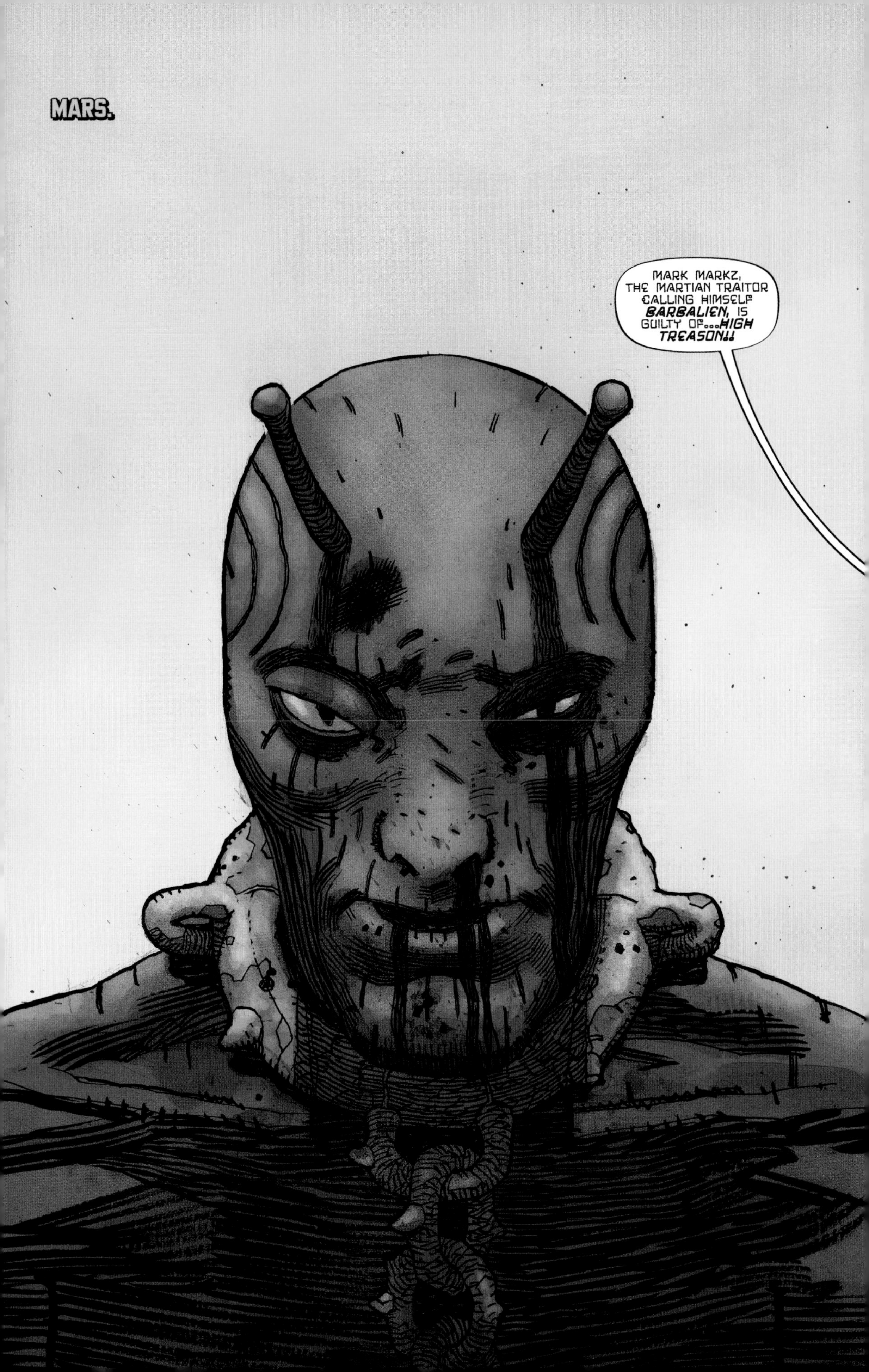
MARS.
MARK MARKZ, THE MARTIAN TRAITOR CALLING HIMSELF BARBALIEN, IS GUILTY OF...HIGH TREASON!!

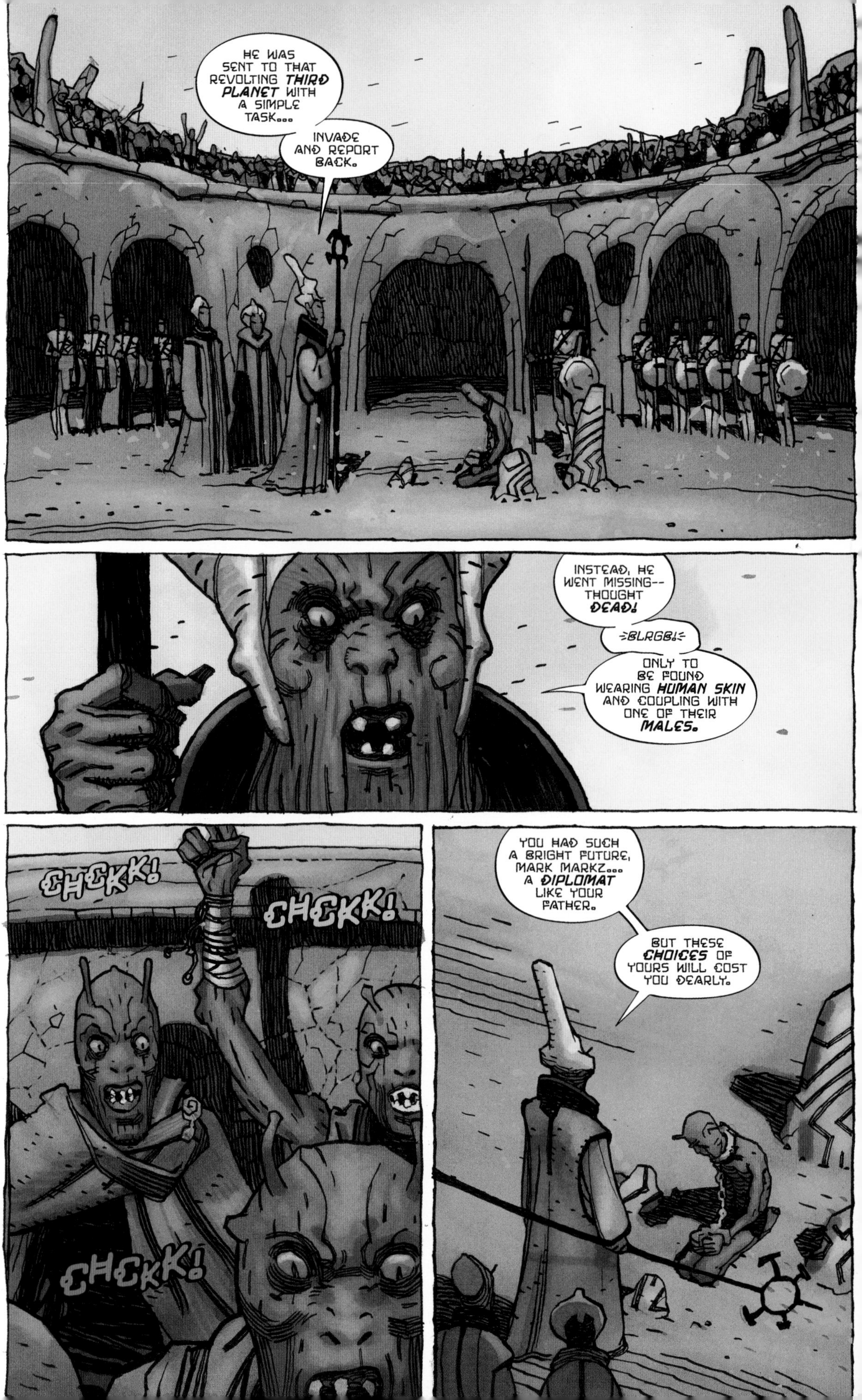
HE WAS SENT TO THAT REVOLTING THIRD PLANET WITH A SIMPLE TASK...
INVADE AND REPORT BACK.
INSTEAD, HE WENT MISSING-- THOUGHT DEAD!
BLRGB!
ONLY TO BE FOUND WEARING HUMAN SKIN AND COUPLING WITH ONE OF THEIR MALES.
CHCKK!
CHCKK!
CHCKK!
YOU HAD SUCH A BRIGHT FUTURE, MARK MARKZ... A DIPLOMAT LIKE YOUR FATHER.
BUT THESE CHOICES OF YOURS WILL COST YOU DEARLY.

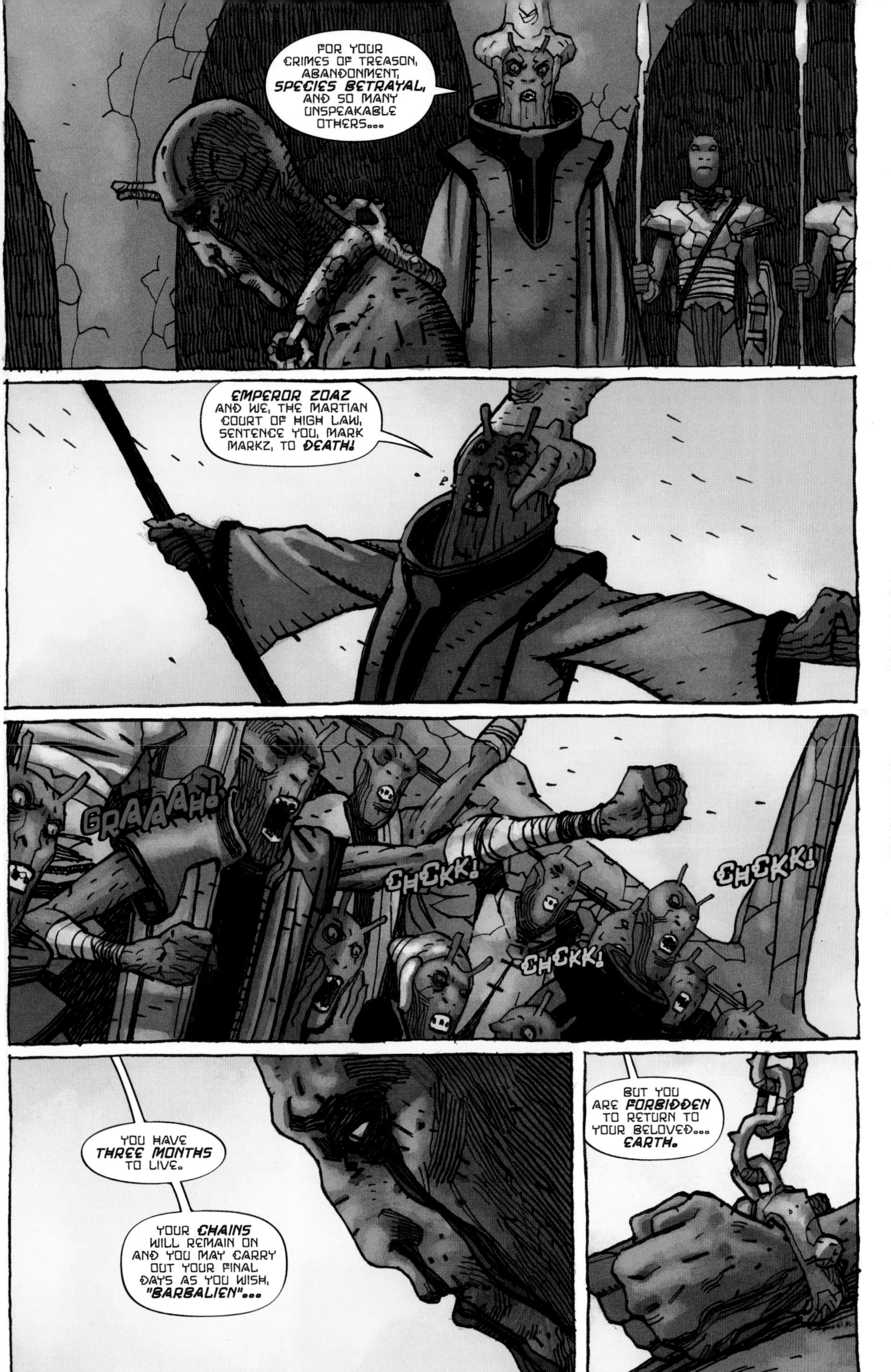
FOR YOUR CRIMES OF TREASON, ABANDONMENT, SPECIES BETRAYAL, AND SO MANY UNSPEAKABLE OTHERS...
EMPEROR ZOAZ AND WE, THE MARTIAN COURT OF HIGH LAW, SENTENCE YOU, MARK MARKZ, TO DEATH!
GRAAAAH!
CHCKK!
CHCKK!
CHCKK!
YOU HAVE THREE MONTHS TO LIVE.
YOUR CHAINS WILL REMAIN ON AND YOU MAY CARRY OUT YOUR FINAL DAYS AS YOU WISH, "BARBALIEN"...
BUT YOU ARE FORBIDDEN TO RETURN TO YOUR BELOVED... EARTH.

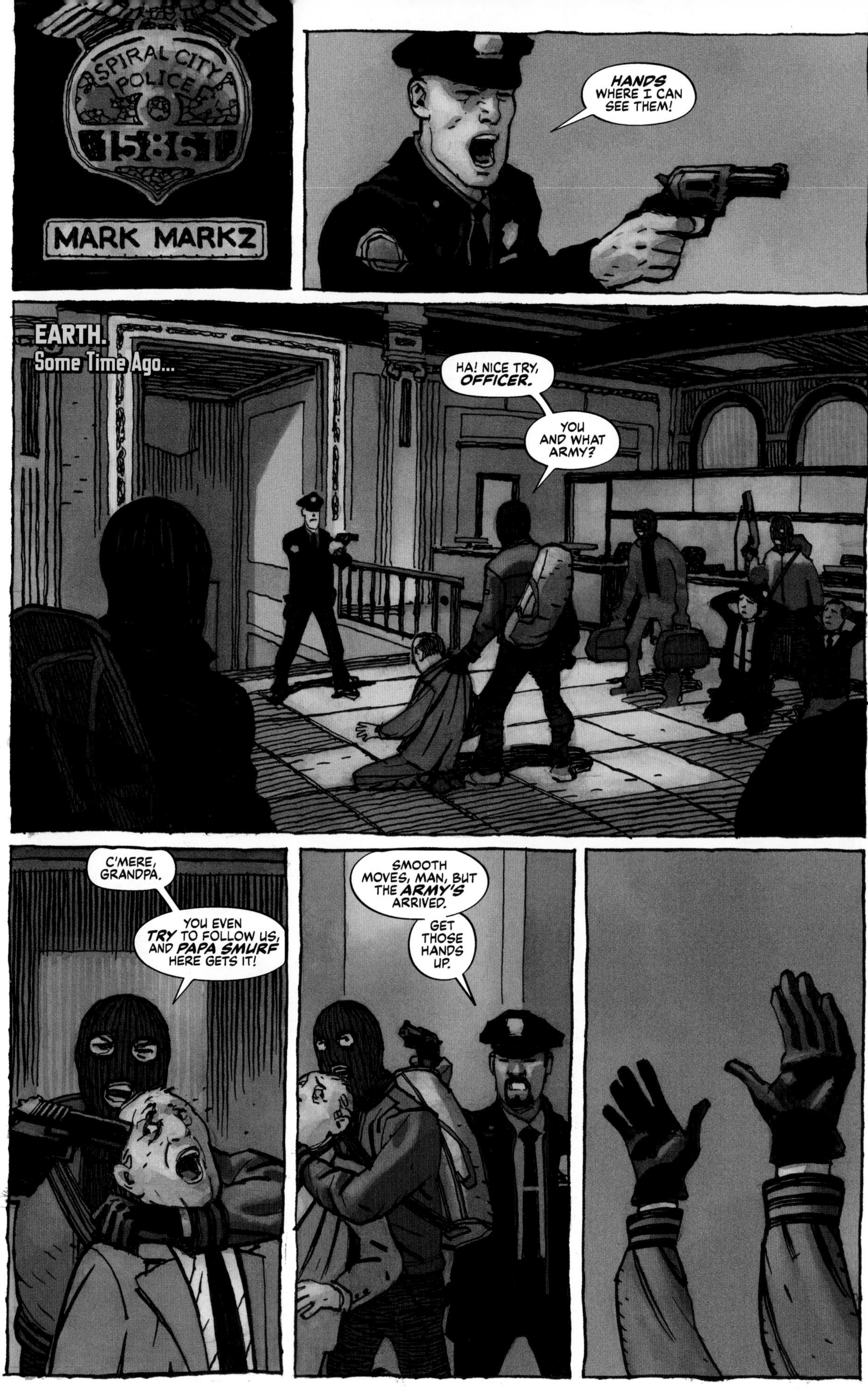
SPIRAL CITY POLICE
1586
MARK MARKZ
HANDS WHERE I CAN SEE THEM!
EARTH.
Some Time Ago...
HA! NICE TRY, OFFICER.
YOU AND WHAT ARMY?
C'MERE, GRANDPA.
YOU EVEN TRY TO FOLLOW US, AND PAPA SMURF HERE GETS IT!
SMOOTH MOVES, MAN, BUT THE ARMY'S ARRIVED.
GET THOSE HANDS UP.

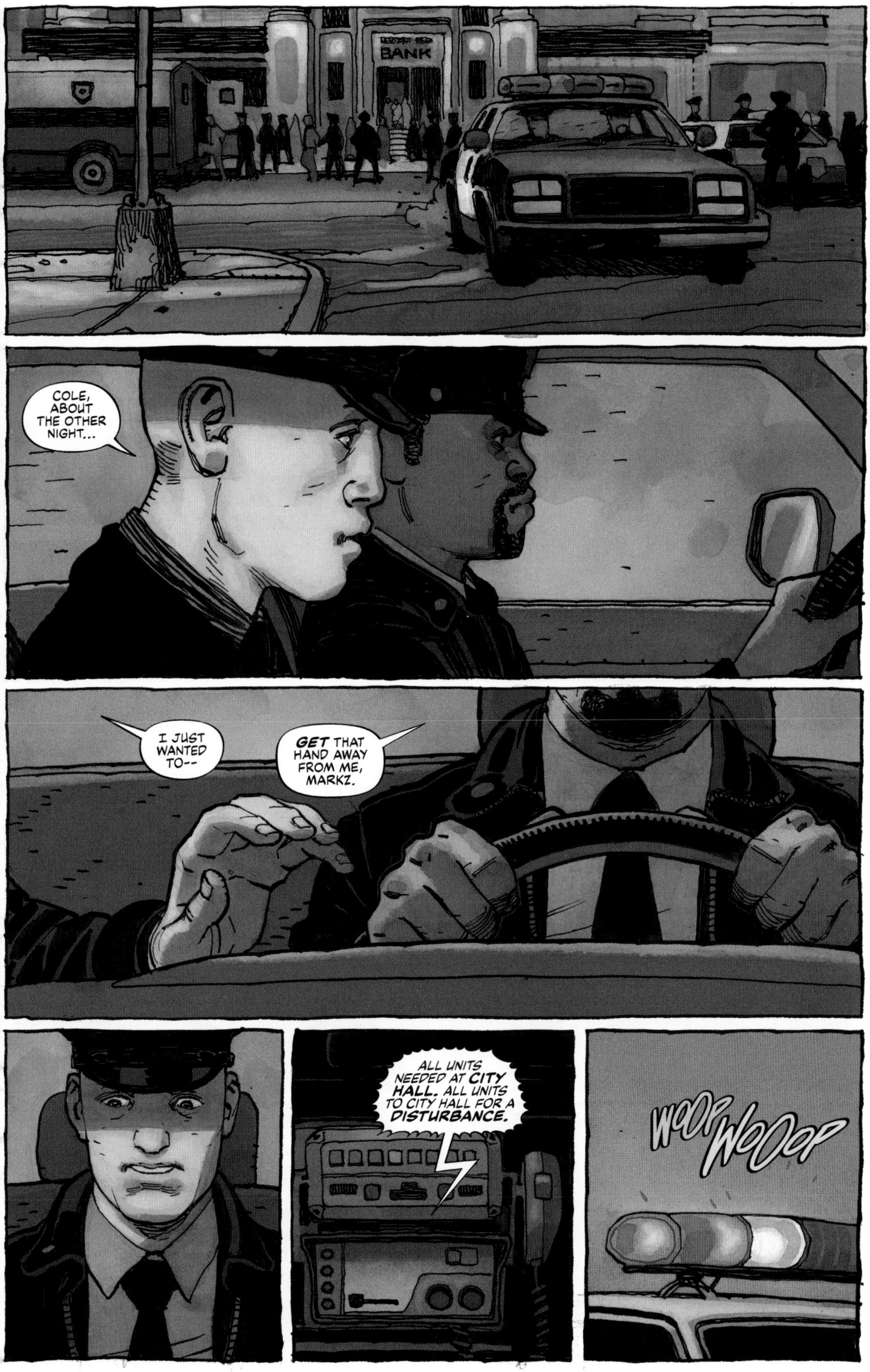
BANK
COLE, ABOUT THE OTHER NIGHT...
I JUST WANTED TO--
GET THAT HAND AWAY FROM ME, MARKZ.
ALL UNITS NEEDED AT CITY HALL. ALL UNITS TO CITY HALL FOR A DISTURBANCE.
WOOP WOOOP

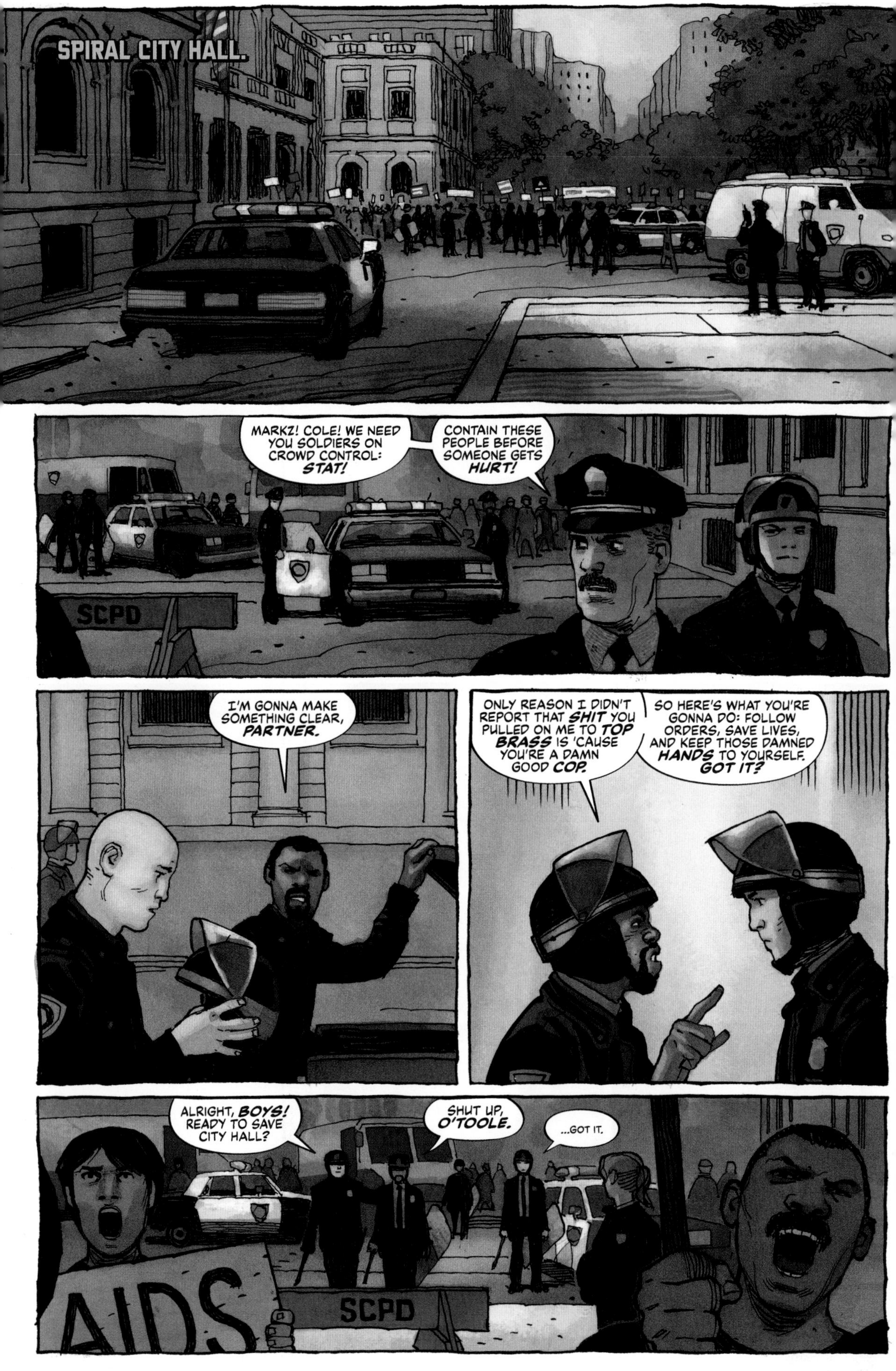
SPIRAL CITY HALL.
MARKZ! COLE! WE NEED YOU SOLDIERS ON CROWD CONTROL: STAT!
CONTAIN THESE PEOPLE BEFORE SOMEONE GETS HURT!
SCPD
I'M GONNA MAKE SOMETHING CLEAR, PARTNER.
ONLY REASON I DIDN'T REPORT THAT SHIT YOU PULLED ON ME TO TOP BRASS IS 'CAUSE YOU'RE A DAMN GOOD COP.
SO HERE'S WHAT YOU'RE GONNA DO: FOLLOW ORDERS, SAVE LIVES, AND KEEP THOSE DAMNED HANDS TO YOURSELF. GOT IT?
ALRIGHT, BOYS! READY TO SAVE CITY HALL?
SHUT UP, O'TOOLE.
...GOT IT.
AIDS
SCPD

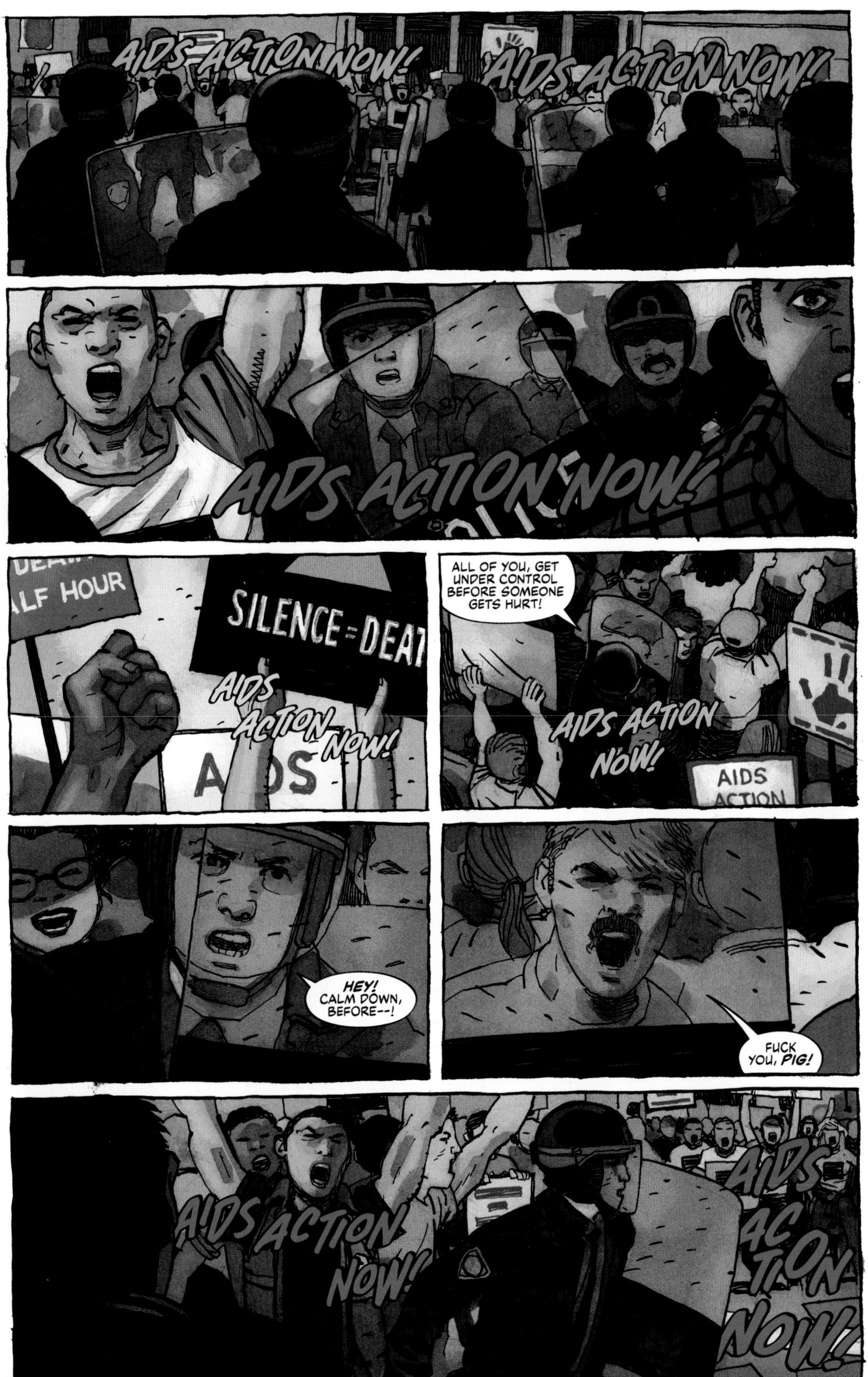

AIDS ACTION NOW!
AIDS ACTION NOW!
AIDS ACTION NOW!
ALF HOUR
SILENCE=DEAT
AIDS ACTION NOW!
AIDS
ALL OF YOU, GET UNDER CONTROL BEFORE SOMEONE GETS HURT!
AIDS ACTION NOW!
AIDS ACTION
HEY! CALM DOWN, BEFORE--!
FUCK YOU, PIG!
AIDS ACTION NOW!
AIDS ACTION NOW!

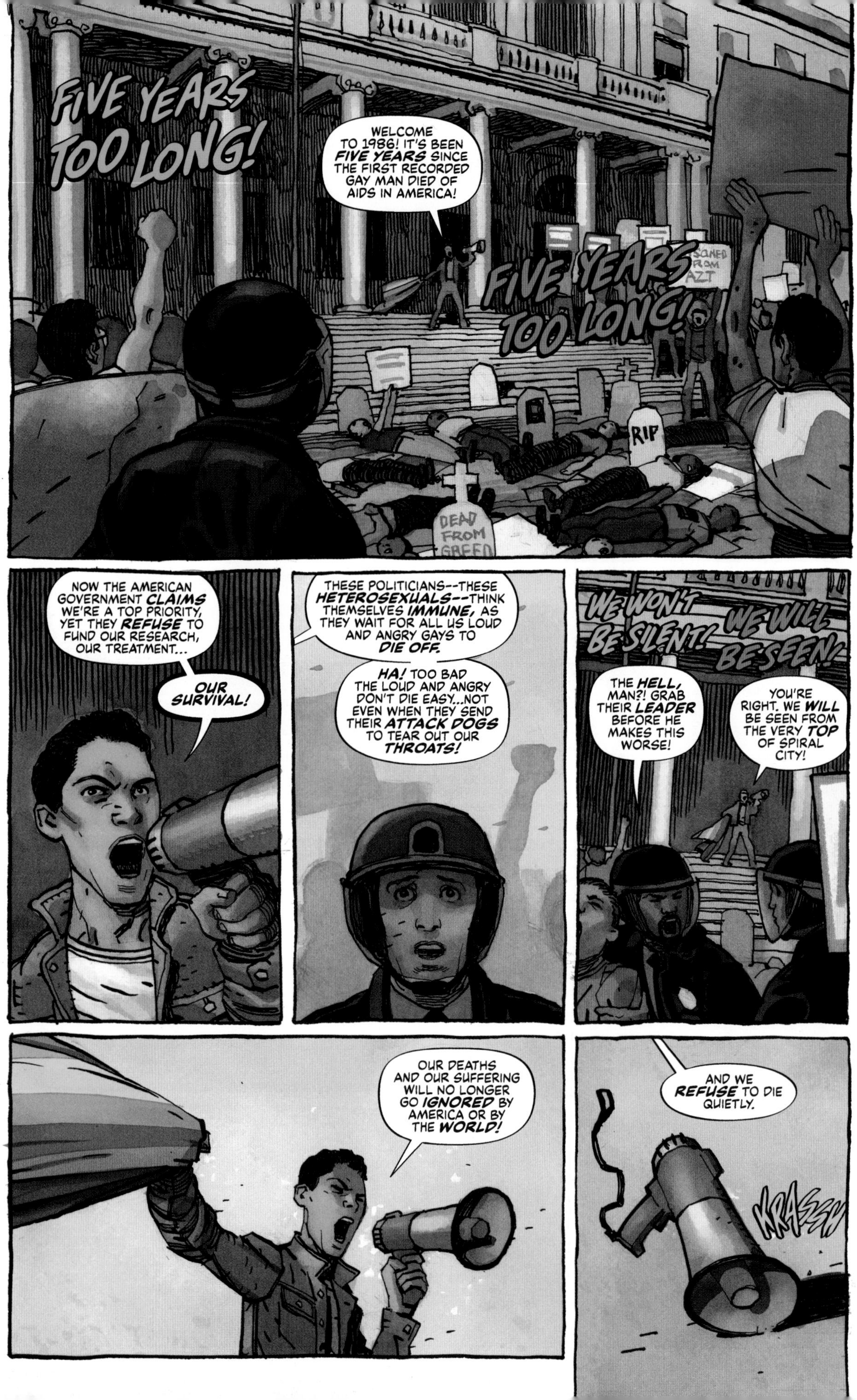
FIVE YEARS TOO LONG!
WELCOME TO 1986! IT'S BEEN FIVE YEARS SINCE THE FIRST RECORDED GAY MAN DIED OF AIDS IN AMERICA!
FIVE YEARS TOO LONG!
RIP
DEAD FROM
NOW THE AMERICAN GOVERNMENT CLAIMS WE'RE A TOP PRIORITY, YET THEY REFUSE TO FUND OUR RESEARCH, OUR TREATMENT...
OUR SURVIVAL!
THESE POLITICIANS--THESE HETEROSEXUALS--THINK THEMSELVES IMMUNE, AS THEY WAIT FOR ALL US LOUD AND ANGRY GAYS TO DIE OFF.
HA! TOO BAD THE LOUD AND ANGRY DON'T DIE EASY...NOT EVEN WHEN THEY SEND THEIR ATTACK DOGS TO TEAR OUT OUR THROATS!
WE WON'T BE SILENT! WE WILL BE SEEN!
THE HELL, MAN?! GRAB THEIR LEADER BEFORE HE MAKES THIS WORSE!
YOU'RE RIGHT. WE WILL BE SEEN FROM THE VERY TOP OF SPIRAL CITY!
OUR DEATHS AND OUR SUFFERING WILL NO LONGER GO IGNORED BY AMERICA OR BY THE WORLD!
AND WE REFUSE TO DIE QUIETLY.
KRASSH

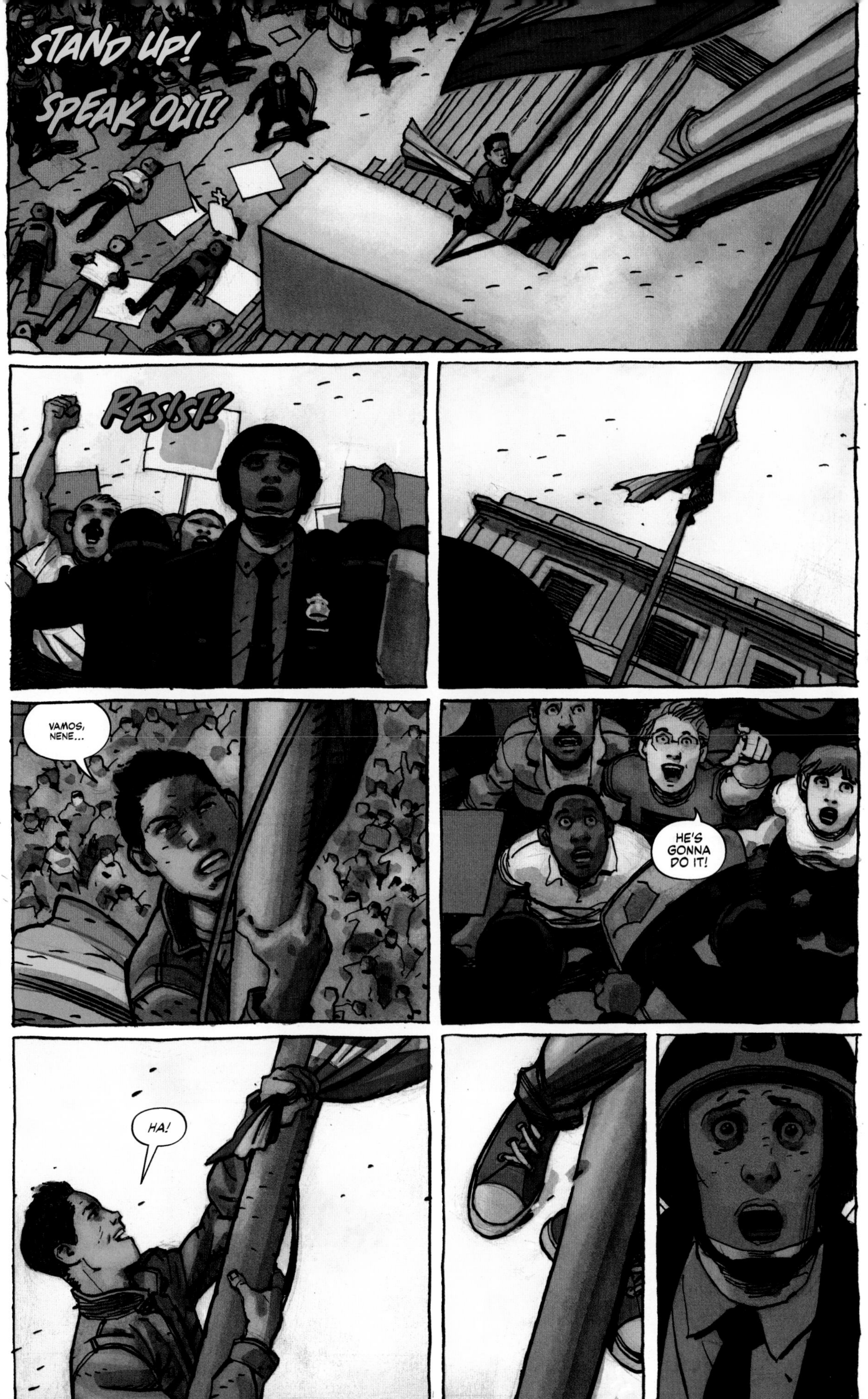
STAND UP!
SPEAK OUT!
RESIST!
VAMOS, NENE...
HE'S GONNA DO IT!
HA!

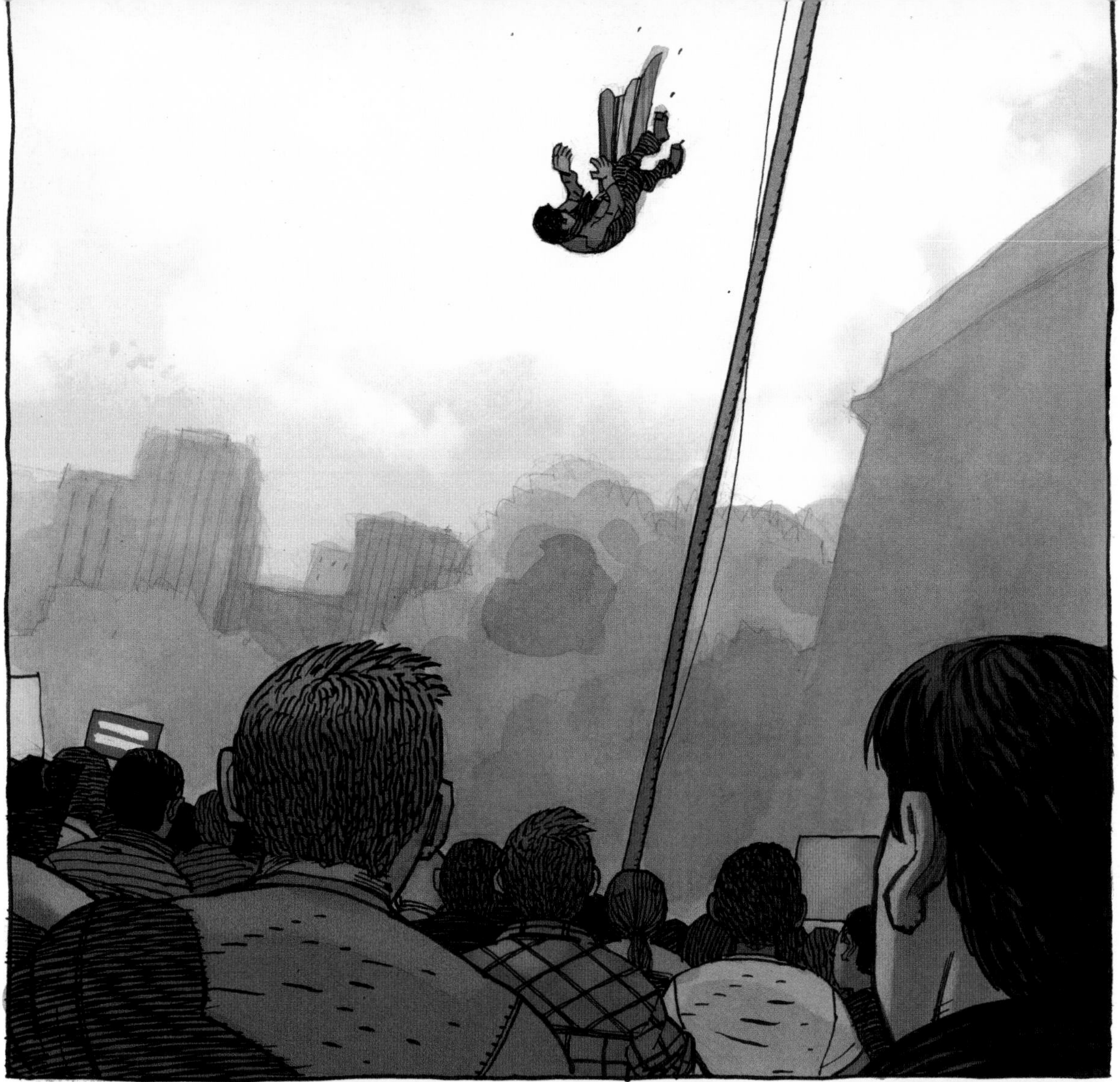

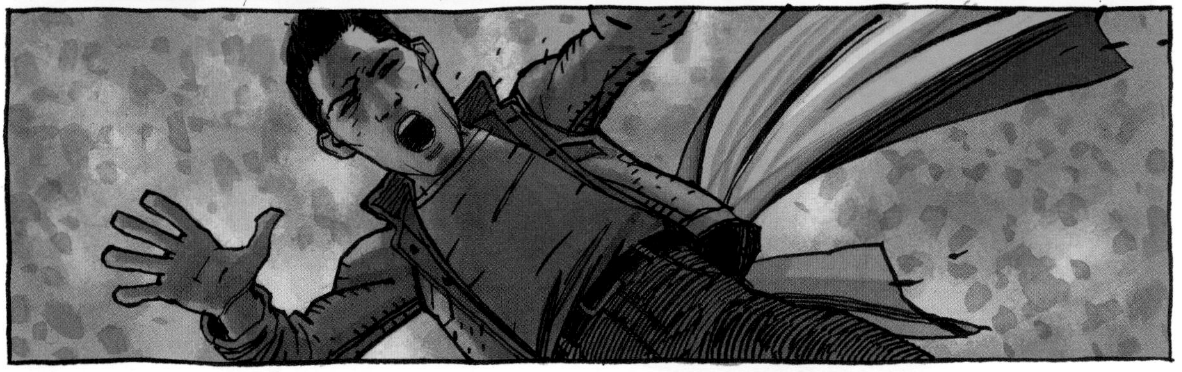

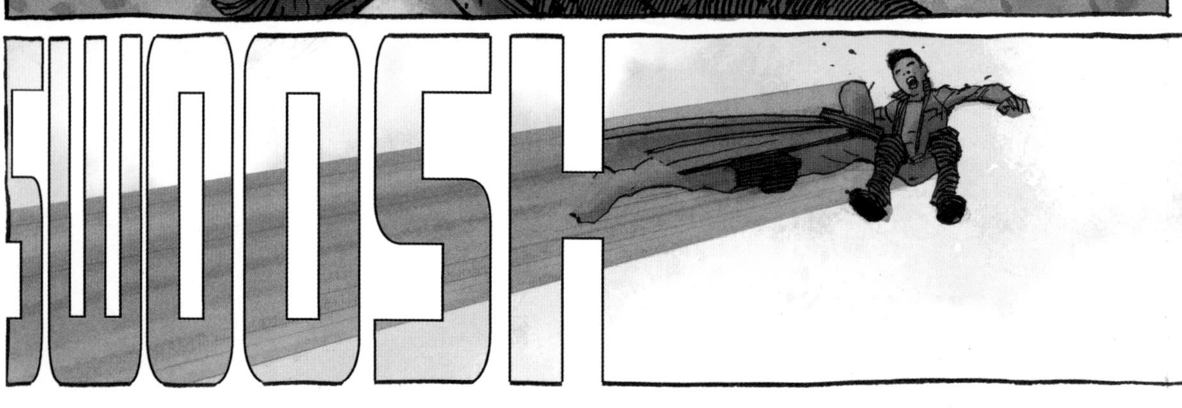
SWOOSH

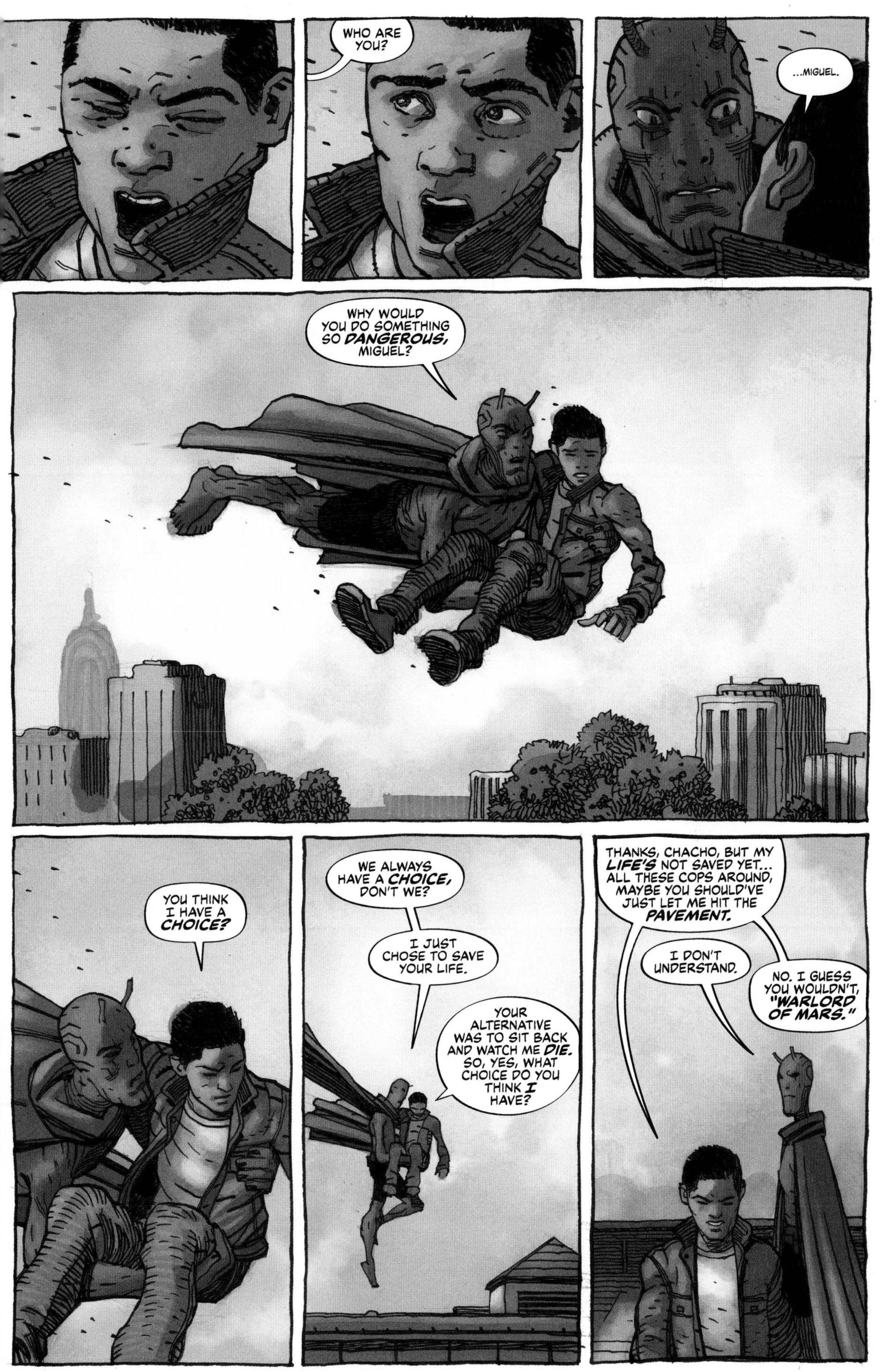
WHO ARE YOU?
...MIGUEL.
WHY WOULD YOU DO SOMETHING SO DANGEROUS, MIGUEL?
YOU THINK I HAVE A CHOICE?
WE ALWAYS HAVE A CHOICE, DON'T WE?
I JUST CHOSE TO SAVE YOUR LIFE.
YOUR ALTERNATIVE WAS TO SIT BACK AND WATCH ME DIE. SO, YES, WHAT CHOICE DO YOU THINK I HAVE?
THANKS, CHACHO, BUT MY LIFE'S NOT SAVED YET... ALL THESE COPS AROUND, MAYBE YOU SHOULD'VE JUST LET ME HIT THE PAVEMENT.
I DON'T UNDERSTAND.
NO. I GUESS YOU WOULDN'T, "WARLORD OF MARS."

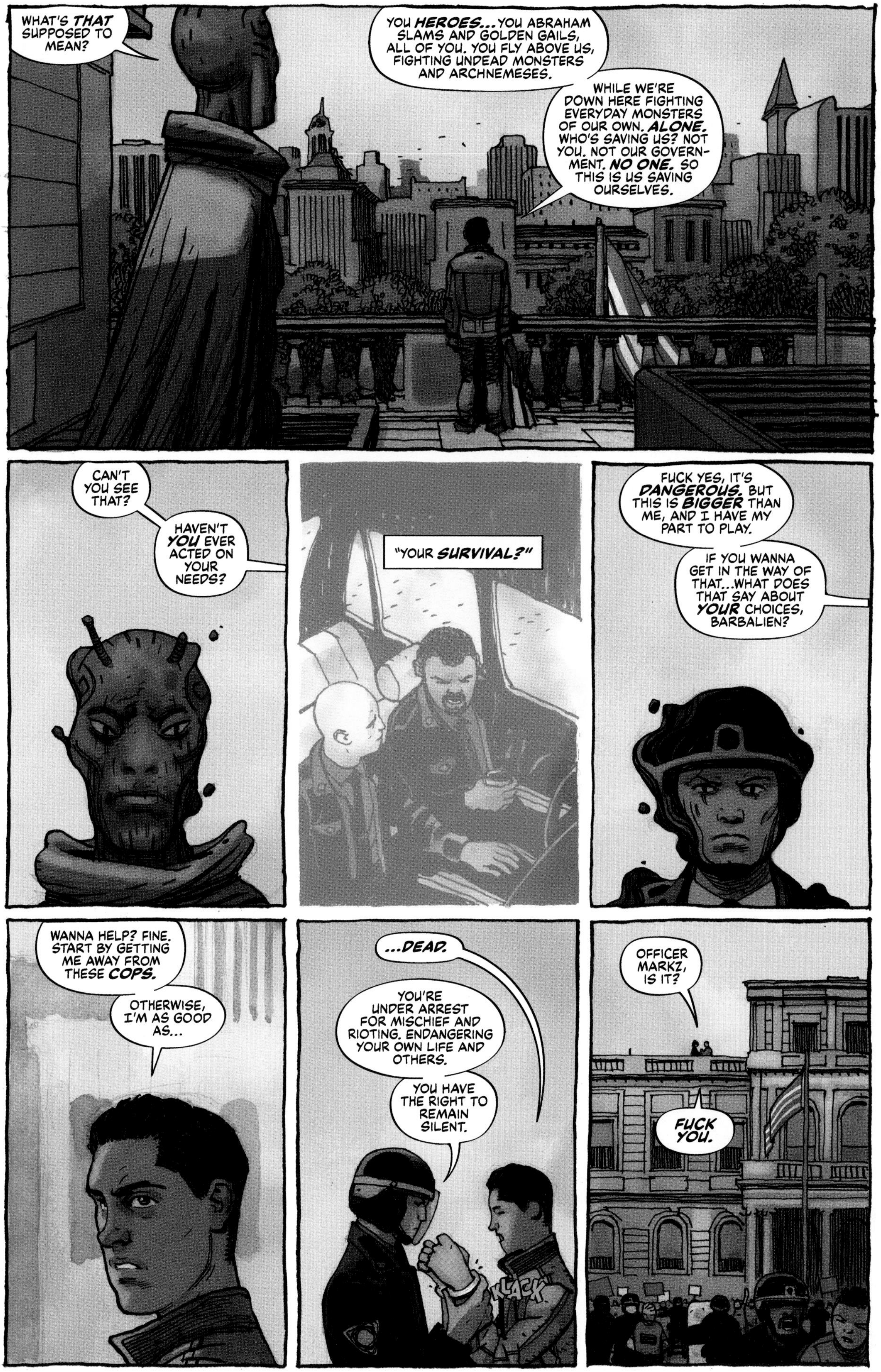

WHAT'S THAT SUPPOSED TO MEAN?
YOU HEROES...YOU ABRAHAM SLAMS AND GOLDEN GAILS, ALL OF YOU. YOU FLY ABOVE US, FIGHTING UNDEAD MONSTERS AND ARCHNEMESES.
WHILE WE'RE DOWN HERE FIGHTING EVERYDAY MONSTERS OF OUR OWN. ALONE. WHO'S SAVING US? NOT YOU. NOT OUR GOVERNMENT. NO ONE. SO THIS IS US SAVING OURSELVES.
CAN'T YOU SEE THAT?
HAVEN'T YOU EVER ACTED ON YOUR NEEDS?
"YOUR SURVIVAL?"
FUCK YES, IT'S DANGEROUS. BUT THIS IS BIGGER THAN ME, AND I HAVE MY PART TO PLAY.
IF YOU WANNA GET IN THE WAY OF THAT...WHAT DOES THAT SAY ABOUT YOUR CHOICES, BARBALIEN?
WANNA HELP? FINE. START BY GETTING ME AWAY FROM THESE COPS.
OTHERWISE, I'M AS GOOD AS...
...DEAD.
YOU'RE UNDER ARREST FOR MISCHIEF AND RIOTING. ENDANGERING YOUR OWN LIFE AND OTHERS.
YOU HAVE THE RIGHT TO REMAIN SILENT.
KLACK
OFFICER MARKZ, IS IT?
FUCK YOU.

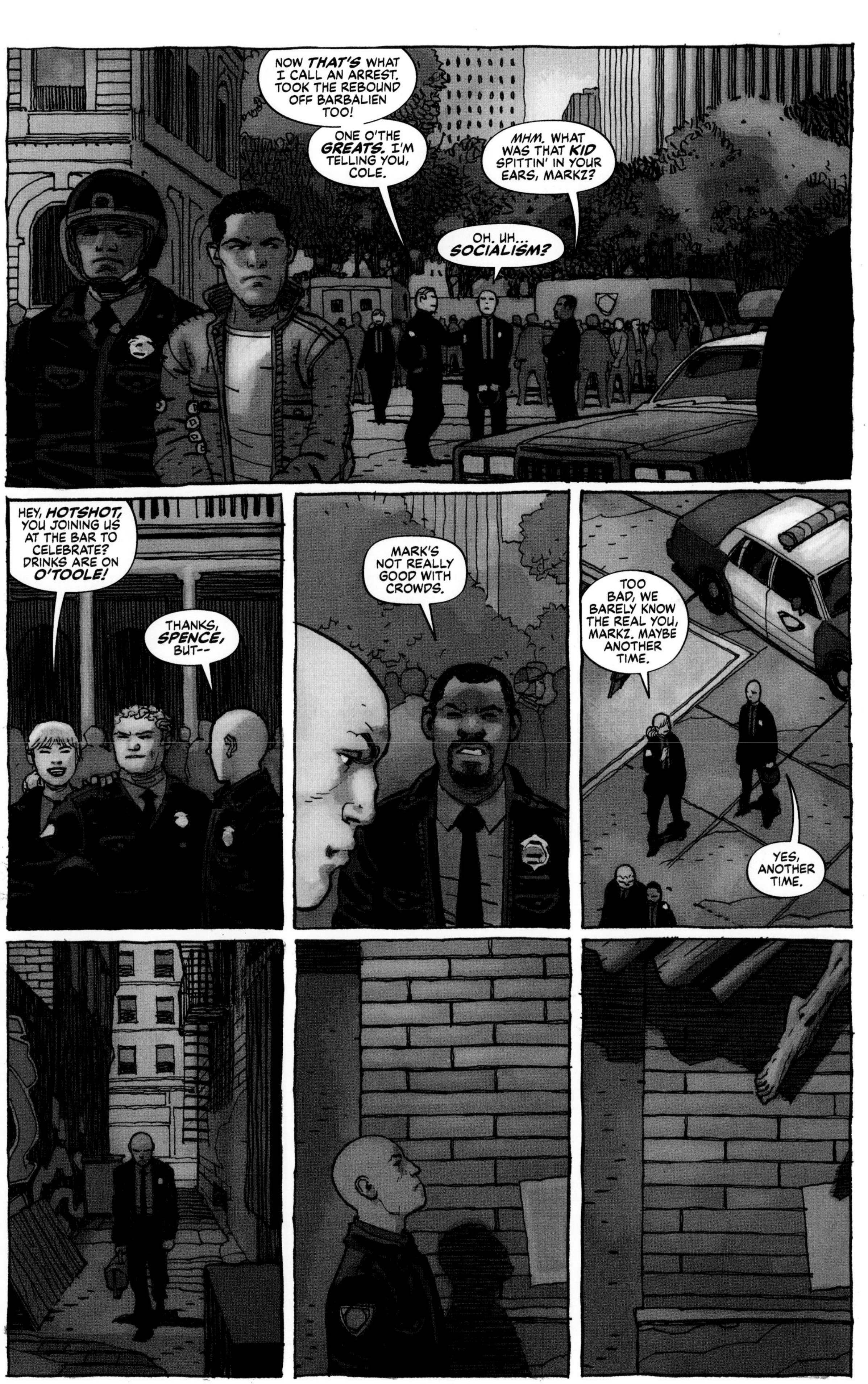
NOW **THAT'S** WHAT I CALL AN ARREST. TOOK THE REBOUND OFF BARBALIEN TOO!
ONE O'THE **GREATS.** I'M TELLING YOU, COLE.
MHM. WHAT WAS THAT **KID** SPITTIN' IN YOUR EARS, MARKZ?
OH. UH... **SOCIALISM?**
HEY, **HOTSHOT,** YOU JOINING US AT THE BAR TO CELEBRATE? DRINKS ARE ON **O'TOOLE!**
THANKS, **SPENCE,** BUT--
MARK'S NOT REALLY GOOD WITH CROWDS.
TOO BAD, WE BARELY KNOW THE REAL YOU, MARKZ. MAYBE ANOTHER TIME.
YES, ANOTHER TIME.

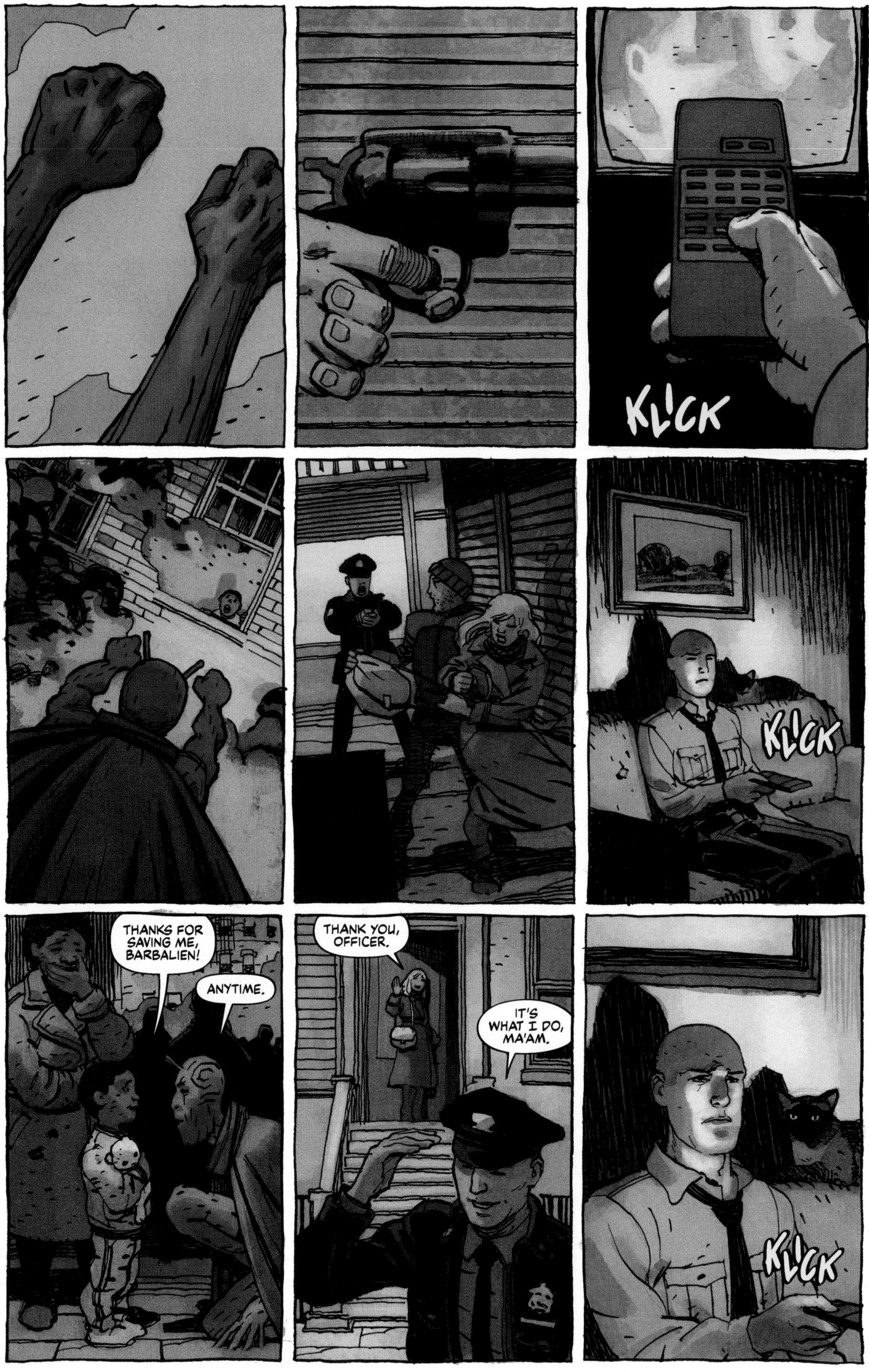
KLICK
KLICK
THANKS FOR SAVING ME, BARBALIEN!
ANYTIME.
THANK YOU, OFFICER.
IT'S WHAT I DO, MA'AM.
KLICK

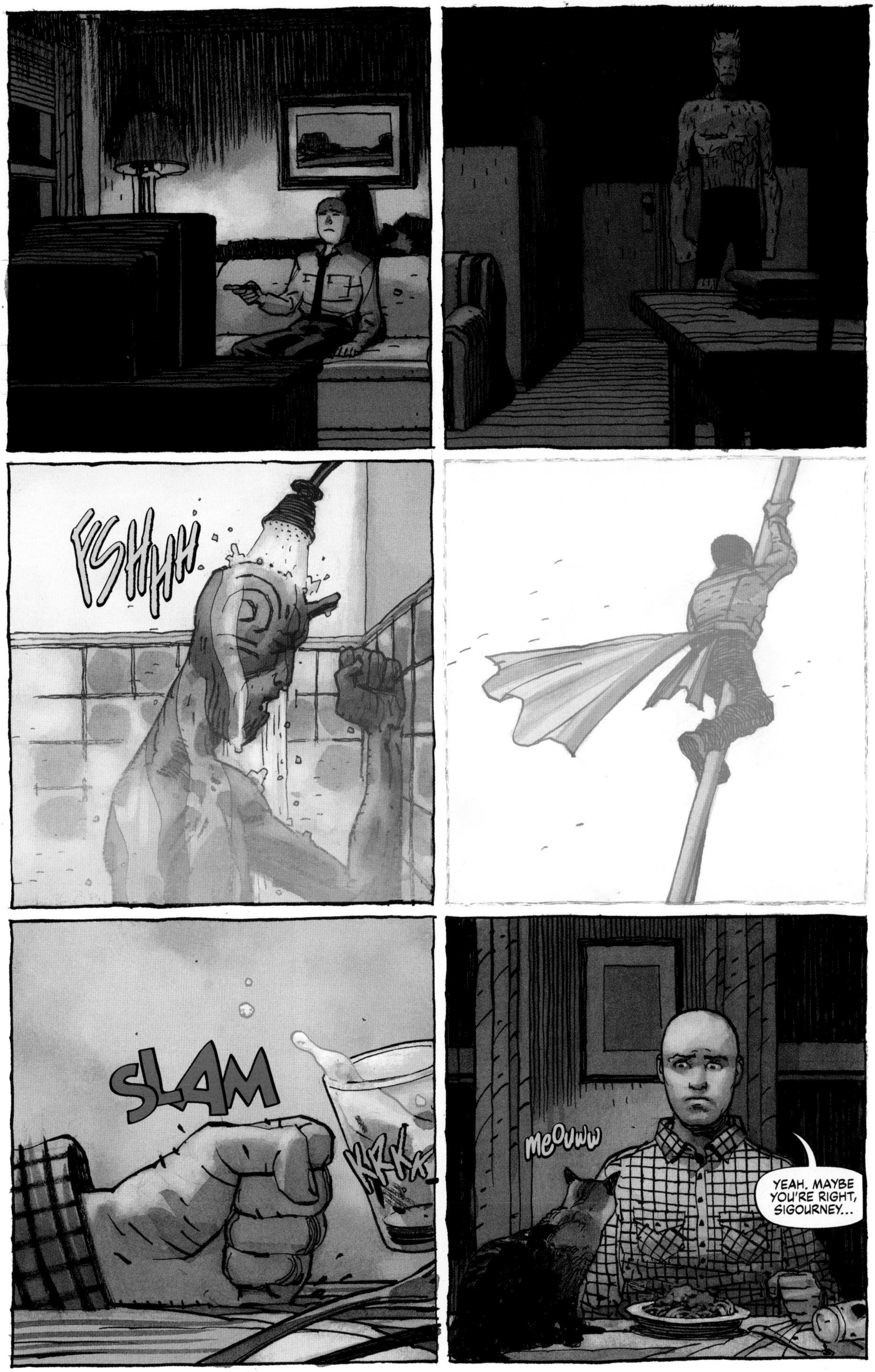
FSHHH
SLAM
KRKK
MEOUWW
YEAH. MAYBE YOU'RE RIGHT, SIGOURNEY...

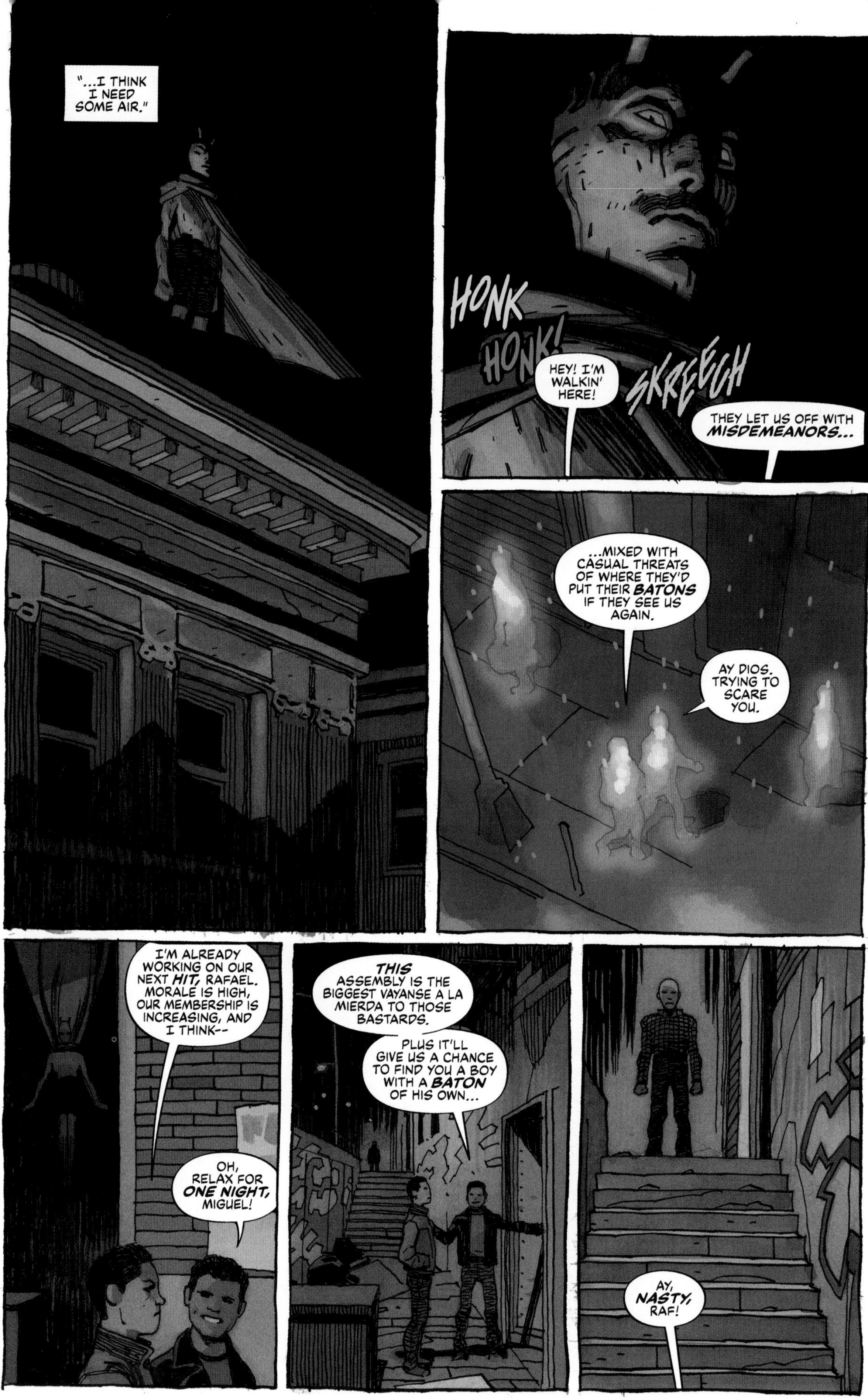

"...I THINK I NEED SOME AIR."
HONK
HONK!
HEY! I'M WALKIN' HERE!
SKREECH
THEY LET US OFF WITH MISDEMEANORS...
...MIXED WITH CASUAL THREATS OF WHERE THEY'D PUT THEIR BATONS IF THEY SEE US AGAIN.
AY DIOS. TRYING TO SCARE YOU.
I'M ALREADY WORKING ON OUR NEXT HIT, RAFAEL. MORALE IS HIGH, OUR MEMBERSHIP IS INCREASING, AND I THINK--
OH, RELAX FOR ONE NIGHT, MIGUEL!
THIS ASSEMBLY IS THE BIGGEST VAYANSE A LA MIERDA TO THOSE BASTARDS.
PLUS IT'LL GIVE US A CHANCE TO FIND YOU A BOY WITH A BATON OF HIS OWN...
AY, NASTY, RAF!

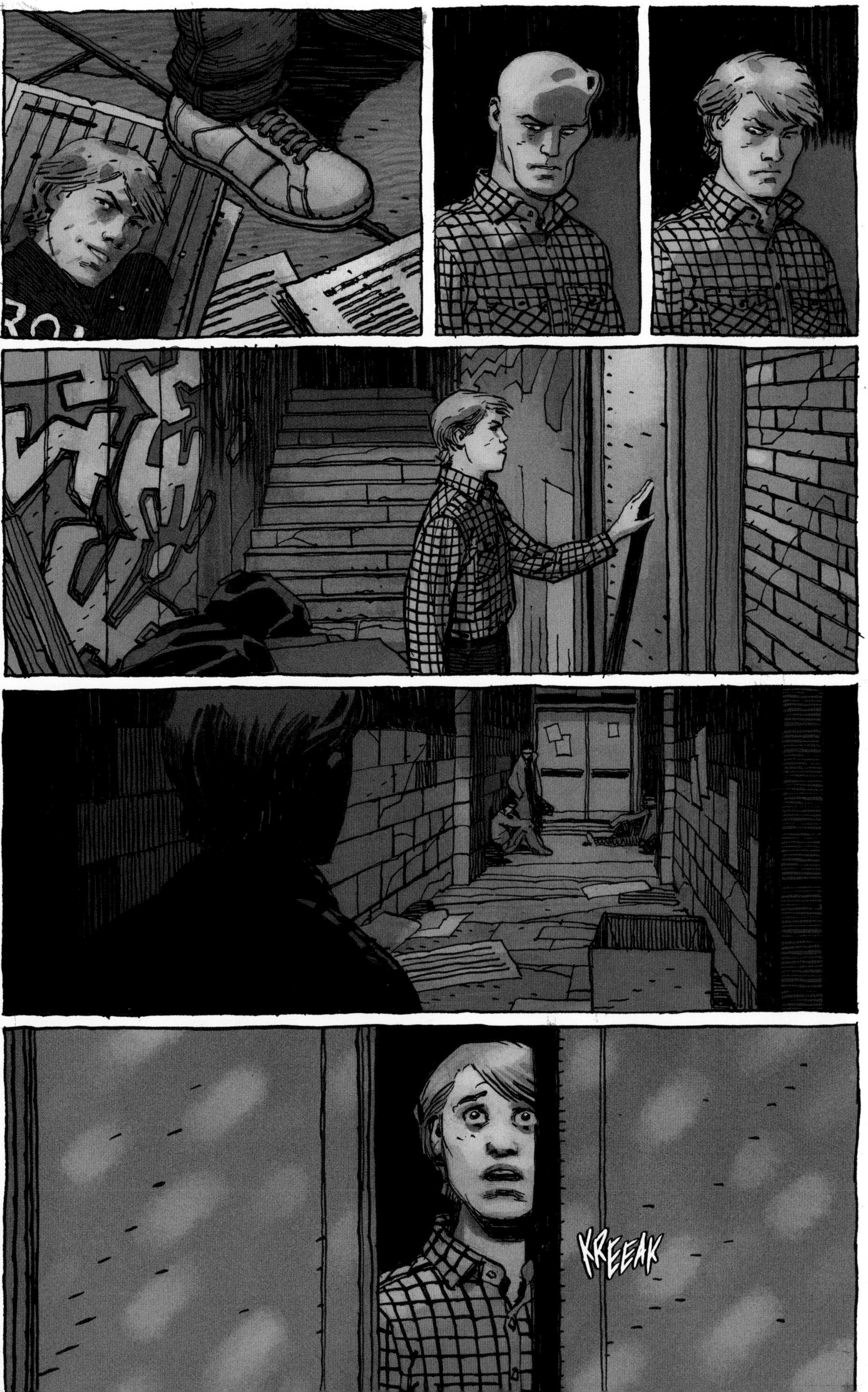
KREEAK

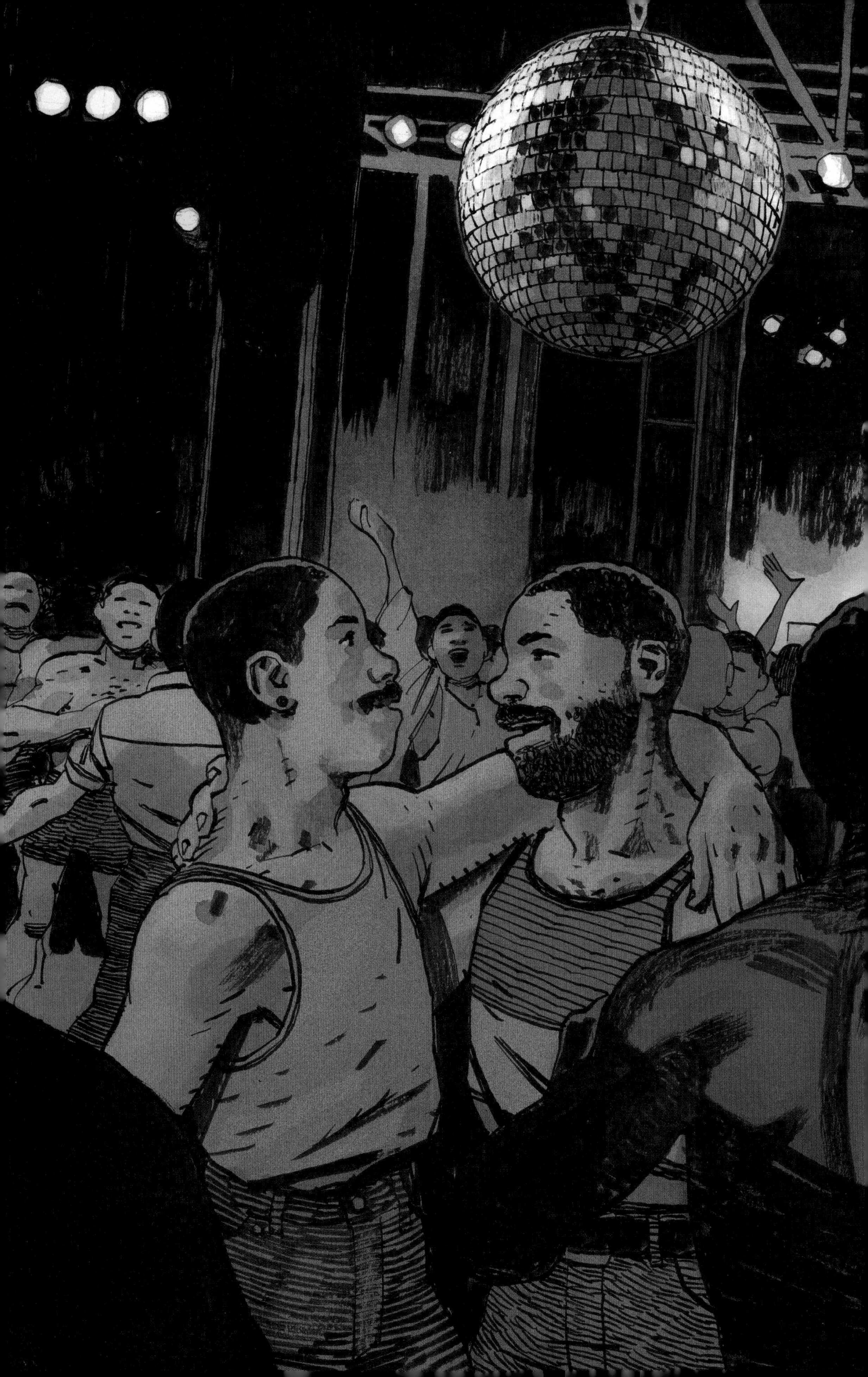

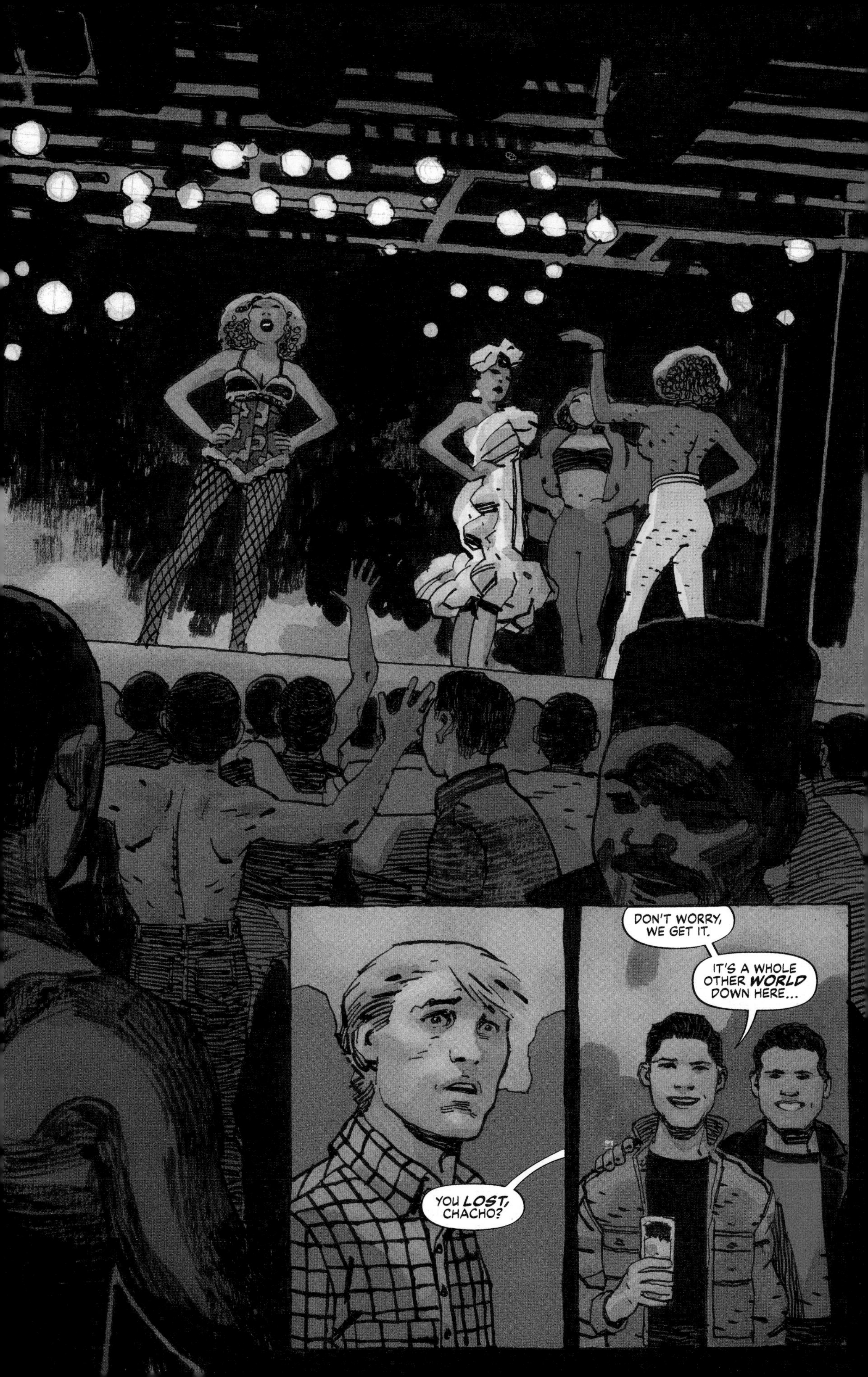
YOU *LOST,* CHACHO?
DON'T WORRY, WE GET IT.
IT'S A WHOLE OTHER *WORLD* DOWN HERE...

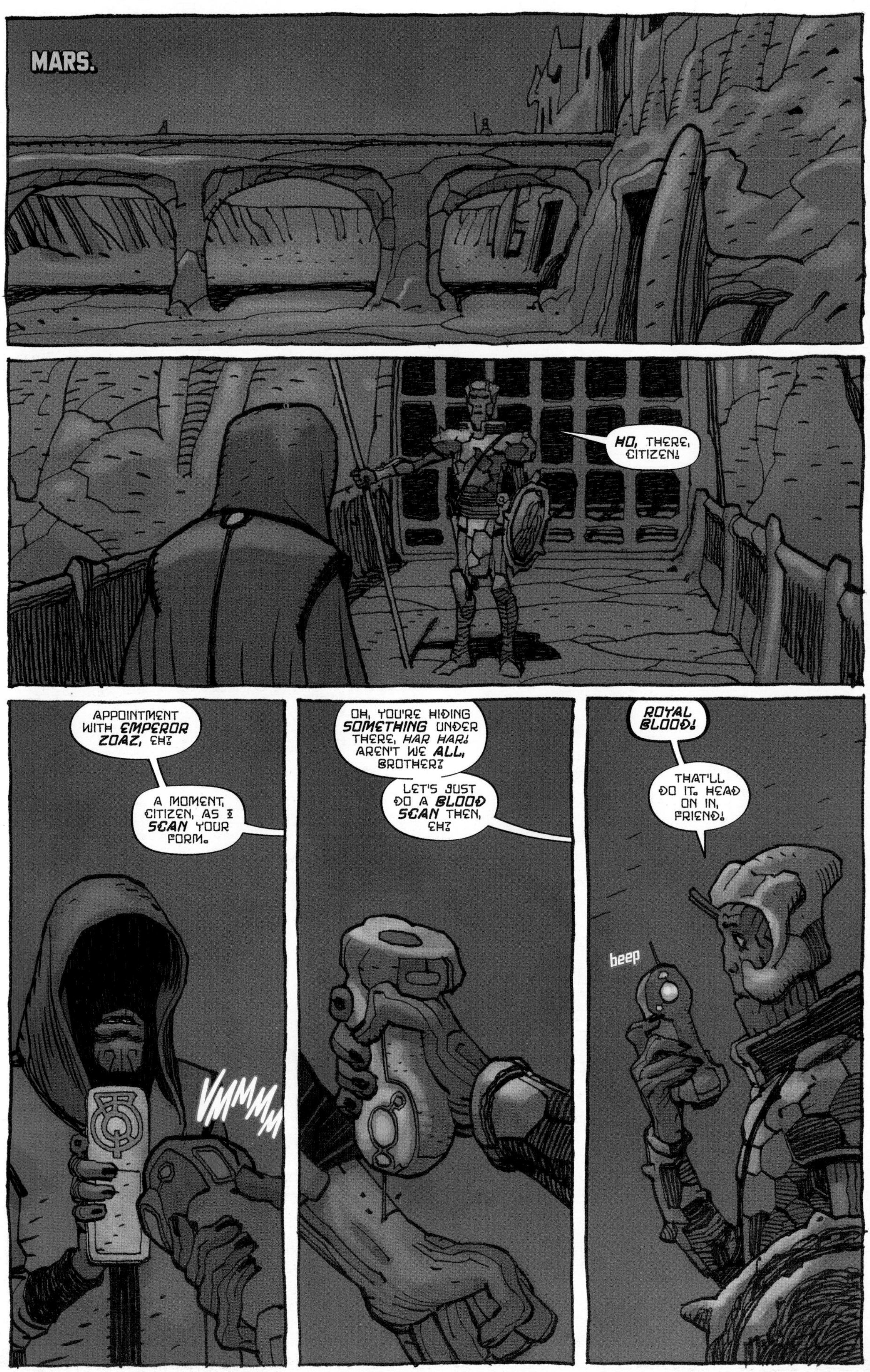
MARS.
HO, THERE, CITIZEN!
APPOINTMENT WITH EMPEROR ZOAZ, EH?
A MOMENT, CITIZEN, AS I SCAN YOUR FORM.
VMMMM
OH, YOU'RE HIDING SOMETHING UNDER THERE, HAR HAR! AREN'T WE ALL, BROTHER?
LET'S JUST DO A BLOOD SCAN THEN, EH?
ROYAL BLOOD!
THAT'LL DO IT. HEAD ON IN, FRIEND!
beep

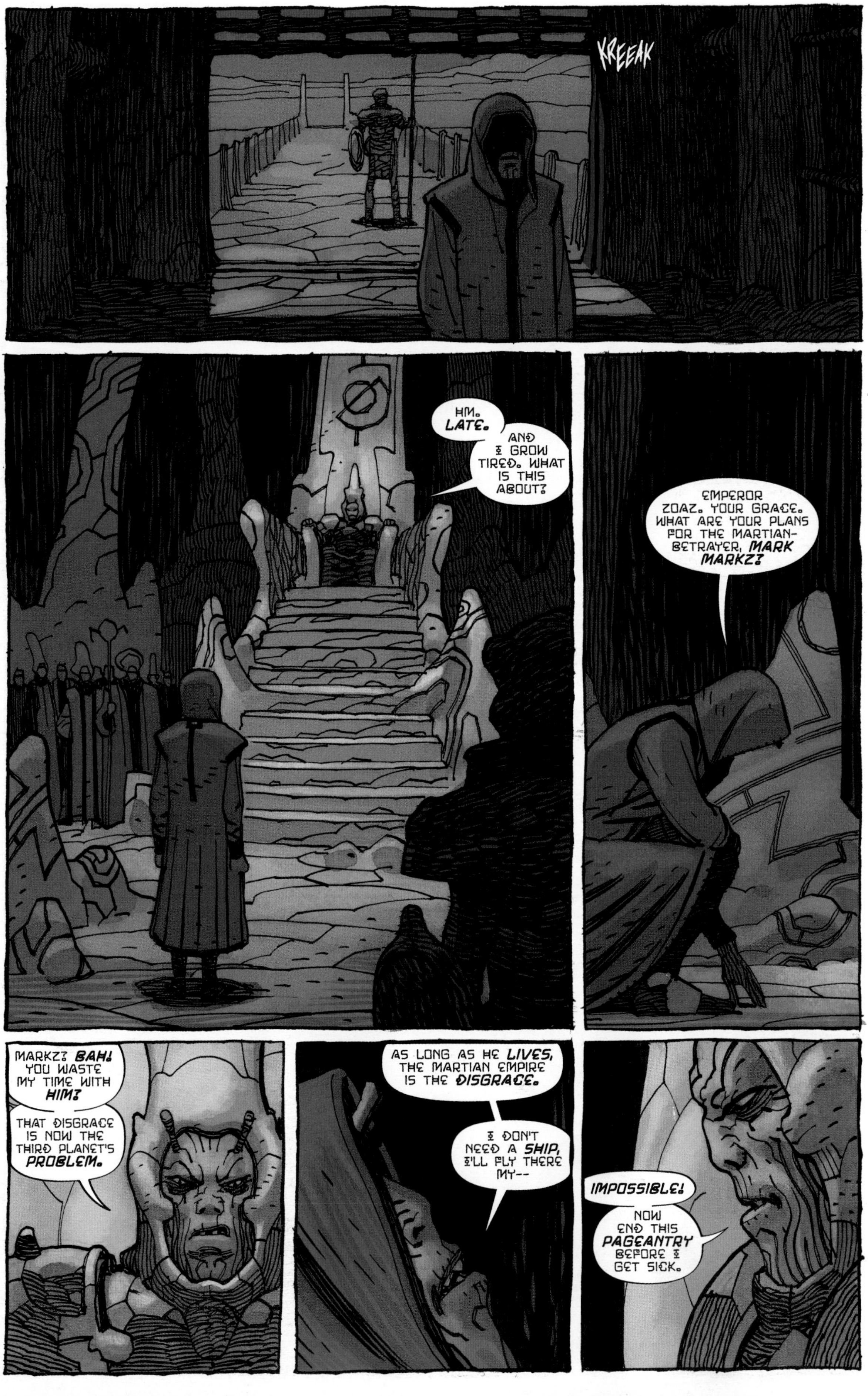
KREEAK
HM. LATE.
AND I GROW TIRED. WHAT IS THIS ABOUT?
EMPEROR ZOAZ. YOUR GRACE. WHAT ARE YOUR PLANS FOR THE MARTIAN-BETRAYER, MARK MARKZ?
MARKZ? BAH! YOU WASTE MY TIME WITH HIM?
THAT DISGRACE IS NOW THE THIRD PLANET'S PROBLEM.
AS LONG AS HE LIVES, THE MARTIAN EMPIRE IS THE DISGRACE.
I DON'T NEED A SHIP, I'LL FLY THERE MY--
IMPOSSIBLE!
NOW END THIS PAGEANTRY BEFORE I GET SICK.

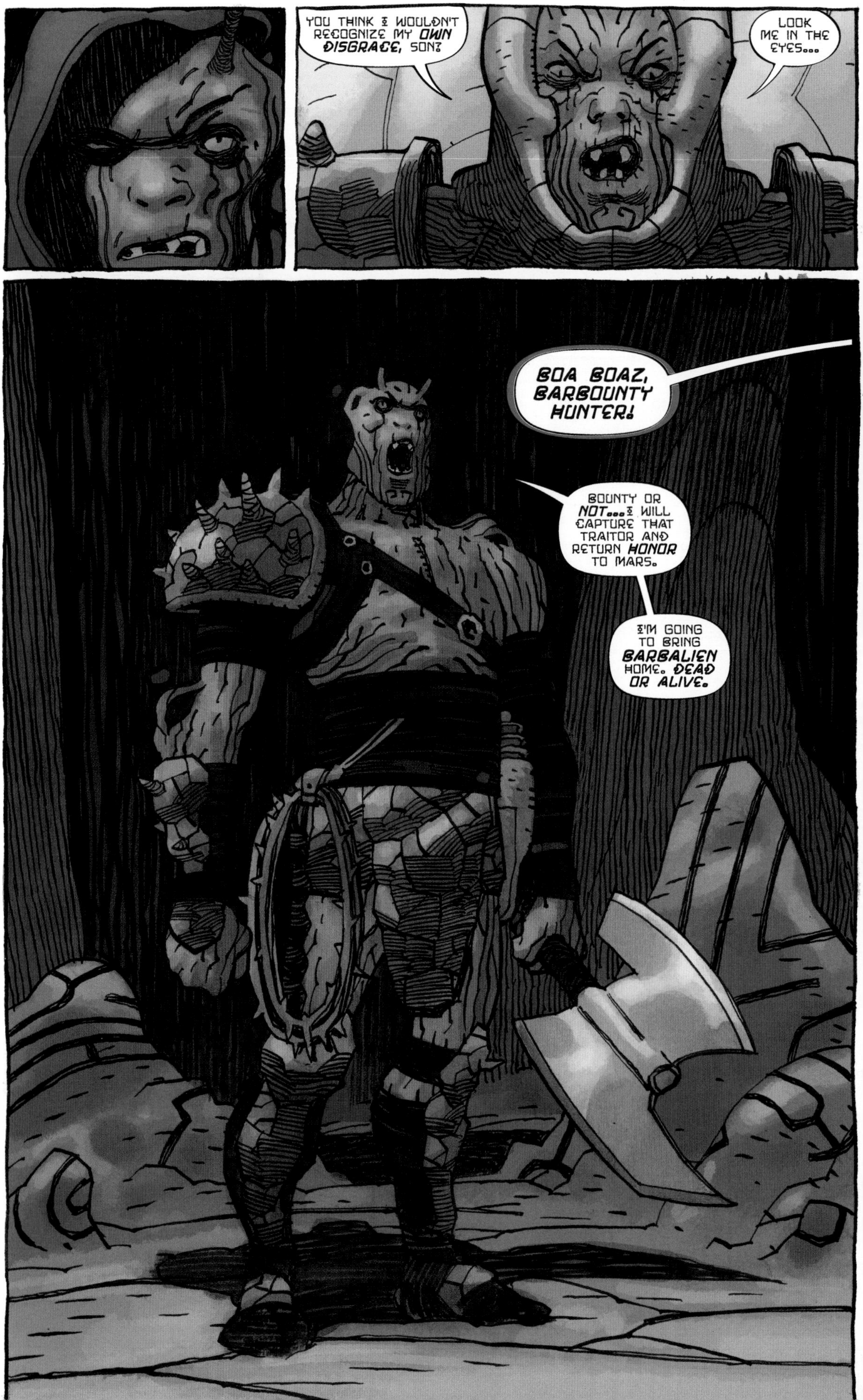
YOU THINK I WOULDN'T RECOGNIZE MY OWN DISGRACE, SON?
LOOK ME IN THE EYES...
BOA BOAZ, BARBOUNTY HUNTER!
BOUNTY OR NOT... I WILL CAPTURE THAT TRAITOR AND RETURN HONOR TO MARS.
I'M GOING TO BRING BARBALIEN HOME. DEAD OR ALIVE.

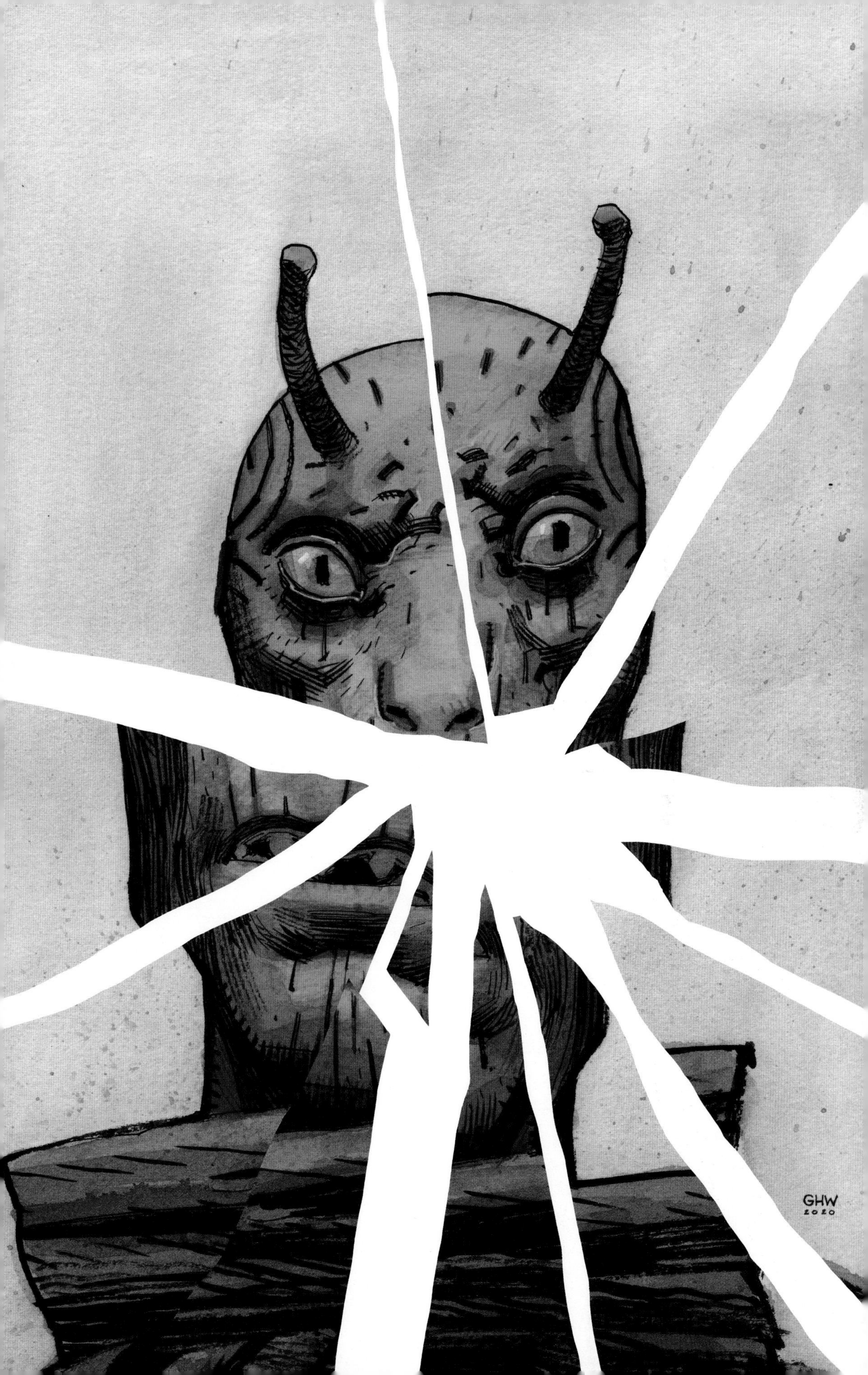
GHW
2020

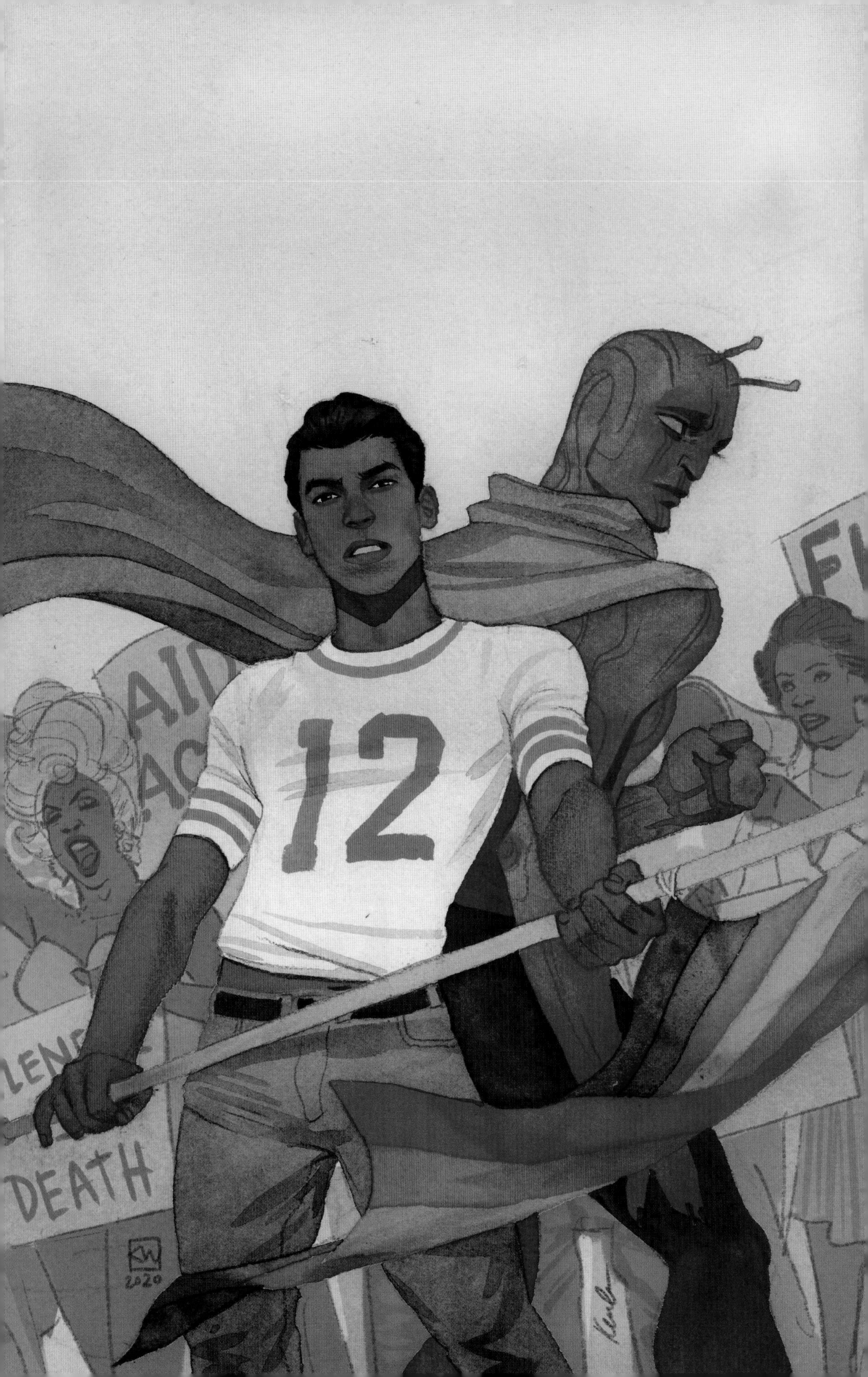
12
DEATH

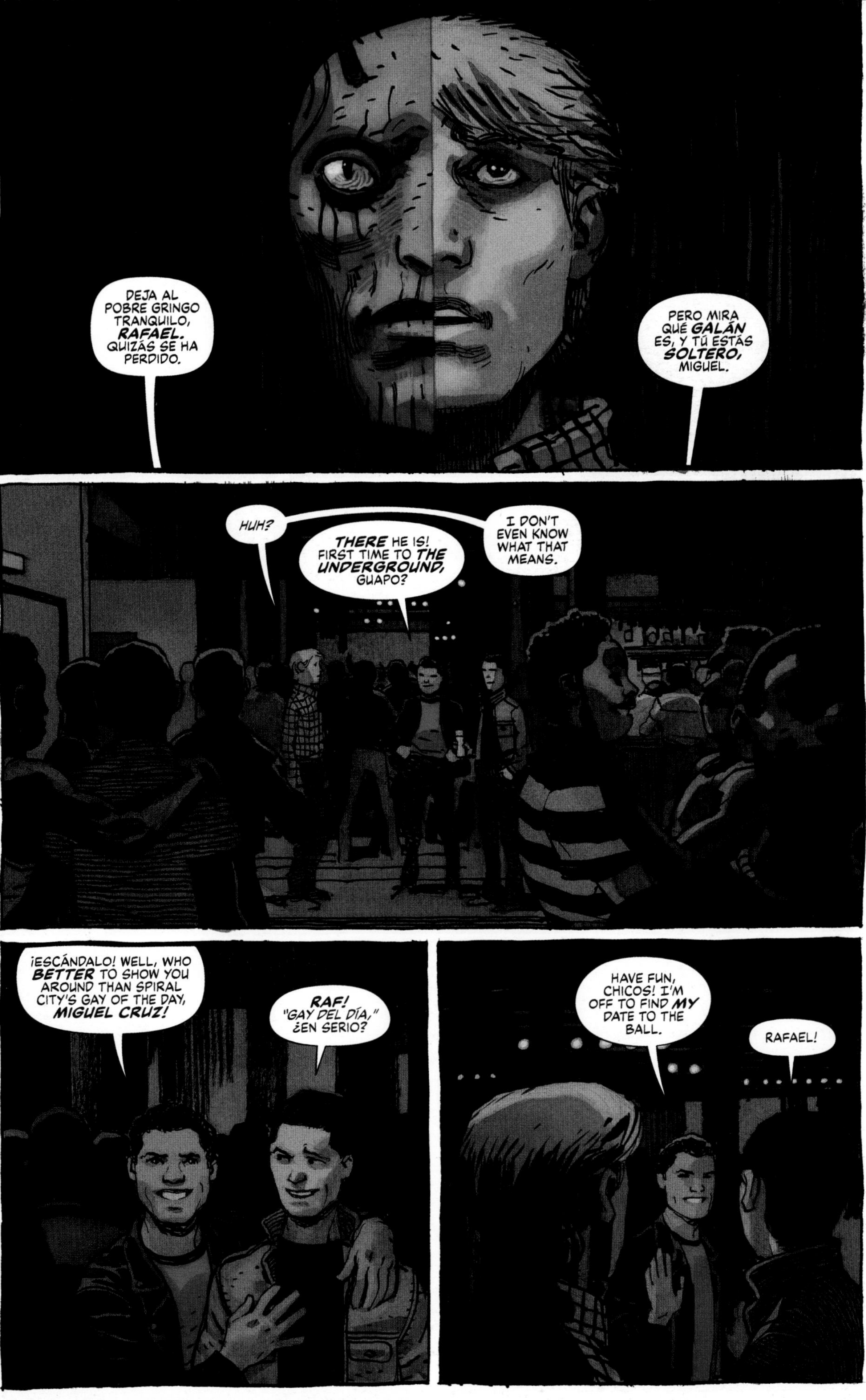
DEJA AL POBRE GRINGO TRANQUILO, RAFAEL. QUIZÁS SE HA PERDIDO.
PERO MIRA QUÉ GALÁN ES, Y TÚ ESTÁS SOLTERO, MIGUEL.
THERE HE IS! FIRST TIME TO THE UNDERGROUND, GUAPO?
HUH?
I DON'T EVEN KNOW WHAT THAT MEANS.
¡ESCÁNDALO! WELL, WHO BETTER TO SHOW YOU AROUND THAN SPIRAL CITY'S GAY OF THE DAY, MIGUEL CRUZ!
RAF! "GAY DEL DÍA," ¿EN SERIO?
HAVE FUN, CHICOS! I'M OFF TO FIND MY DATE TO THE BALL.
RAFAEL!

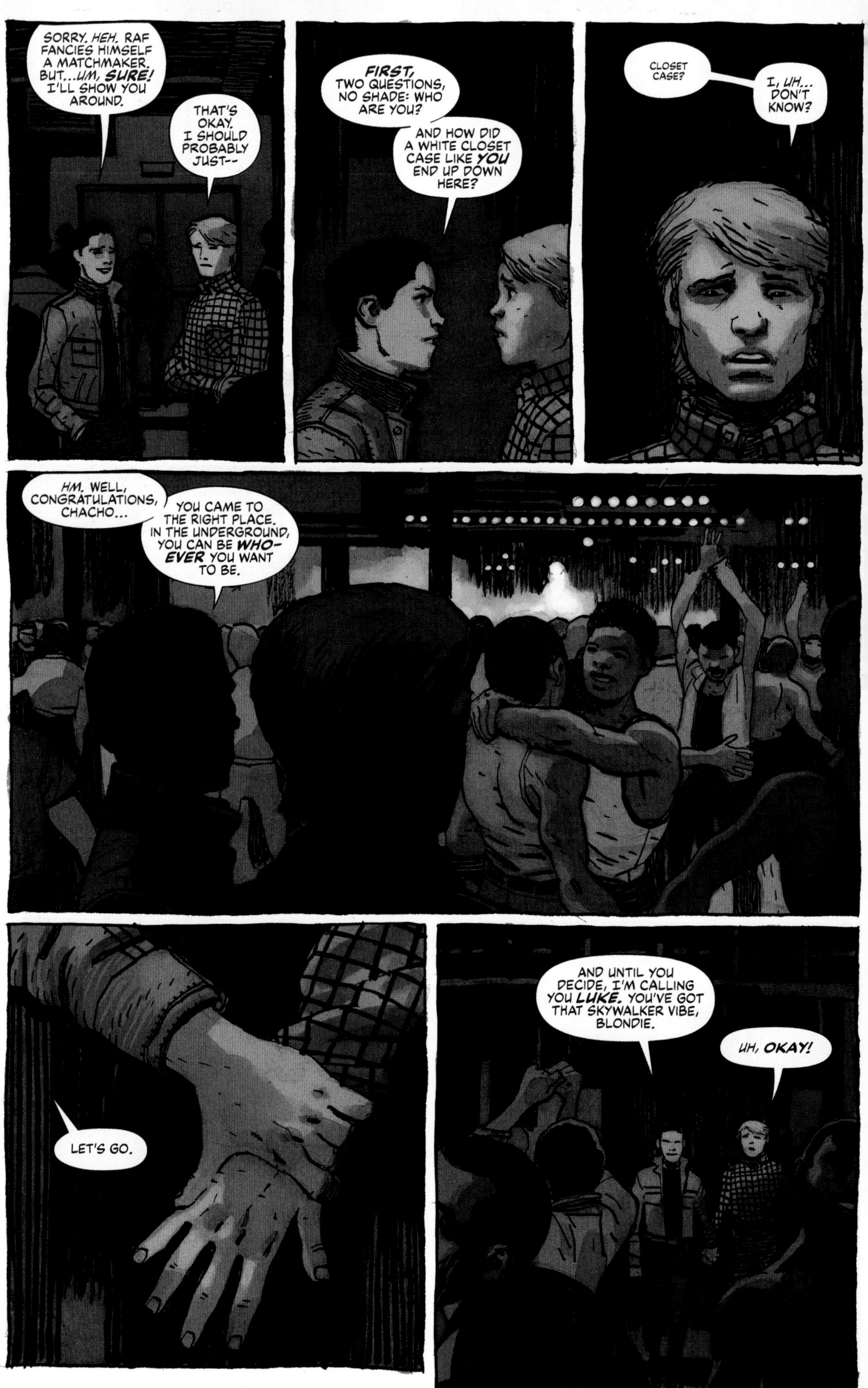
SORRY. HEH. RAF FANCIES HIMSELF A MATCHMAKER. BUT...UM, SURE! I'LL SHOW YOU AROUND.
THAT'S OKAY. I SHOULD PROBABLY JUST--
FIRST, TWO QUESTIONS, NO SHADE: WHO ARE YOU?
AND HOW DID A WHITE CLOSET CASE LIKE YOU END UP DOWN HERE?
CLOSET CASE?
I, UH... DON'T KNOW?
HM. WELL, CONGRATULATIONS, CHACHO...
YOU CAME TO THE RIGHT PLACE. IN THE UNDERGROUND, YOU CAN BE WHO-EVER YOU WANT TO BE.
LET'S GO.
AND UNTIL YOU DECIDE, I'M CALLING YOU LUKE. YOU'VE GOT THAT SKYWALKER VIBE, BLONDIE.
UH, OKAY!

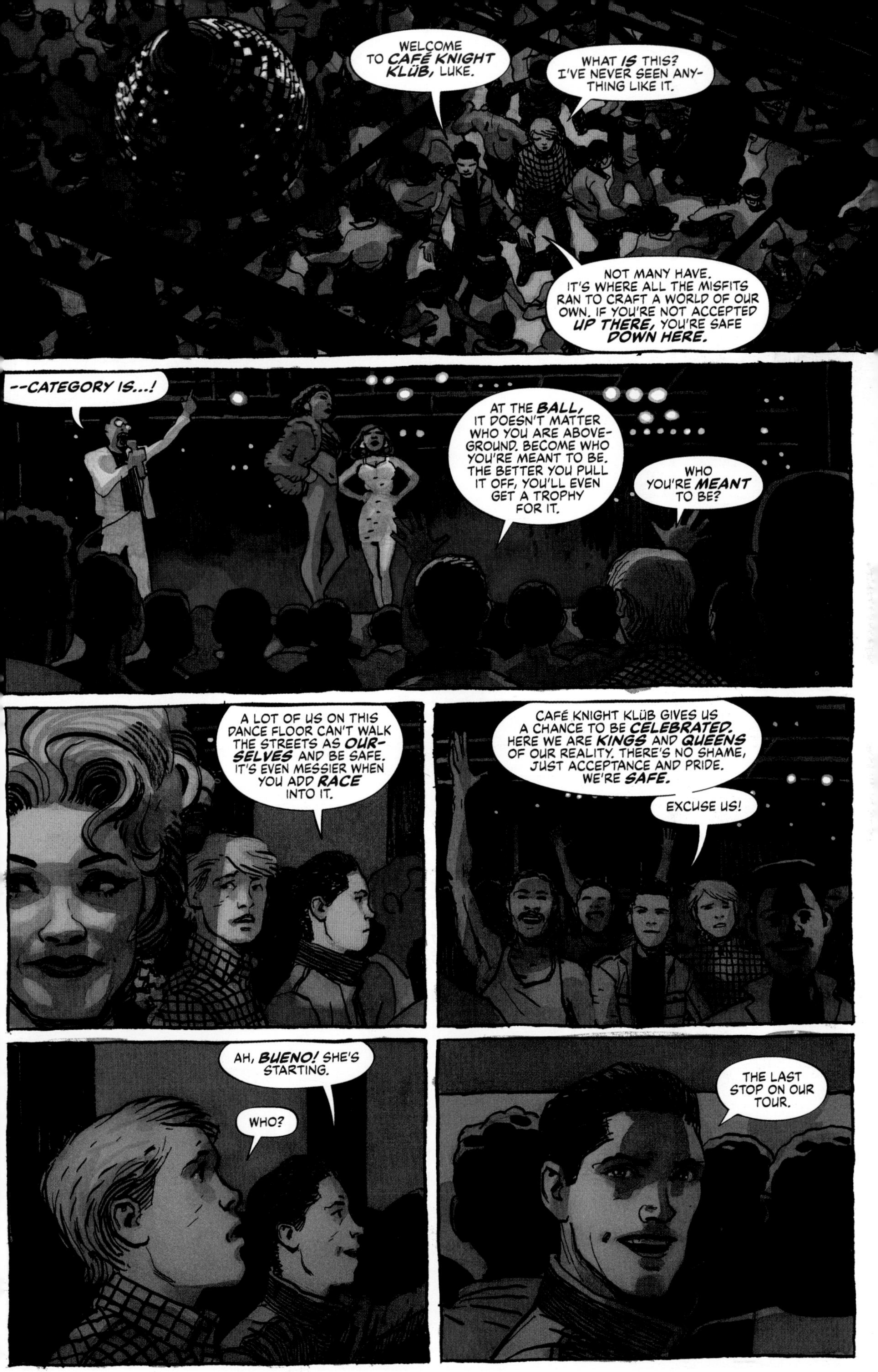
WELCOME TO CAFÉ KNIGHT KLÜB, LUKE.
WHAT IS THIS? I'VE NEVER SEEN ANYTHING LIKE IT.
NOT MANY HAVE. IT'S WHERE ALL THE MISFITS RAN TO CRAFT A WORLD OF OUR OWN. IF YOU'RE NOT ACCEPTED UP THERE, YOU'RE SAFE DOWN HERE.
--CATEGORY IS...!
AT THE BALL, IT DOESN'T MATTER WHO YOU ARE ABOVEGROUND. BECOME WHO YOU'RE MEANT TO BE. THE BETTER YOU PULL IT OFF, YOU'LL EVEN GET A TROPHY FOR IT.
WHO YOU'RE MEANT TO BE?
A LOT OF US ON THIS DANCE FLOOR CAN'T WALK THE STREETS AS OURSELVES AND BE SAFE. IT'S EVEN MESSIER WHEN YOU ADD RACE INTO IT.
CAFÉ KNIGHT KLÜB GIVES US A CHANCE TO BE CELEBRATED. HERE WE ARE KINGS AND QUEENS OF OUR REALITY. THERE'S NO SHAME, JUST ACCEPTANCE AND PRIDE. WE'RE SAFE.
EXCUSE US!
AH, BUENO! SHE'S STARTING.
WHO?
THE LAST STOP ON OUR TOUR.

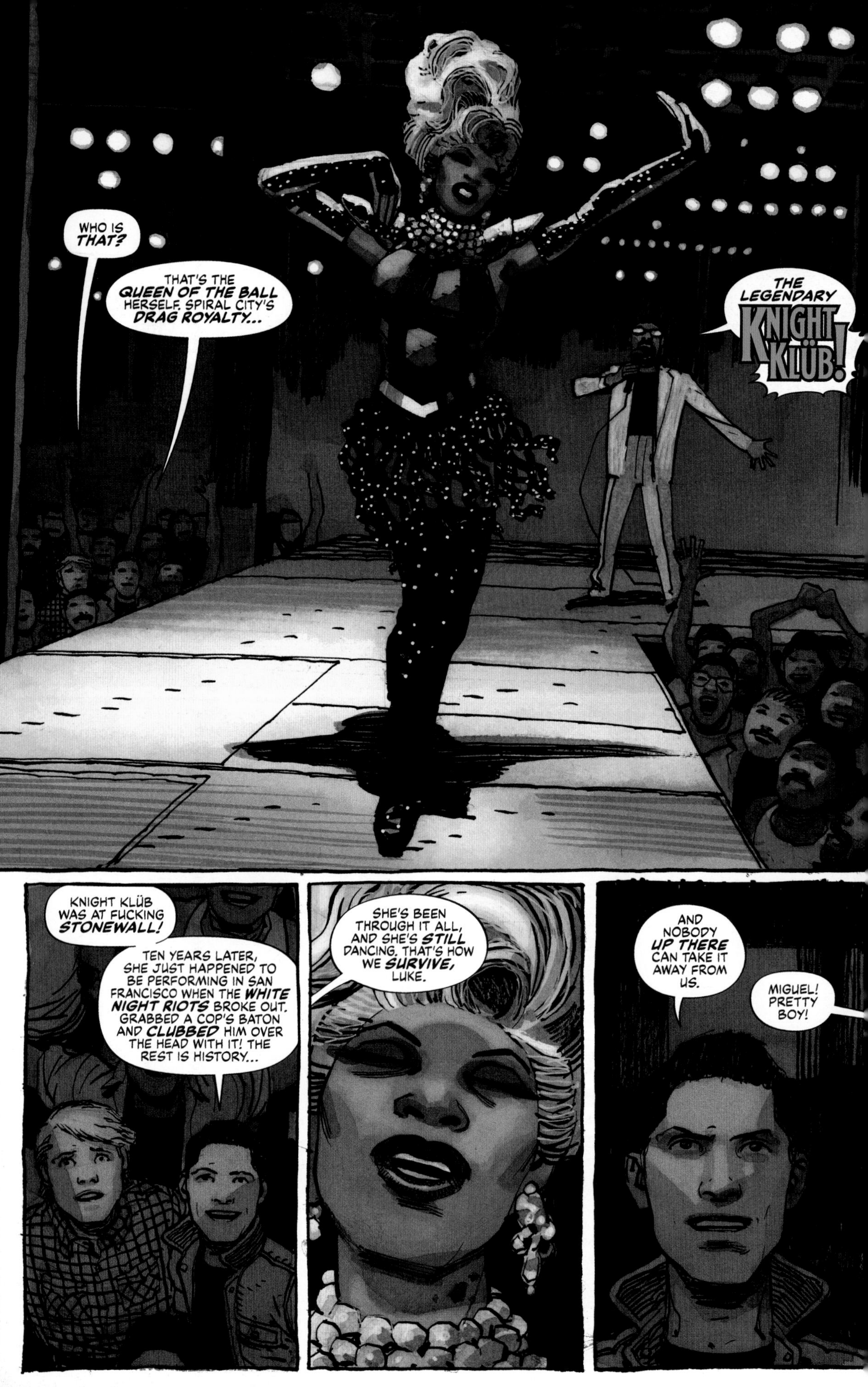
WHO IS THAT?
THAT'S THE QUEEN OF THE BALL HERSELF. SPIRAL CITY'S DRAG ROYALTY...
THE LEGENDARY KNIGHT KLÜB!
KNIGHT KLÜB WAS AT FUCKING STONEWALL!
TEN YEARS LATER, SHE JUST HAPPENED TO BE PERFORMING IN SAN FRANCISCO WHEN THE WHITE NIGHT RIOTS BROKE OUT. GRABBED A COP'S BATON AND CLUBBED HIM OVER THE HEAD WITH IT! THE REST IS HISTORY...
SHE'S BEEN THROUGH IT ALL, AND SHE'S STILL DANCING. THAT'S HOW WE SURVIVE, LUKE.
AND NOBODY UP THERE CAN TAKE IT AWAY FROM US.
MIGUEL! PRETTY BOY!

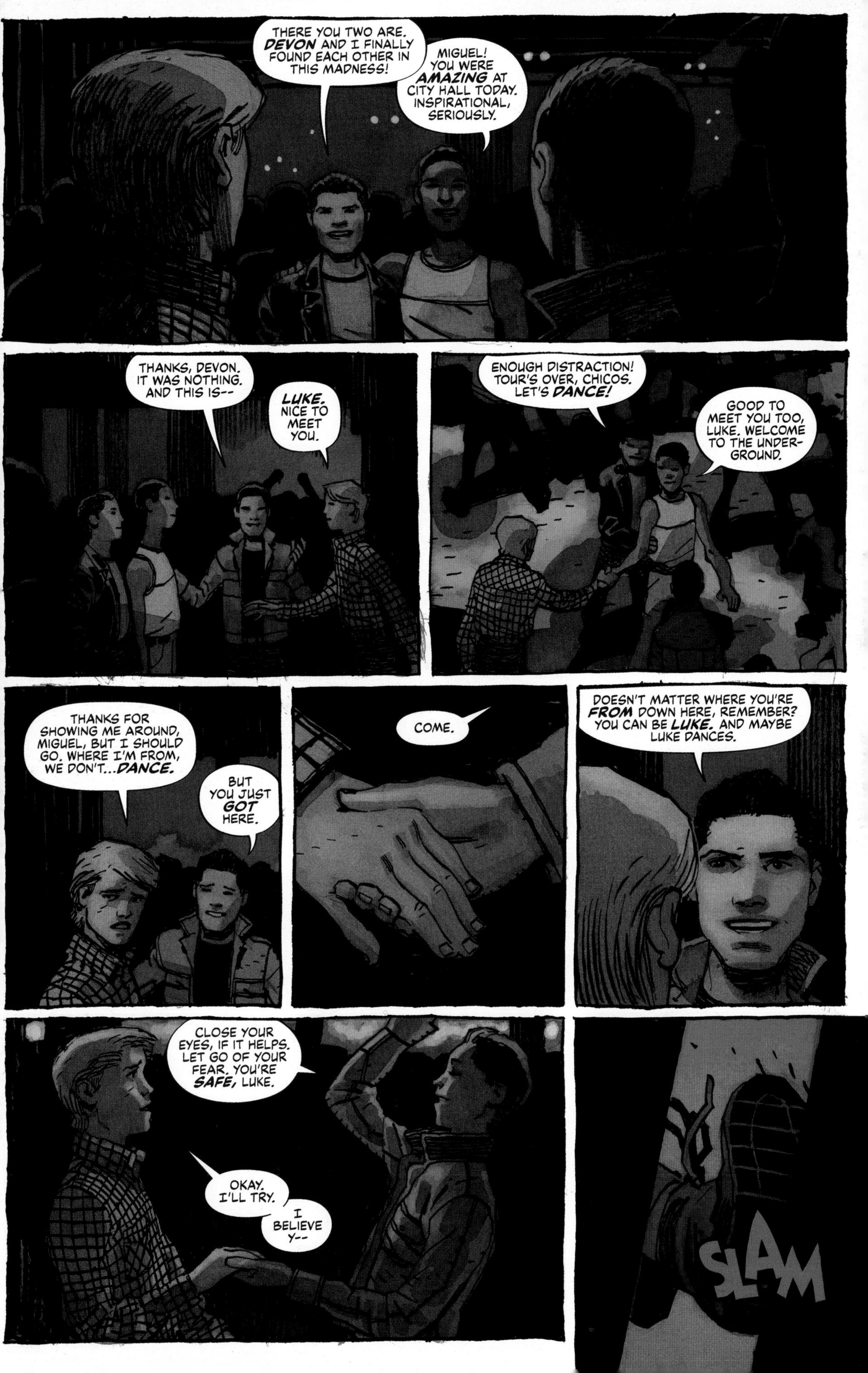
THERE YOU TWO ARE. DEVON AND I FINALLY FOUND EACH OTHER IN THIS MADNESS!
MIGUEL! YOU WERE AMAZING AT CITY HALL TODAY. INSPIRATIONAL, SERIOUSLY.
THANKS, DEVON. IT WAS NOTHING. AND THIS IS--
LUKE. NICE TO MEET YOU.
ENOUGH DISTRACTION! TOUR'S OVER, CHICOS. LET'S DANCE!
GOOD TO MEET YOU TOO, LUKE. WELCOME TO THE UNDER-GROUND.
THANKS FOR SHOWING ME AROUND, MIGUEL, BUT I SHOULD GO. WHERE I'M FROM, WE DON'T...DANCE.
BUT YOU JUST GOT HERE.
COME.
DOESN'T MATTER WHERE YOU'RE FROM DOWN HERE, REMEMBER? YOU CAN BE LUKE. AND MAYBE LUKE DANCES.
CLOSE YOUR EYES, IF IT HELPS. LET GO OF YOUR FEAR. YOU'RE SAFE, LUKE.
OKAY. I'LL TRY.
I BELIEVE Y--
SLAM

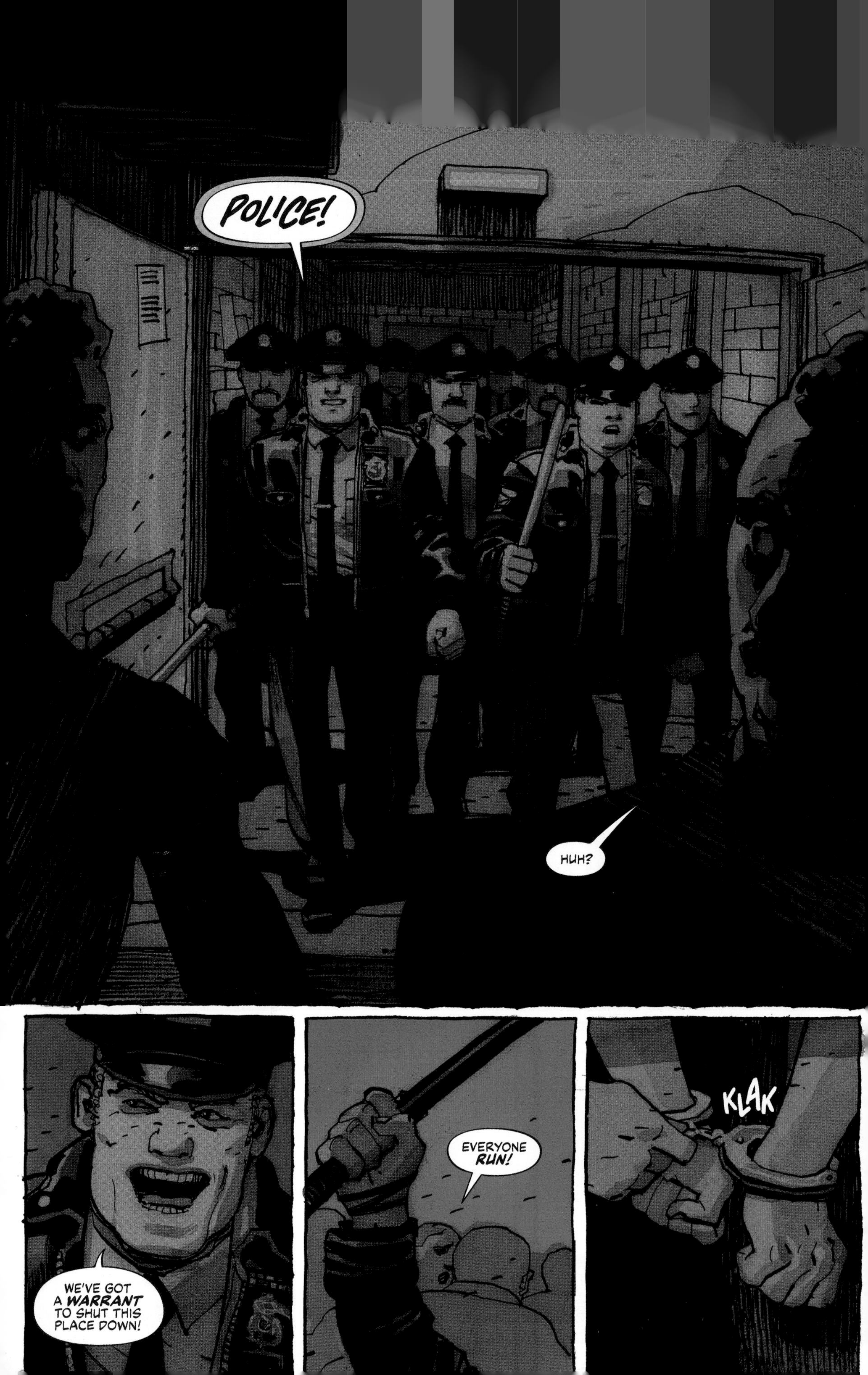
POLICE!
HUH?
WE'VE GOT A WARRANT TO SHUT THIS PLACE DOWN!
EVERYONE RUN!
KLAK

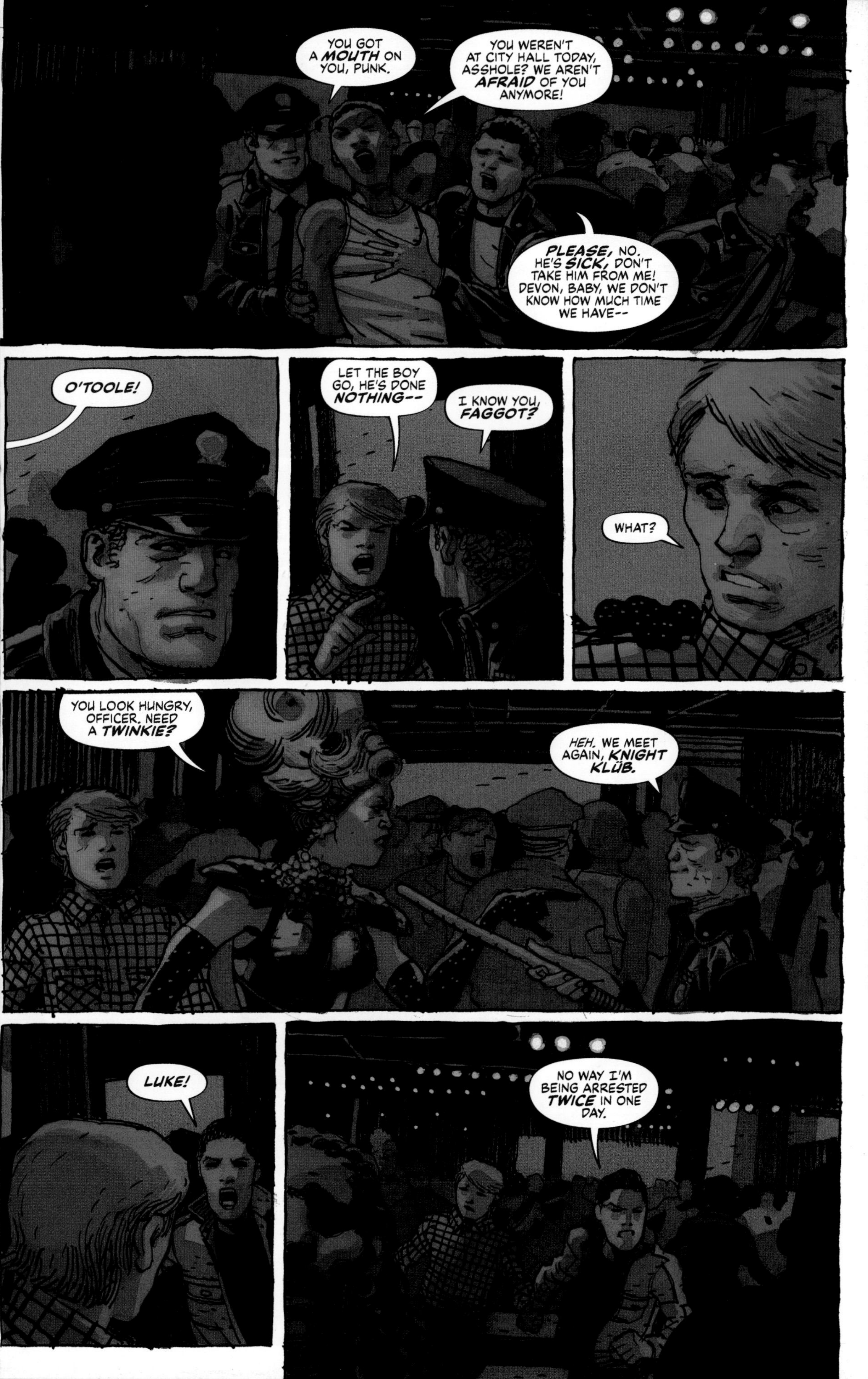
YOU GOT A MOUTH ON YOU, PUNK.
YOU WEREN'T AT CITY HALL TODAY, ASSHOLE? WE AREN'T AFRAID OF YOU ANYMORE!
PLEASE, NO. HE'S SICK, DON'T TAKE HIM FROM ME! DEVON, BABY, WE DON'T KNOW HOW MUCH TIME WE HAVE--
O'TOOLE!
LET THE BOY GO, HE'S DONE NOTHING--
I KNOW YOU, FAGGOT?
WHAT?
YOU LOOK HUNGRY, OFFICER. NEED A TWINKIE?
HEH. WE MEET AGAIN, KNIGHT KLÜB.
LUKE!
NO WAY I'M BEING ARRESTED TWICE IN ONE DAY.

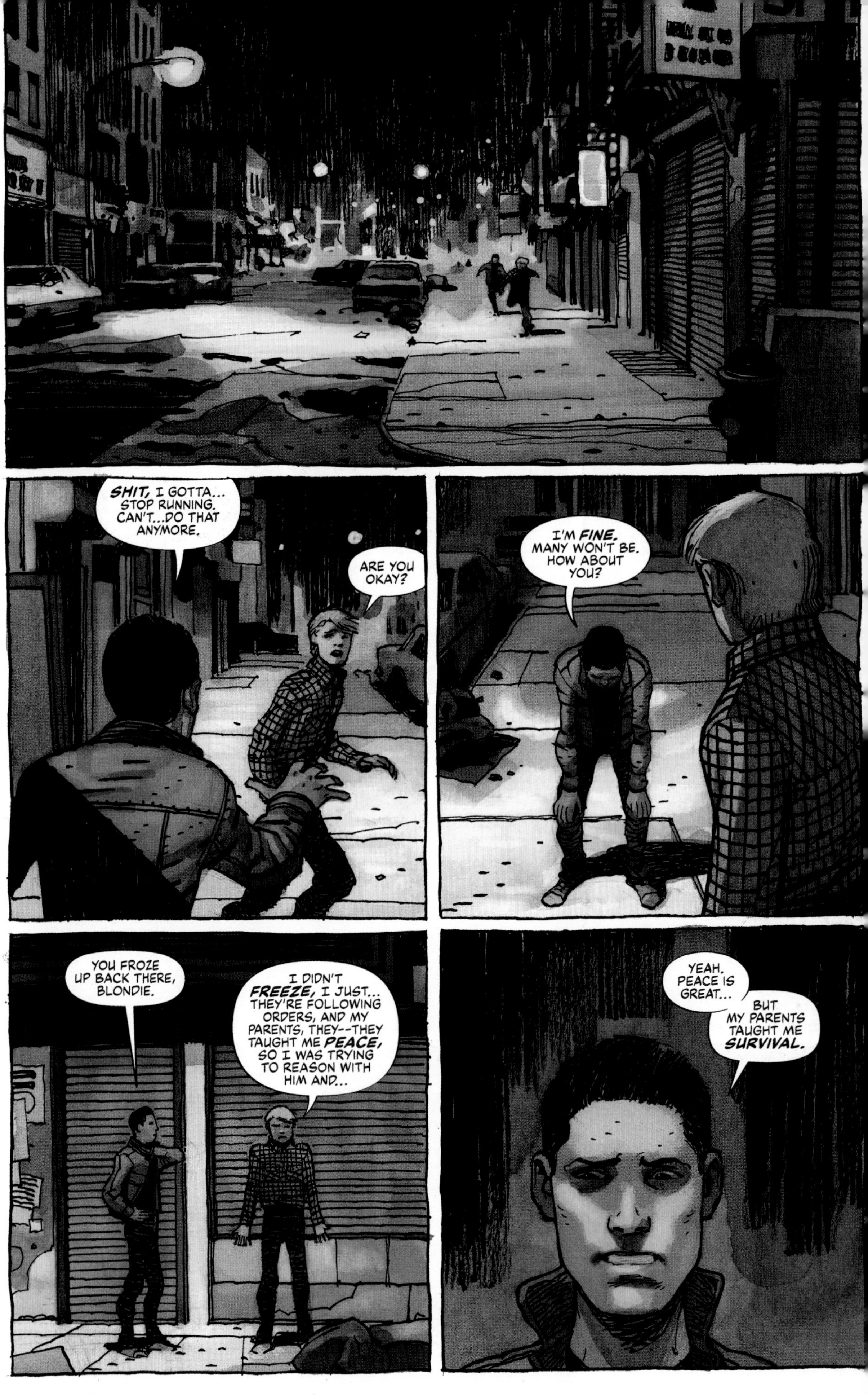
SHIT, I GOTTA... STOP RUNNING. CAN'T...DO THAT ANYMORE.
ARE YOU OKAY?
I'M FINE. MANY WON'T BE. HOW ABOUT YOU?
YOU FROZE UP BACK THERE, BLONDIE.
I DIDN'T FREEZE, I JUST... THEY'RE FOLLOWING ORDERS, AND MY PARENTS, THEY--THEY TAUGHT ME PEACE, SO I WAS TRYING TO REASON WITH HIM AND...
YEAH. PEACE IS GREAT...
BUT MY PARENTS TAUGHT ME SURVIVAL.

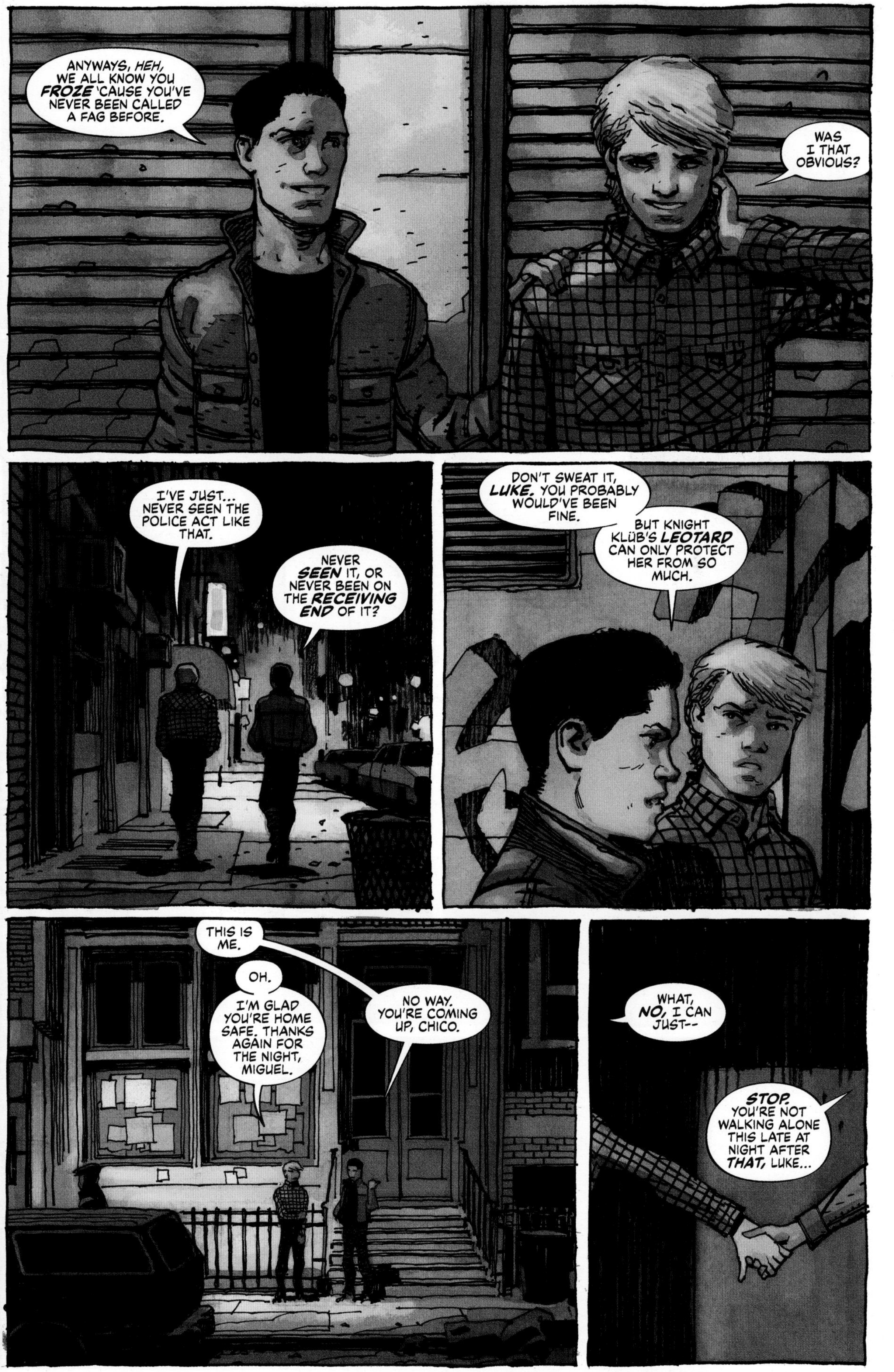

ANYWAYS, HEH, WE ALL KNOW YOU FROZE 'CAUSE YOU'VE NEVER BEEN CALLED A FAG BEFORE.
WAS I THAT OBVIOUS?
I'VE JUST... NEVER SEEN THE POLICE ACT LIKE THAT.
NEVER SEEN IT, OR NEVER BEEN ON THE RECEIVING END OF IT?
DON'T SWEAT IT, LUKE. YOU PROBABLY WOULD'VE BEEN FINE.
BUT KNIGHT KLÜB'S LEOTARD CAN ONLY PROTECT HER FROM SO MUCH.
THIS IS ME.
OH.
I'M GLAD YOU'RE HOME SAFE. THANKS AGAIN FOR THE NIGHT, MIGUEL.
NO WAY. YOU'RE COMING UP, CHICO.
WHAT, NO, I CAN JUST--
STOP. YOU'RE NOT WALKING ALONE THIS LATE AT NIGHT AFTER THAT, LUKE...

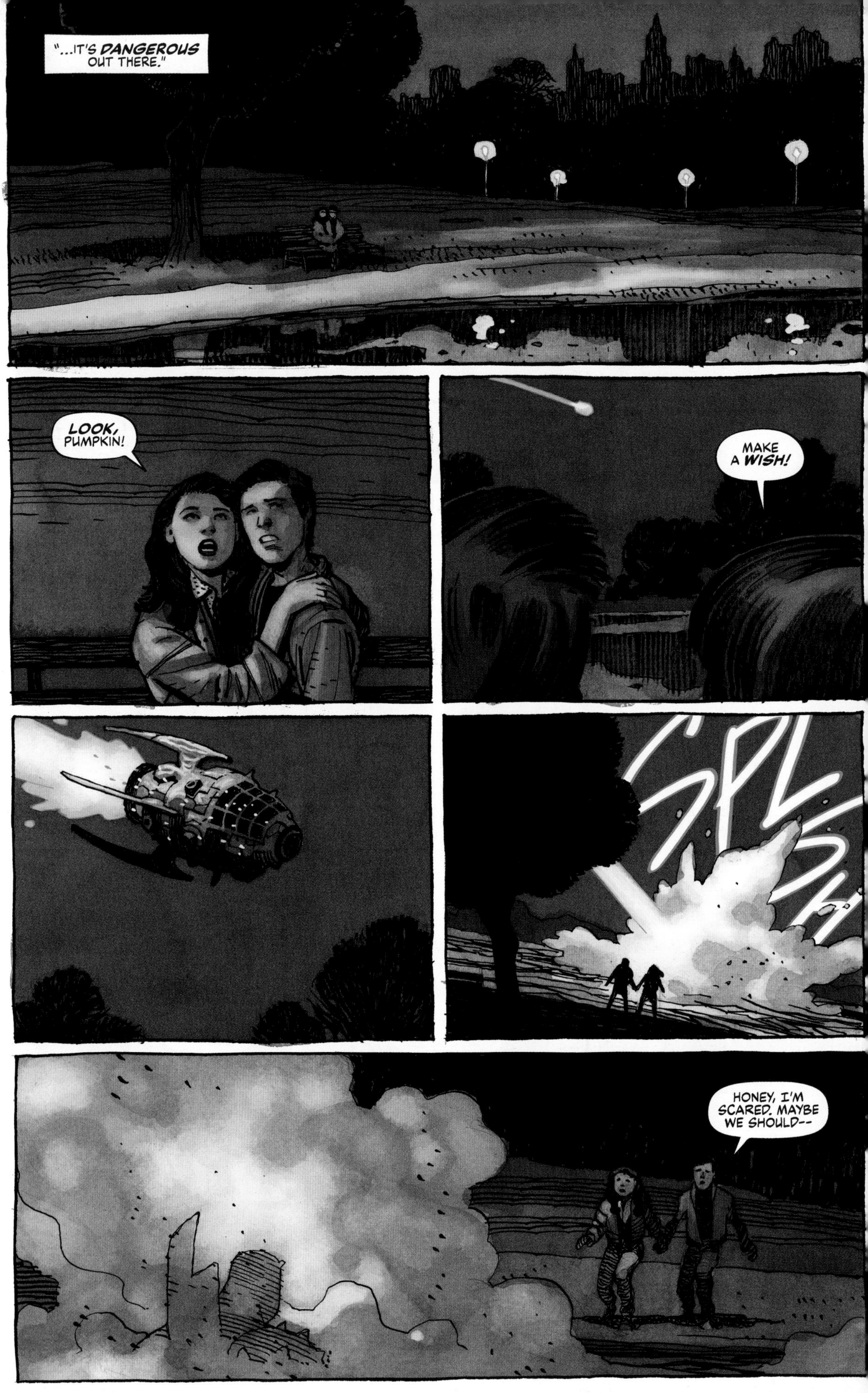
"...IT'S DANGEROUS OUT THERE."
LOOK, PUMPKIN!
MAKE A WISH!
SPLSH
HONEY, I'M SCARED. MAYBE WE SHOULD--

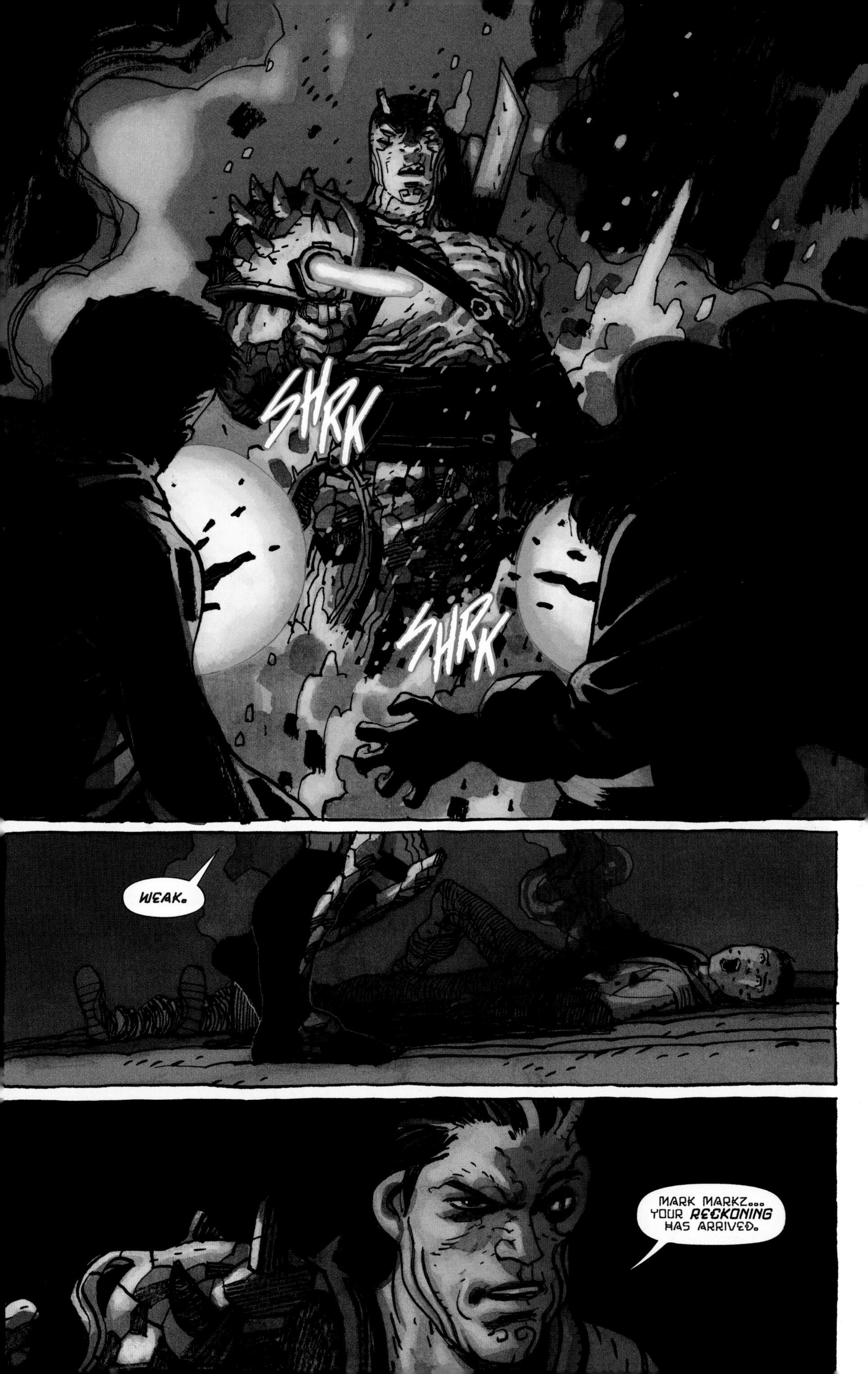
SHRK
SHRK
WEAK.
MARK MARKZ... YOUR RECKONING HAS ARRIVED.

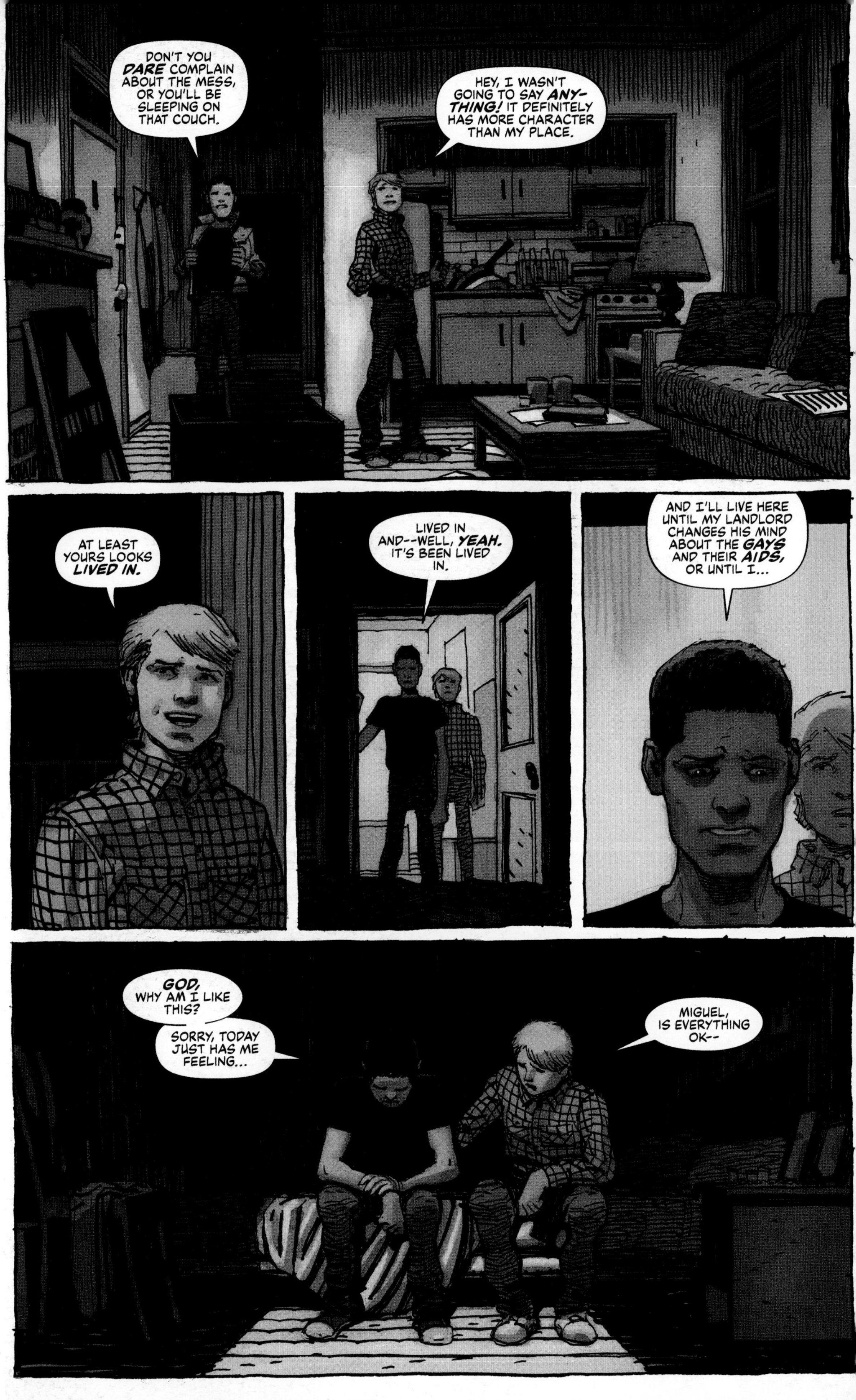
DON'T YOU DARE COMPLAIN ABOUT THE MESS, OR YOU'LL BE SLEEPING ON THAT COUCH.
HEY, I WASN'T GOING TO SAY ANY-THING! IT DEFINITELY HAS MORE CHARACTER THAN MY PLACE.
AT LEAST YOURS LOOKS LIVED IN.
LIVED IN AND--WELL, YEAH. IT'S BEEN LIVED IN.
AND I'LL LIVE HERE UNTIL MY LANDLORD CHANGES HIS MIND ABOUT THE GAYS AND THEIR AIDS, OR UNTIL I...
GOD, WHY AM I LIKE THIS?
SORRY, TODAY JUST HAS ME FEELING...
MIGUEL, IS EVERYTHING OK--

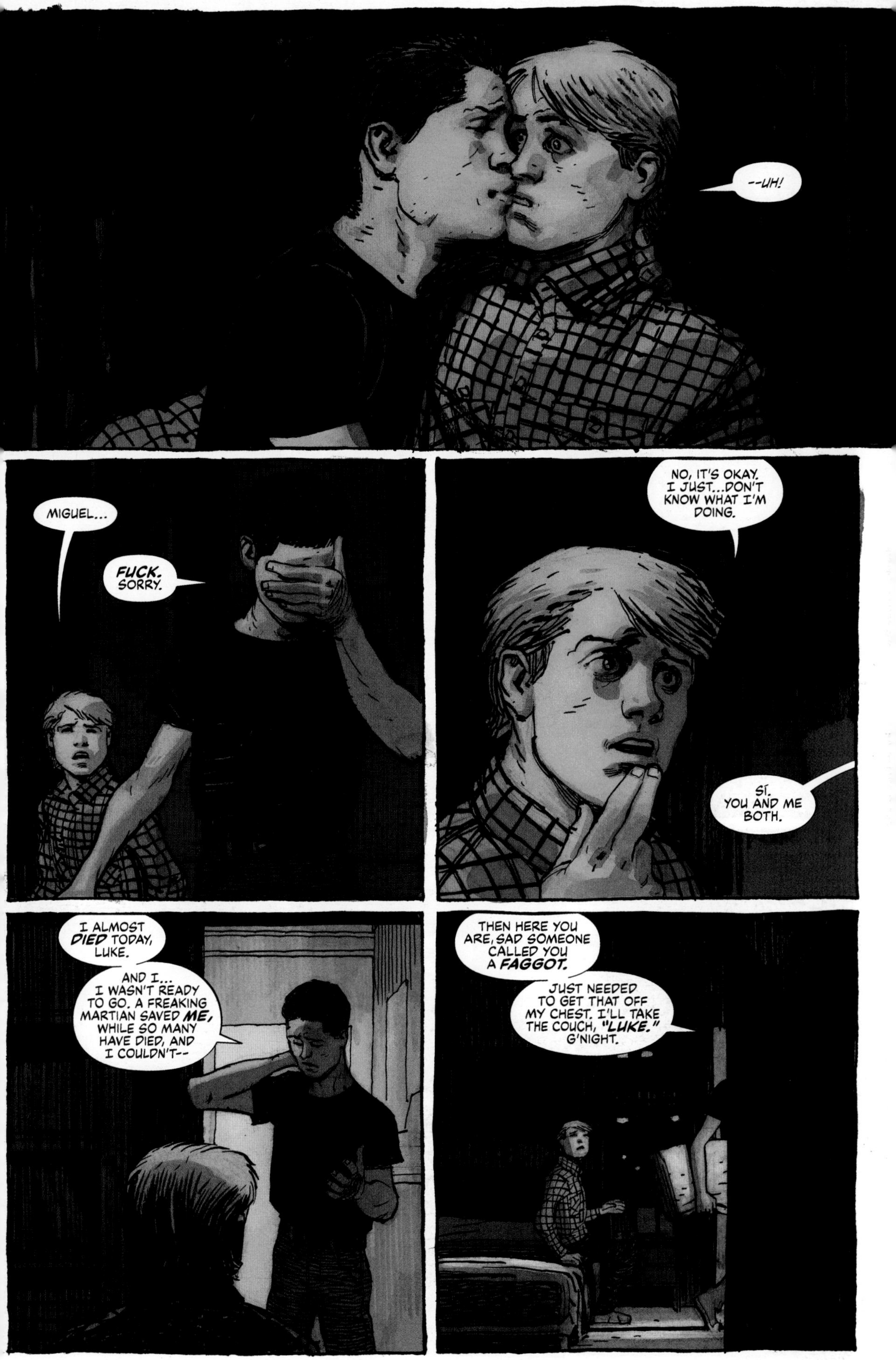
--UH!
MIGUEL...
FUCK. SORRY.
NO, IT'S OKAY. I JUST...DON'T KNOW WHAT I'M DOING.
SÍ. YOU AND ME BOTH.
I ALMOST DIED TODAY, LUKE.
AND I... I WASN'T READY TO GO. A FREAKING MARTIAN SAVED ME, WHILE SO MANY HAVE DIED, AND I COULDN'T--
THEN HERE YOU ARE, SAD SOMEONE CALLED YOU A FAGGOT.
JUST NEEDED TO GET THAT OFF MY CHEST. I'LL TAKE THE COUCH, "LUKE." G'NIGHT.

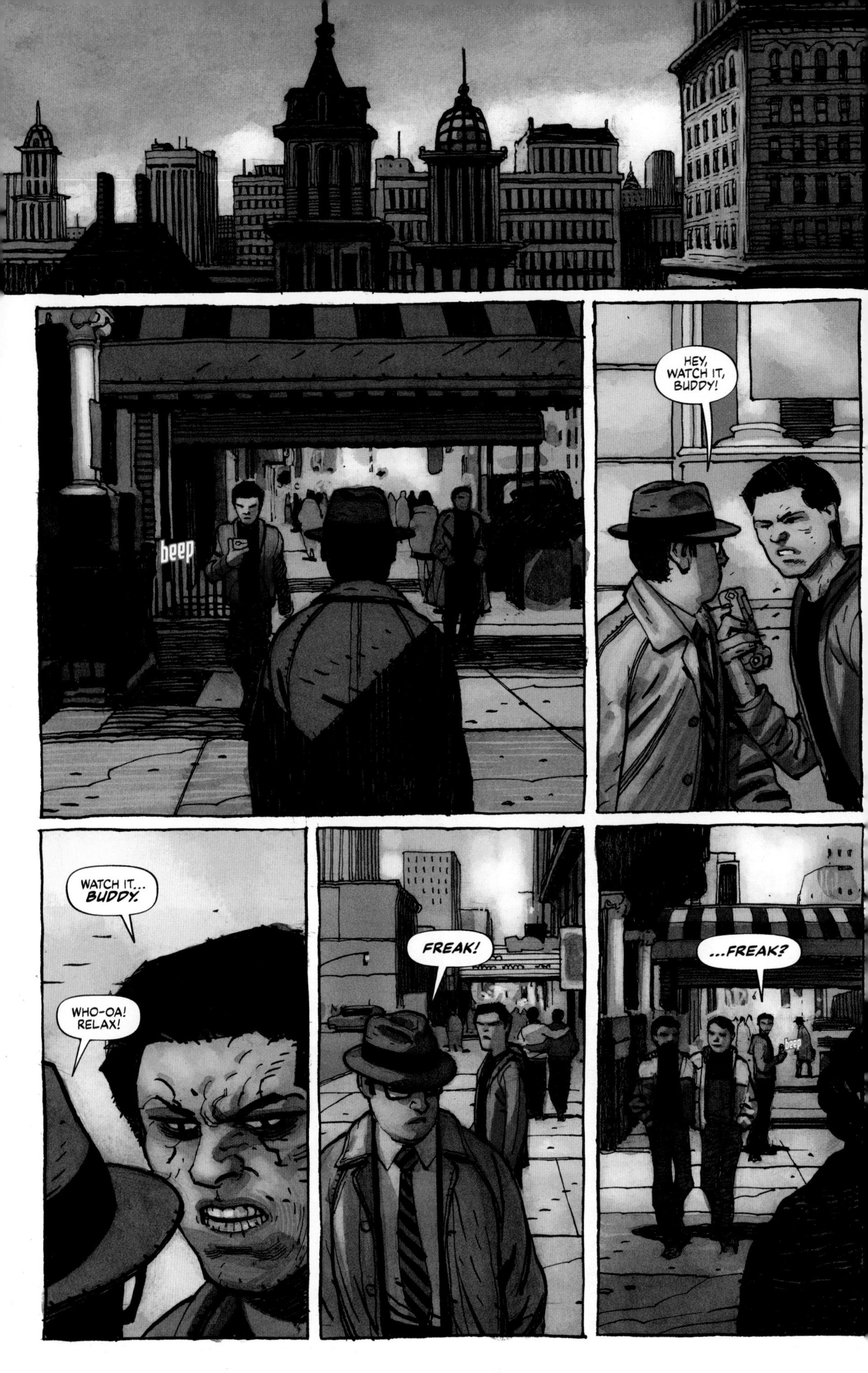

beep
HEY, WATCH IT, BUDDY!
WATCH IT... BUDDY.
WHO-OA! RELAX!
FREAK!
...FREAK?
beep

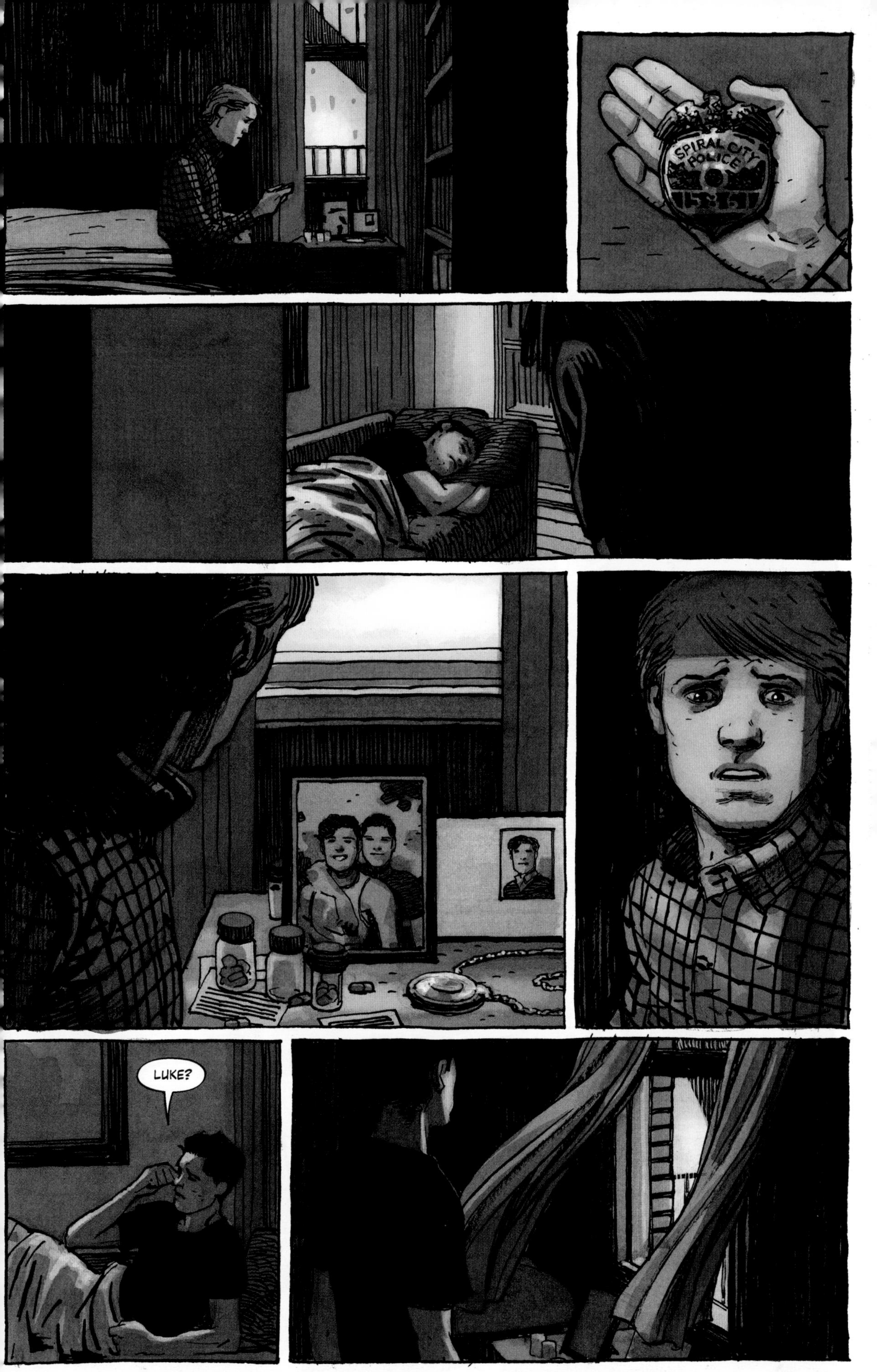
SPIRAL CITY POLICE
LUKE?

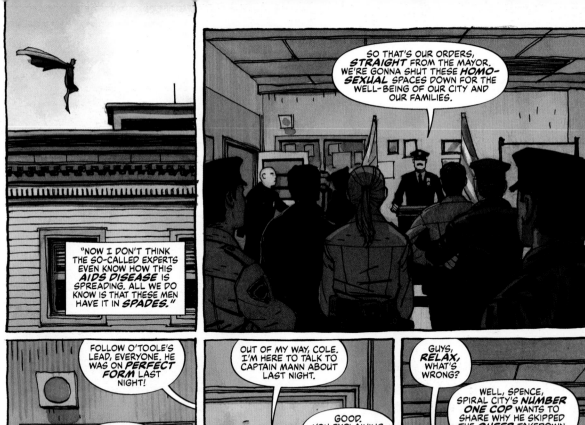

SO THAT'S OUR ORDERS, *STRAIGHT* FROM THE MAYOR. WE'RE GONNA SHUT THESE *HOMO-SEXUAL* SPACES DOWN FOR THE WELL-BEING OF OUR CITY AND OUR FAMILIES.

"NOW I DON'T THINK THE SO-CALLED EXPERTS EVEN KNOW HOW THIS *AIDS DISEASE* IS SPREADING. ALL WE DO KNOW IS THAT THESE MEN HAVE IT IN *SPADES.*"

FOLLOW O'TOOLE'S LEAD, EVERYONE. HE WAS ON *PERFECT FORM* LAST NIGHT!

THE HELL, MARKZ?

OUT OF MY WAY, COLE. I'M HERE TO TALK TO CAPTAIN MANN ABOUT LAST NIGHT.

GOOD. YOU EXPLAINING WHERE YOU WERE, *PARTNER?*

GUYS, *RELAX,* WHAT'S WRONG?

WELL, SPENCE, SPIRAL CITY'S *NUMBER ONE COP* WANTS TO SHARE WHY HE SKIPPED THE *QUEER* TAKEDOWN LAST NIGHT.

SAY ANY MORE, AND I'LL--

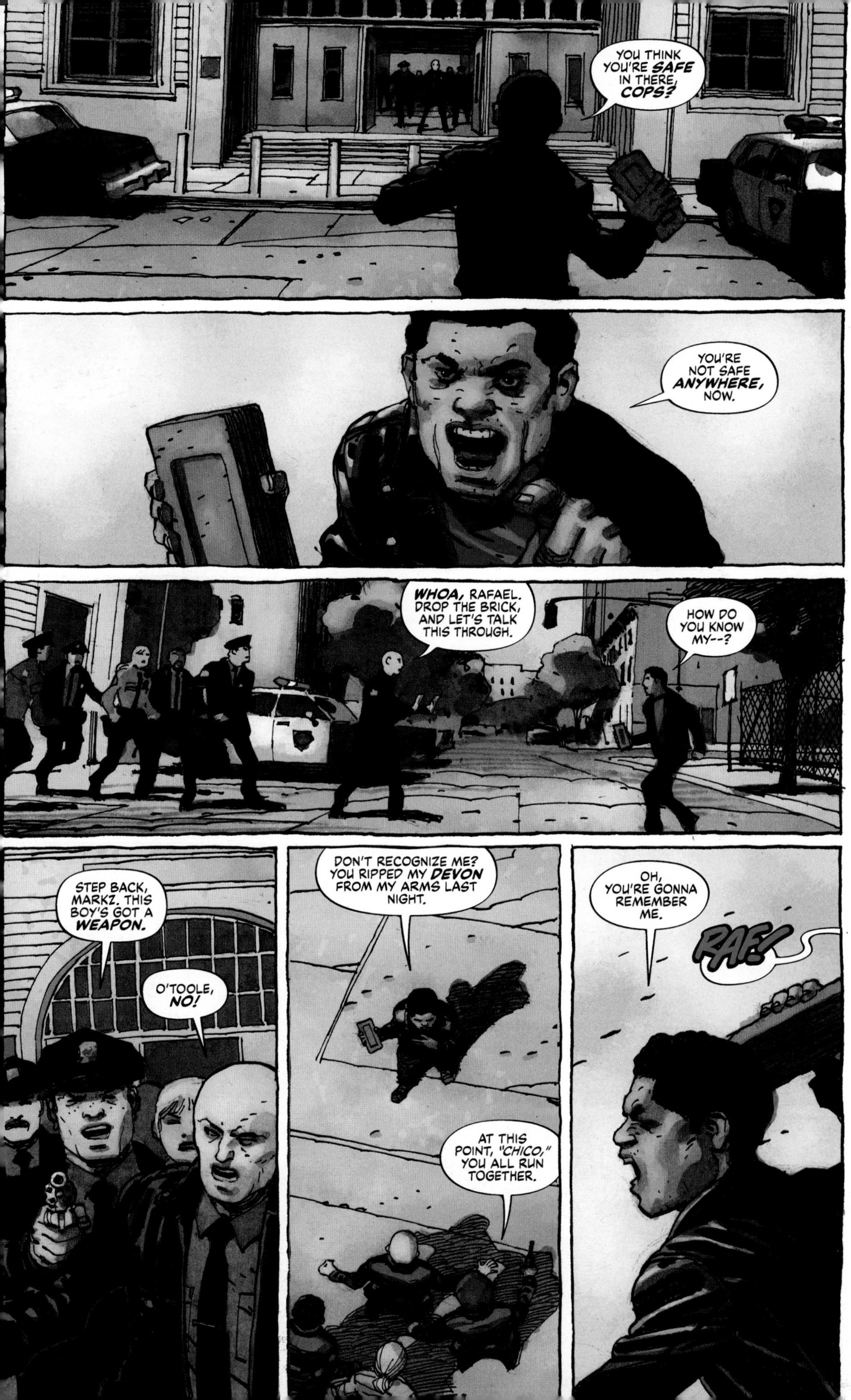
YOU THINK YOU'RE SAFE IN THERE, COPS?
YOU'RE NOT SAFE ANYWHERE, NOW.
WHOA, RAFAEL. DROP THE BRICK, AND LET'S TALK THIS THROUGH.
HOW DO YOU KNOW MY--?
STEP BACK, MARKZ. THIS BOY'S GOT A WEAPON.
O'TOOLE, NO!
DON'T RECOGNIZE ME? YOU RIPPED MY DEVON FROM MY ARMS LAST NIGHT.
AT THIS POINT, "CHICO," YOU ALL RUN TOGETHER.
OH, YOU'RE GONNA REMEMBER ME.
RAF!

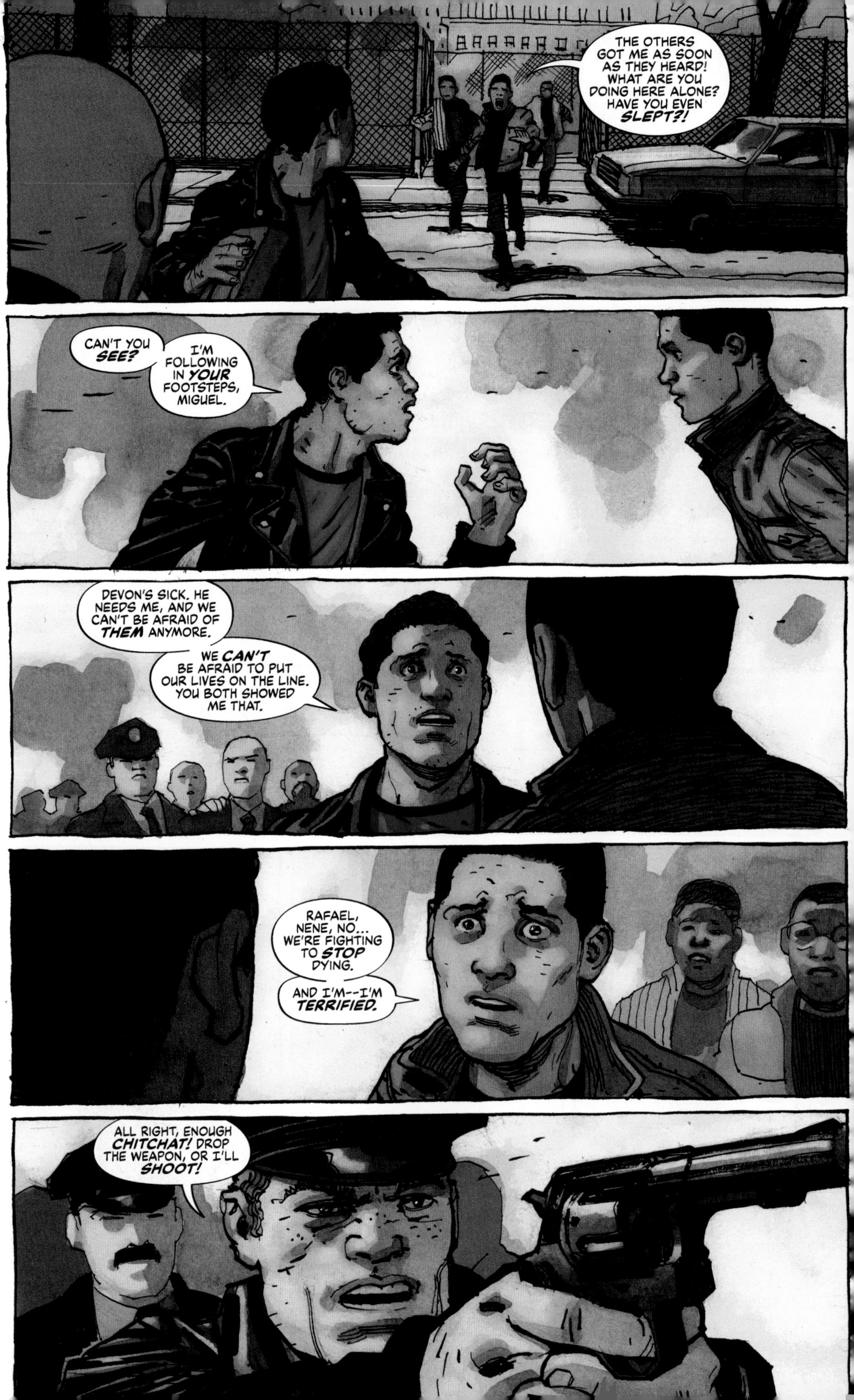
THE OTHERS GOT ME AS SOON AS THEY HEARD! WHAT ARE YOU DOING HERE ALONE? HAVE YOU EVEN SLEPT?!
CAN'T YOU SEE?
I'M FOLLOWING IN YOUR FOOTSTEPS, MIGUEL.
DEVON'S SICK. HE NEEDS ME, AND WE CAN'T BE AFRAID OF THEM ANYMORE.
WE CAN'T BE AFRAID TO PUT OUR LIVES ON THE LINE. YOU BOTH SHOWED ME THAT.
RAFAEL, NENE, NO... WE'RE FIGHTING TO STOP DYING.
AND I'M--I'M TERRIFIED.
ALL RIGHT, ENOUGH CHITCHAT! DROP THE WEAPON, OR I'LL SHOOT!

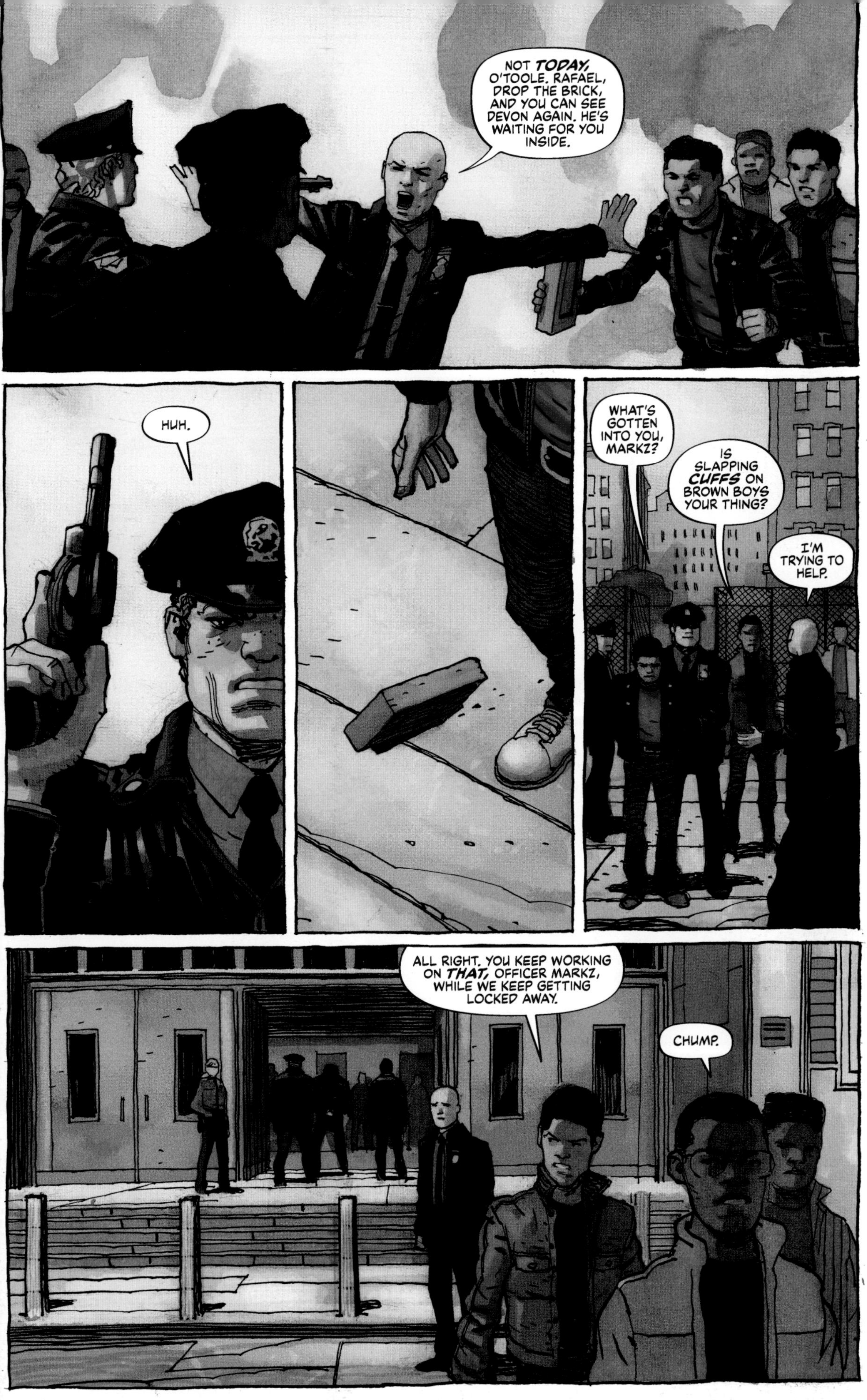
NOT TODAY, O'TOOLE. RAFAEL, DROP THE BRICK, AND YOU CAN SEE DEVON AGAIN. HE'S WAITING FOR YOU INSIDE.
HUH.
WHAT'S GOTTEN INTO YOU, MARKZ?
IS SLAPPING CUFFS ON BROWN BOYS YOUR THING?
I'M TRYING TO HELP.
ALL RIGHT. YOU KEEP WORKING ON THAT, OFFICER MARKZ, WHILE WE KEEP GETTING LOCKED AWAY.
CHUMP.

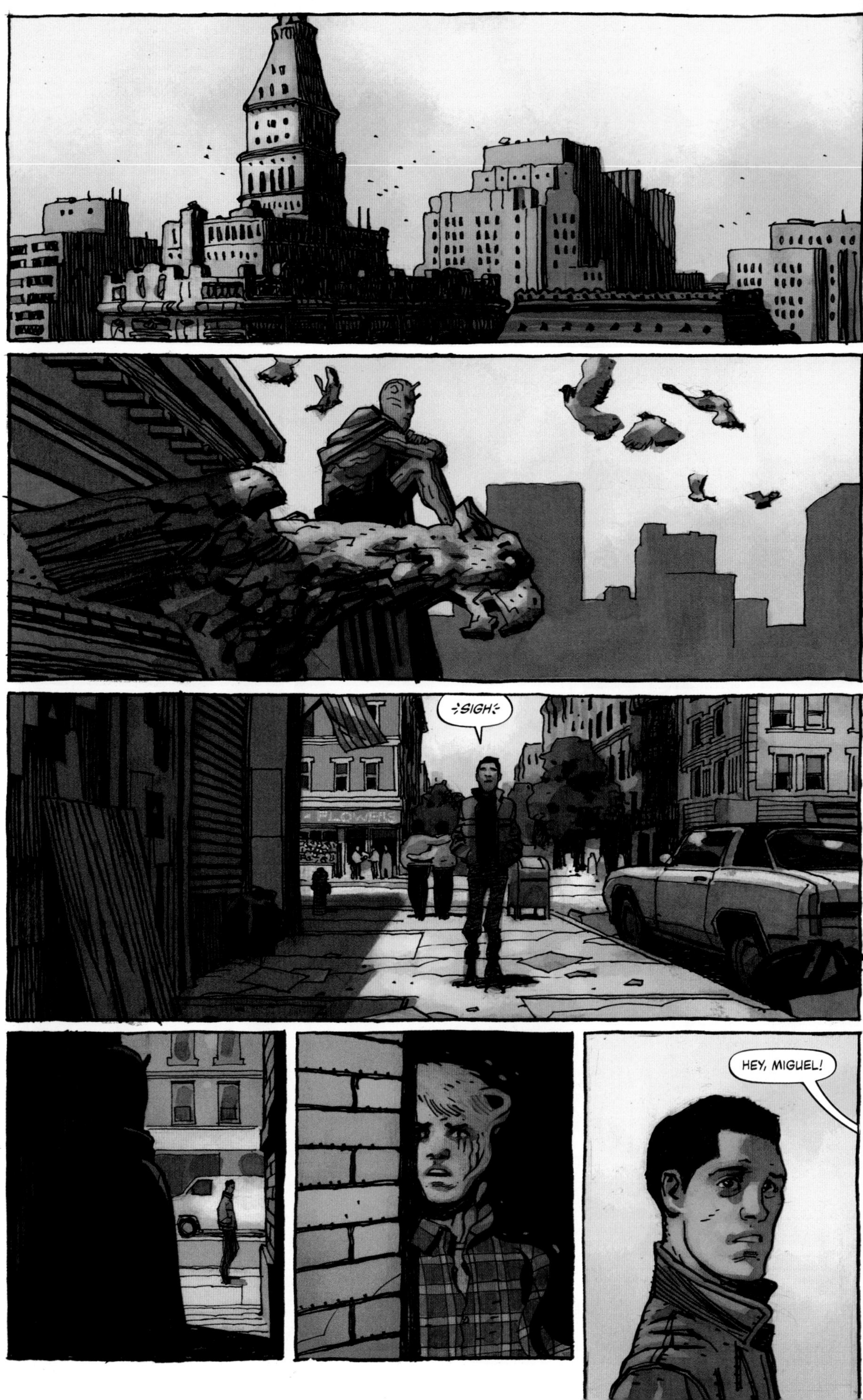
-SIGH-
HEY, MIGUEL!

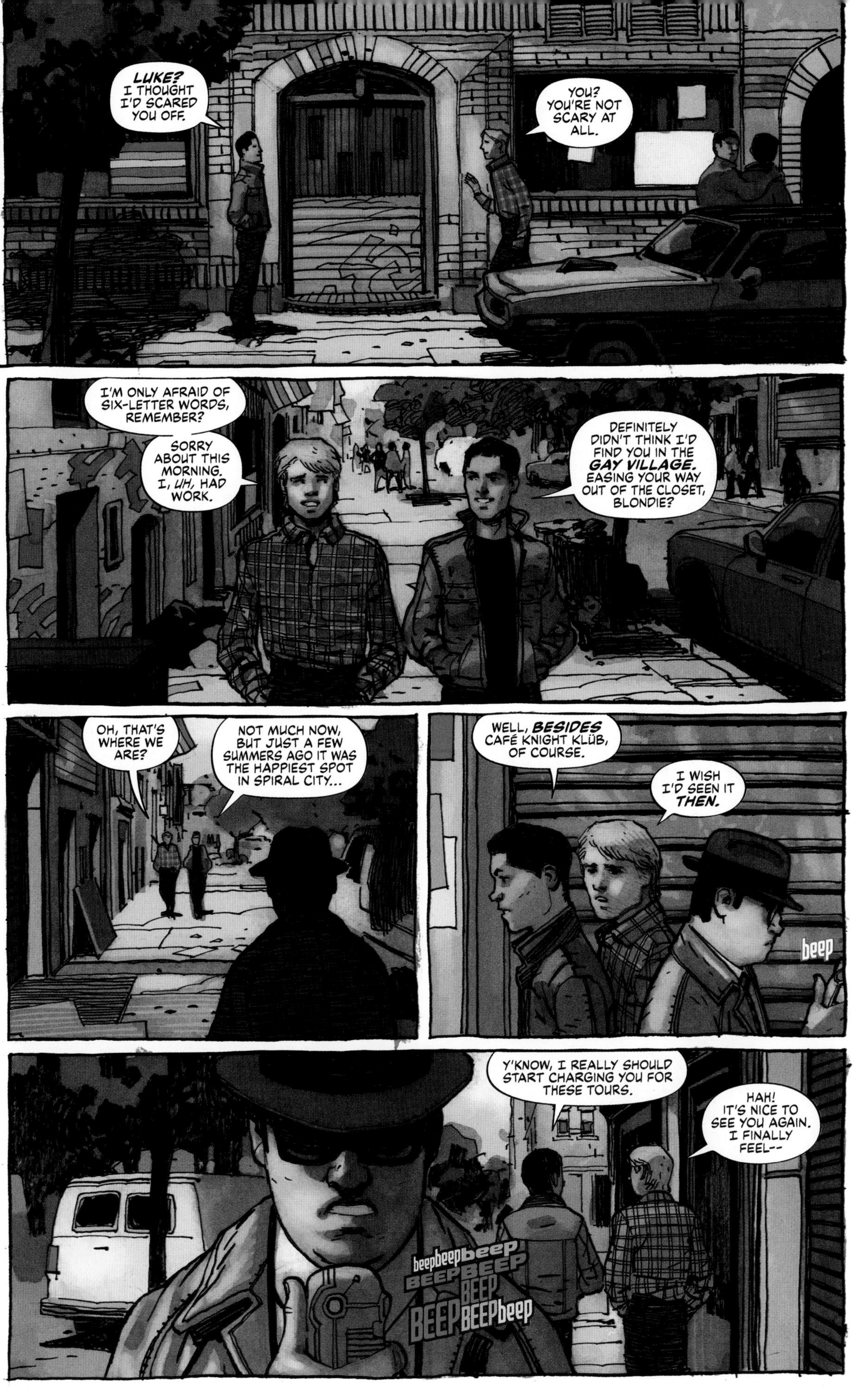
LUKE? I THOUGHT I'D SCARED YOU OFF.
YOU? YOU'RE NOT SCARY AT ALL.
I'M ONLY AFRAID OF SIX-LETTER WORDS, REMEMBER?
SORRY ABOUT THIS MORNING. I, UH, HAD WORK.
DEFINITELY DIDN'T THINK I'D FIND YOU IN THE GAY VILLAGE. EASING YOUR WAY OUT OF THE CLOSET, BLONDIE?
OH, THAT'S WHERE WE ARE?
NOT MUCH NOW, BUT JUST A FEW SUMMERS AGO IT WAS THE HAPPIEST SPOT IN SPIRAL CITY...
WELL, BESIDES CAFÉ KNIGHT KLÜB, OF COURSE.
I WISH I'D SEEN IT THEN.
beep
Y'KNOW, I REALLY SHOULD START CHARGING YOU FOR THESE TOURS.
HAH! IT'S NICE TO SEE YOU AGAIN. I FINALLY FEEL--
beepbeepbeep BEEPBEEP BEEP BEEP BEEPbeep

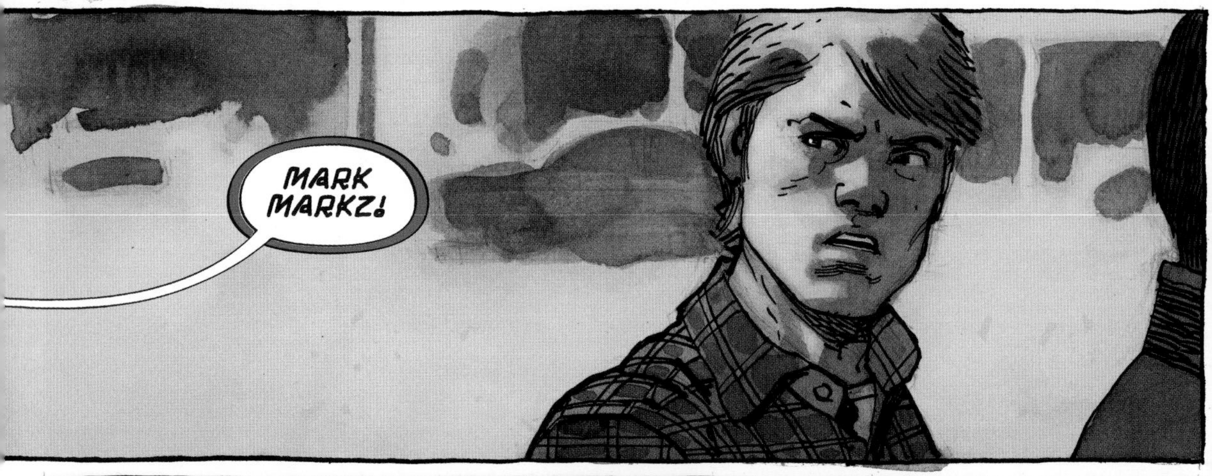
MARK MARKZ!

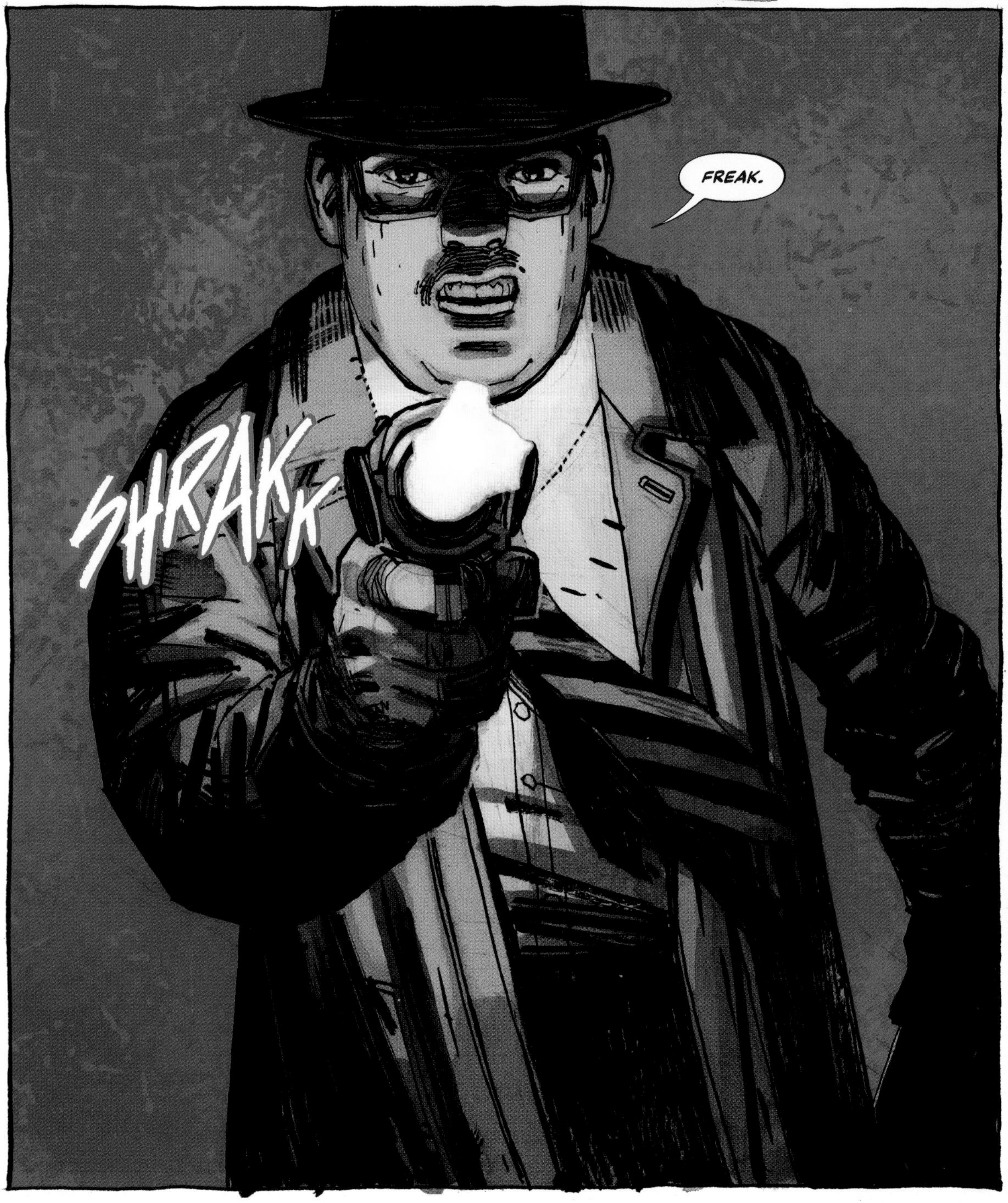
FREAK.
SHRAKK

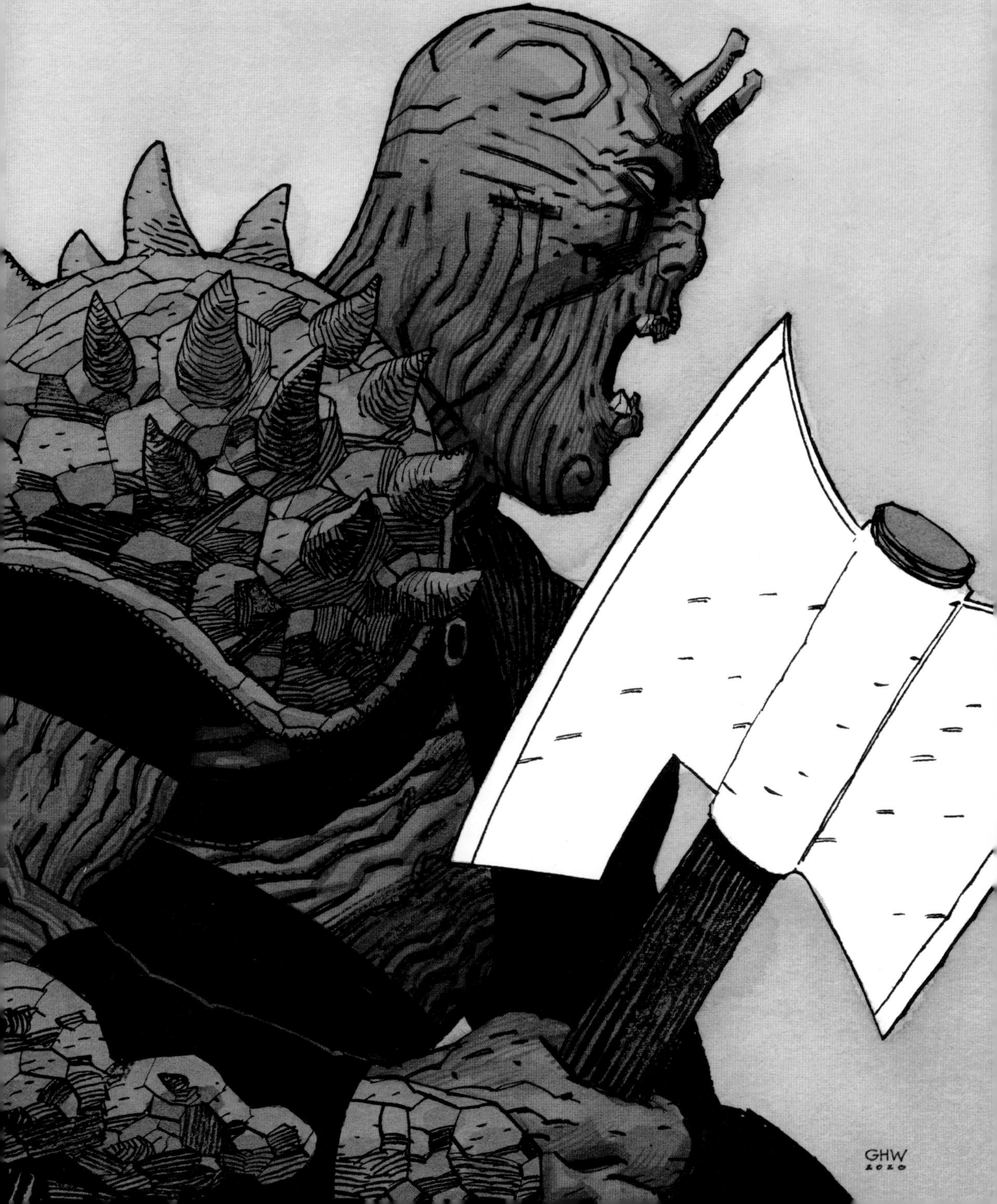
GHW
2020

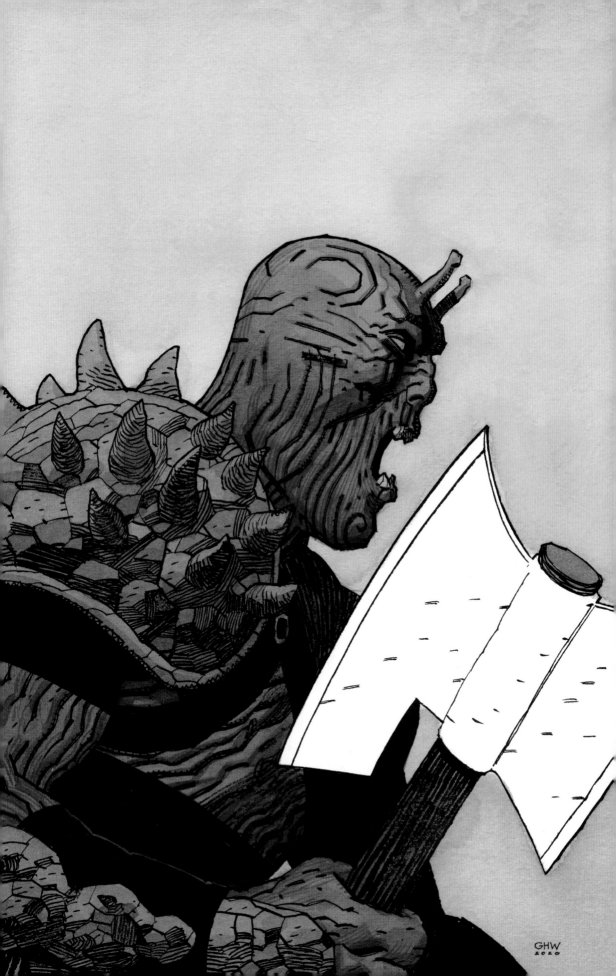

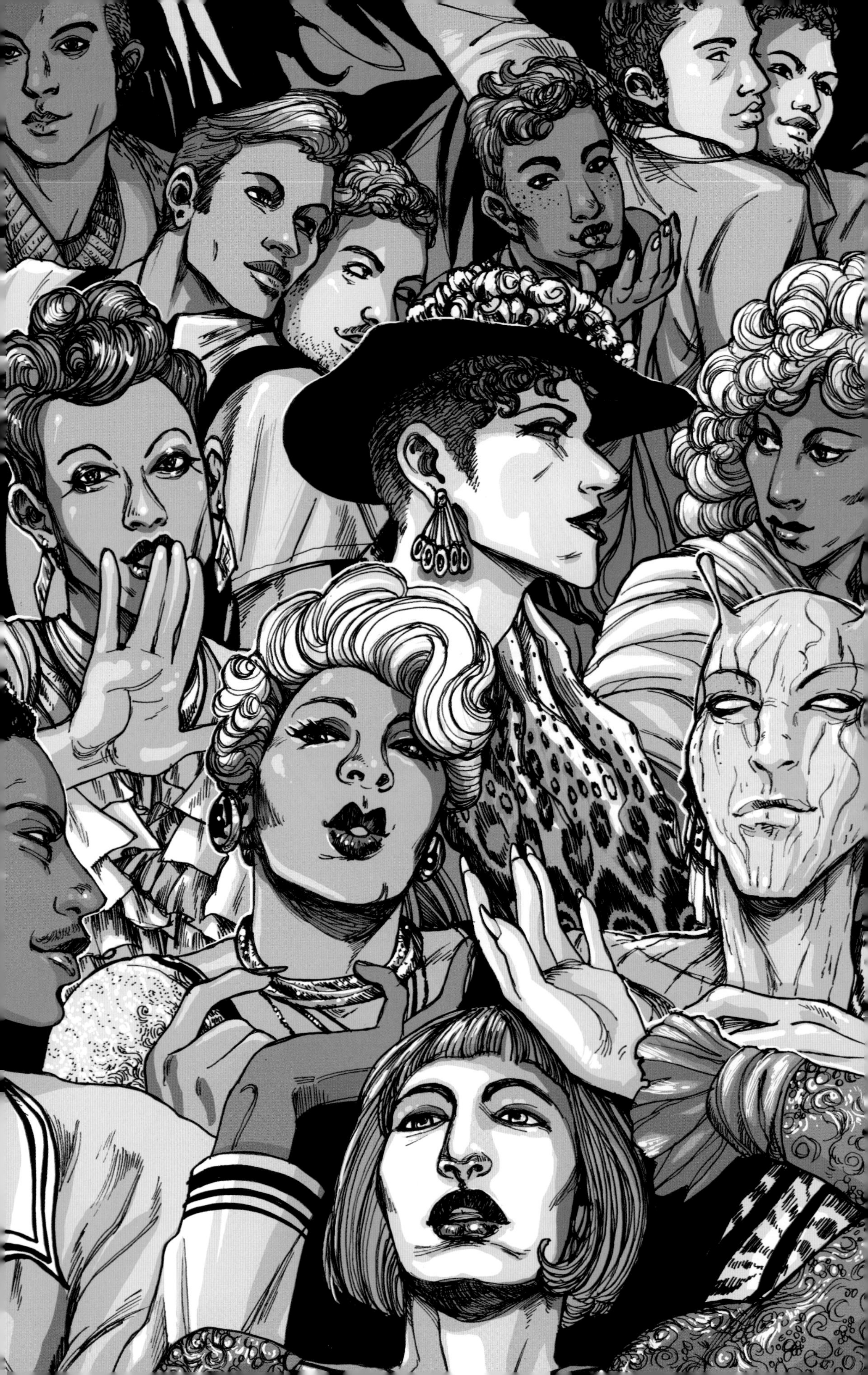

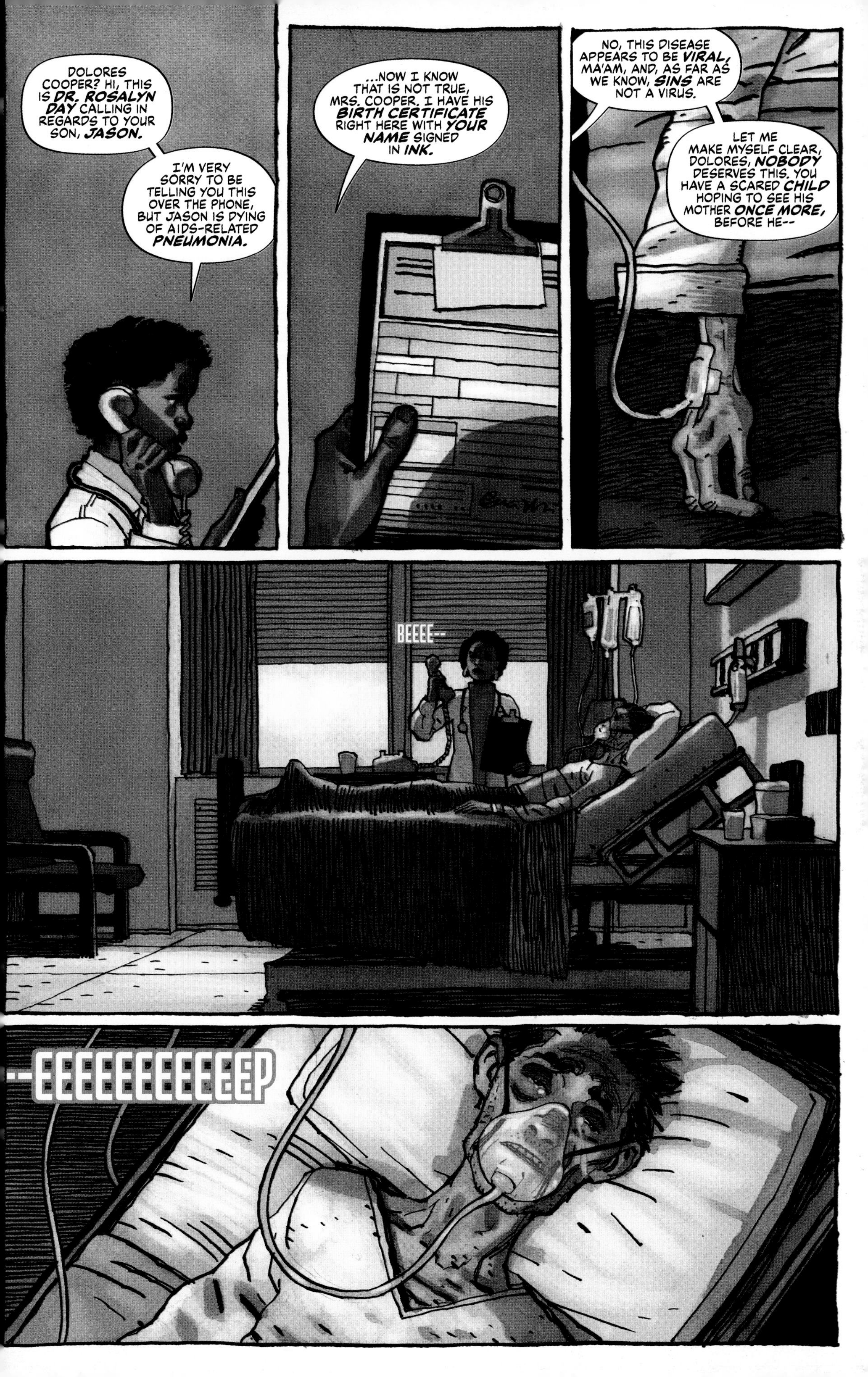
DOLORES COOPER? HI, THIS IS DR. ROSALYN DAY CALLING IN REGARDS TO YOUR SON, JASON.
I'M VERY SORRY TO BE TELLING YOU THIS OVER THE PHONE, BUT JASON IS DYING OF AIDS-RELATED PNEUMONIA.
...NOW I KNOW THAT IS NOT TRUE, MRS. COOPER. I HAVE HIS BIRTH CERTIFICATE RIGHT HERE WITH YOUR NAME SIGNED IN INK.
NO, THIS DISEASE APPEARS TO BE VIRAL, MA'AM, AND, AS FAR AS WE KNOW, SINS ARE NOT A VIRUS.
LET ME MAKE MYSELF CLEAR, DOLORES, NOBODY DESERVES THIS. YOU HAVE A SCARED CHILD HOPING TO SEE HIS MOTHER ONCE MORE, BEFORE HE--
BEEEE--
--EEEEEEEEEEEEP

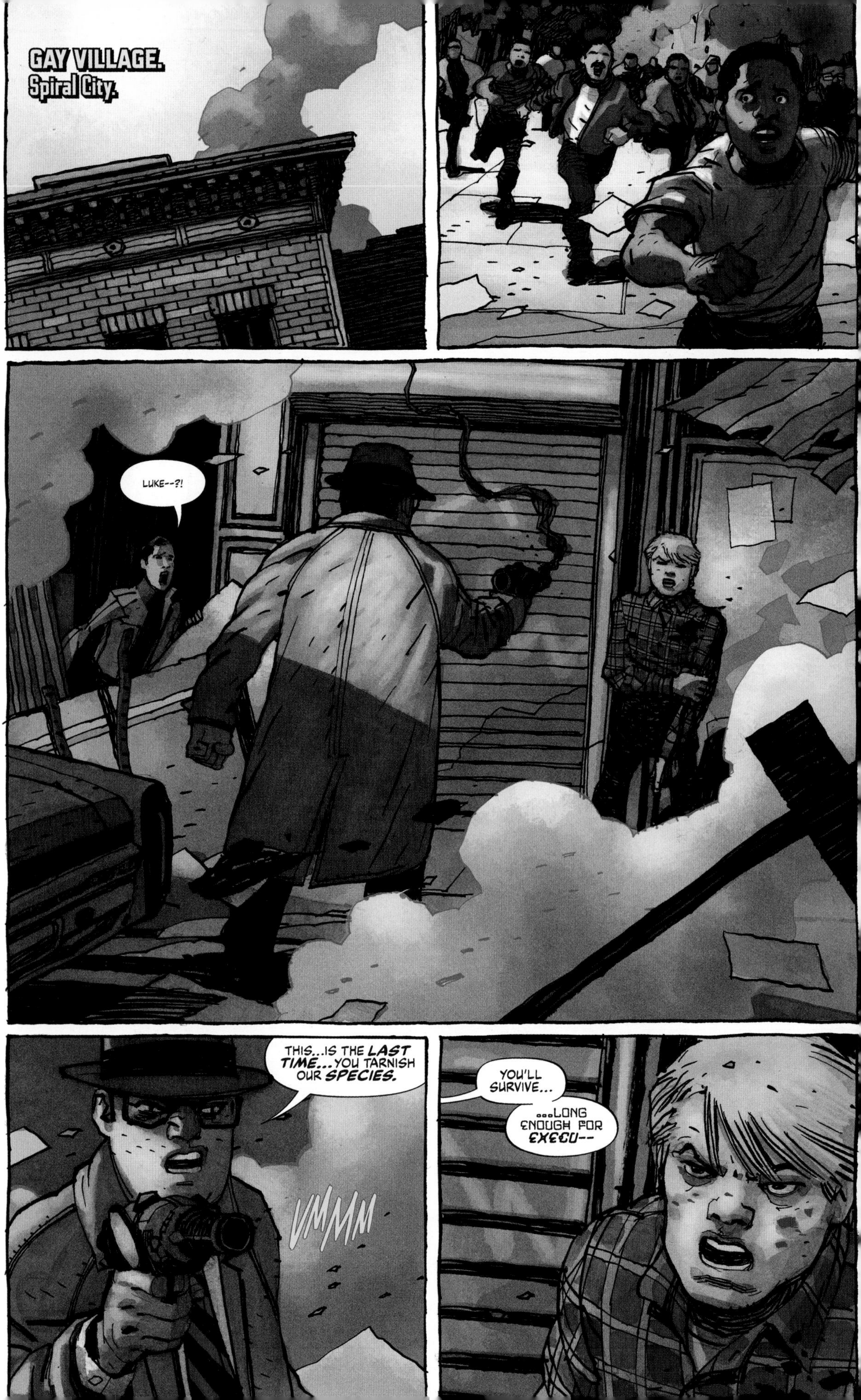
GAY VILLAGE.
Spiral City.
LUKE--?!
THIS...IS THE LAST TIME...YOU TARNISH OUR SPECIES.
VMMM
YOU'LL SURVIVE...
...LONG ENOUGH FOR EXECU--

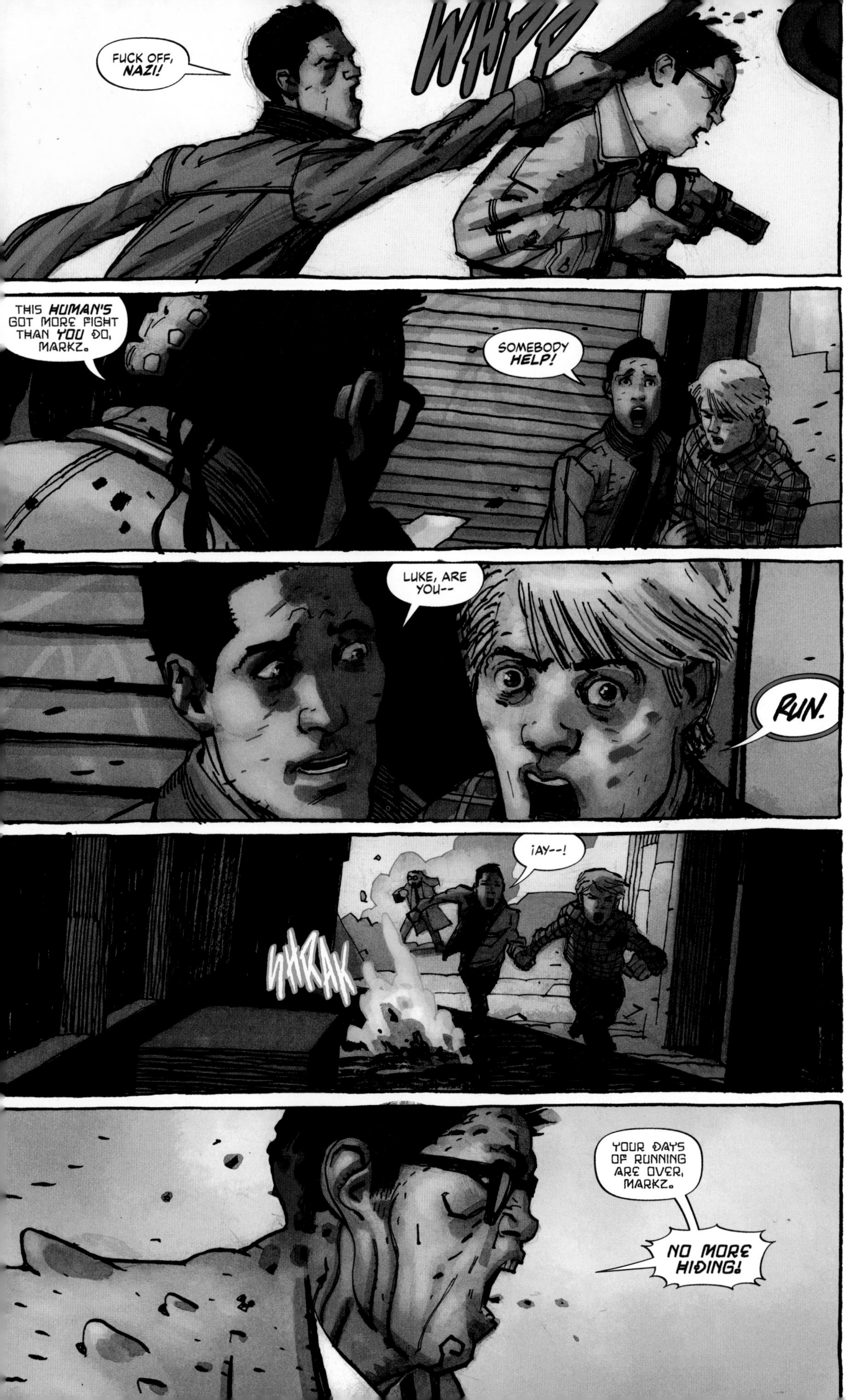

FUCK OFF, NAZI!
WHPP
THIS HUMAN'S GOT MORE FIGHT THAN YOU DO, MARKZ.
SOMEBODY HELP!
LUKE, ARE YOU--
RUN.
¡AY--!
SHRAK
YOUR DAYS OF RUNNING ARE OVER, MARKZ.
NO MORE HIDING!

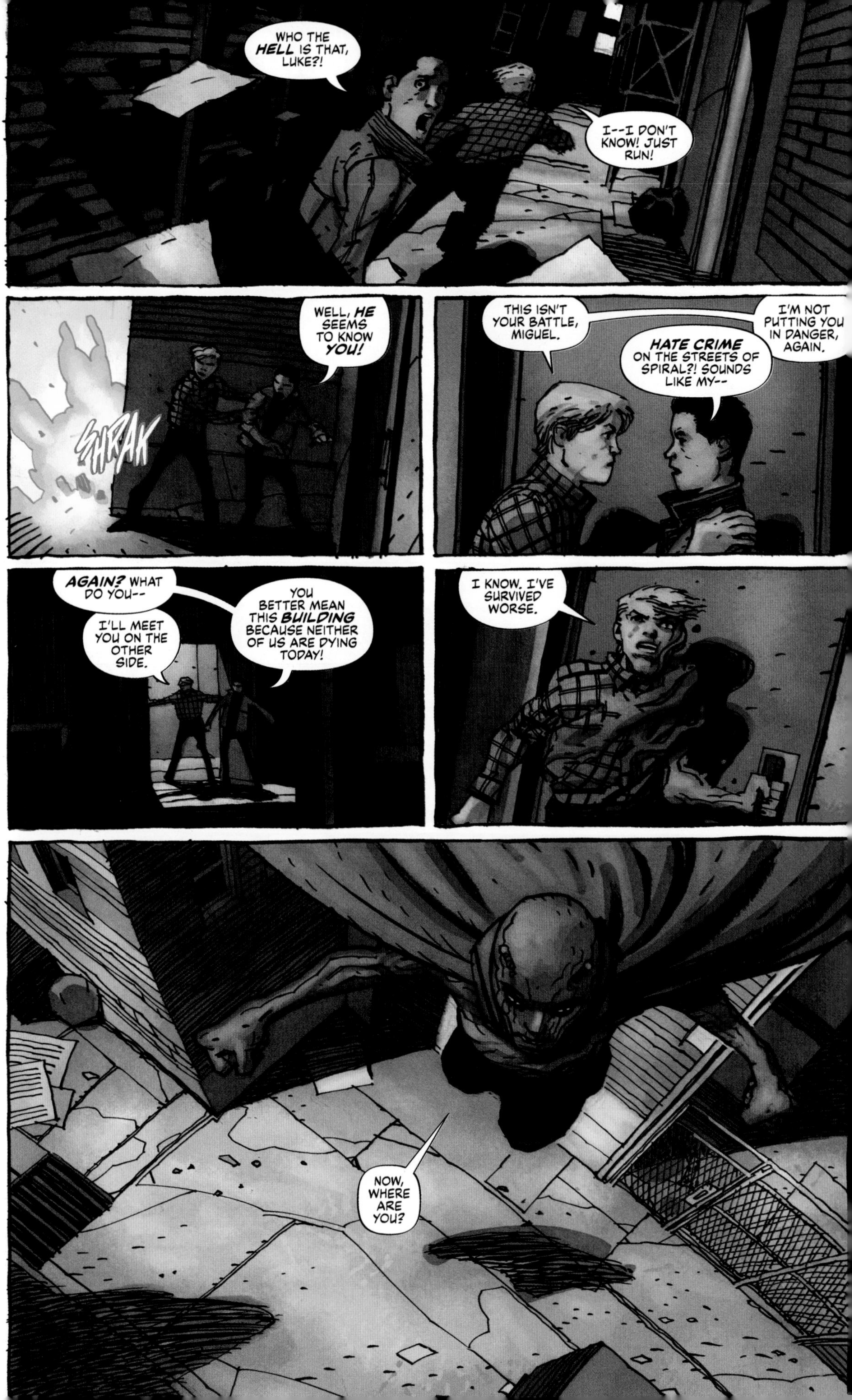
WHO THE **HELL** IS THAT, LUKE?!
I--I DON'T KNOW! JUST RUN!
WELL, **HE** SEEMS TO KNOW **YOU!**
SHRAK
THIS ISN'T YOUR BATTLE, MIGUEL.
I'M NOT PUTTING YOU IN DANGER, AGAIN.
HATE CRIME ON THE STREETS OF SPIRAL?! SOUNDS LIKE MY--
AGAIN? WHAT DO YOU--
I'LL MEET YOU ON THE OTHER SIDE.
YOU BETTER MEAN THIS **BUILDING** BECAUSE NEITHER OF US ARE DYING TODAY!
I KNOW. I'VE SURVIVED WORSE.
NOW, WHERE ARE YOU?

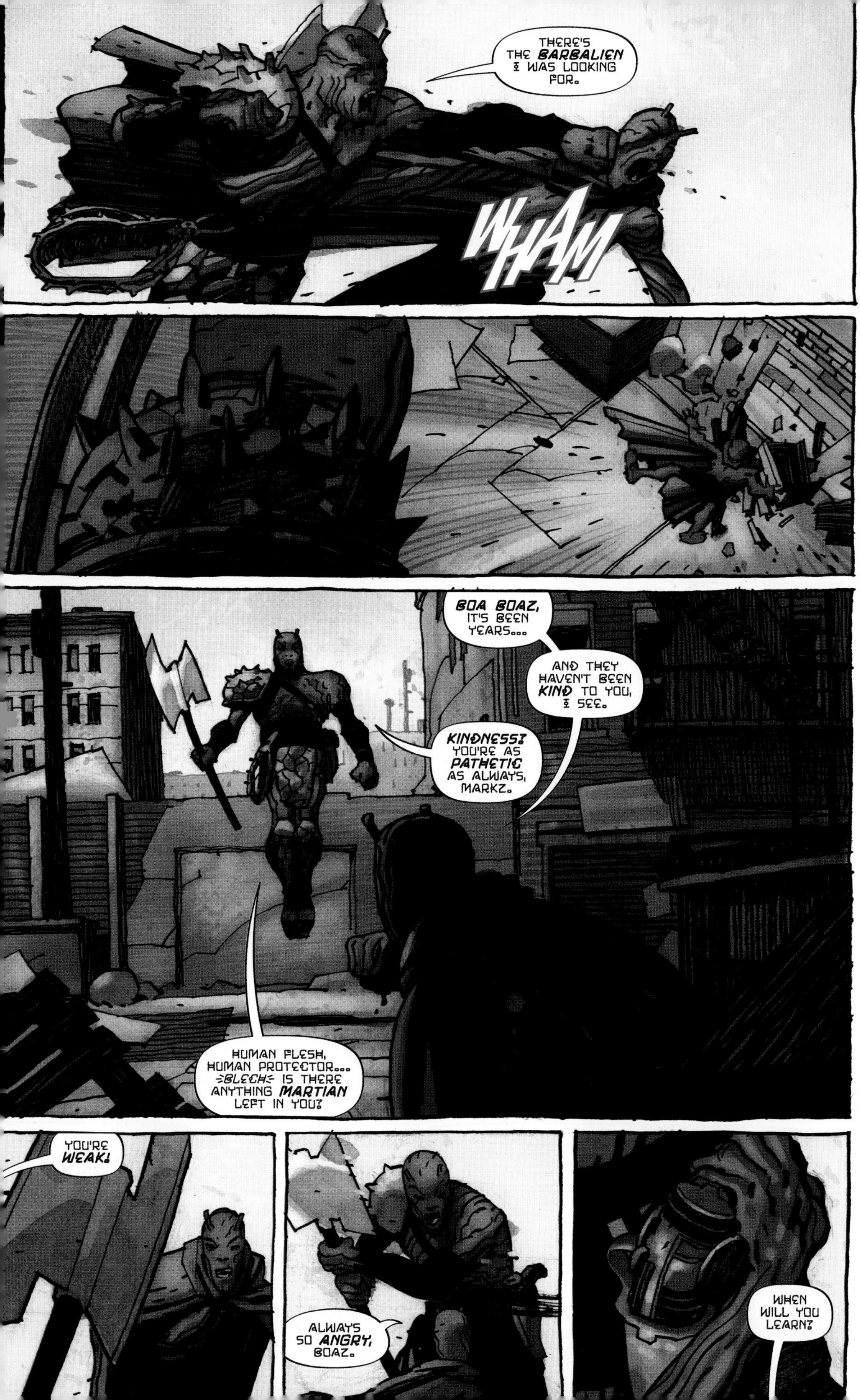

THERE'S THE BARBALIEN I WAS LOOKING FOR.
WHAM
BOA BOAZ, IT'S BEEN YEARS...
AND THEY HAVEN'T BEEN KIND TO YOU, I SEE.
KINDNESS? YOU'RE AS PATHETIC AS ALWAYS, MARKZ.
HUMAN FLESH, HUMAN PROTECTOR... =BLECH= IS THERE ANYTHING MARTIAN LEFT IN YOU?
YOU'RE WEAK!
ALWAYS SO ANGRY, BOAZ.
WHEN WILL YOU LEARN?

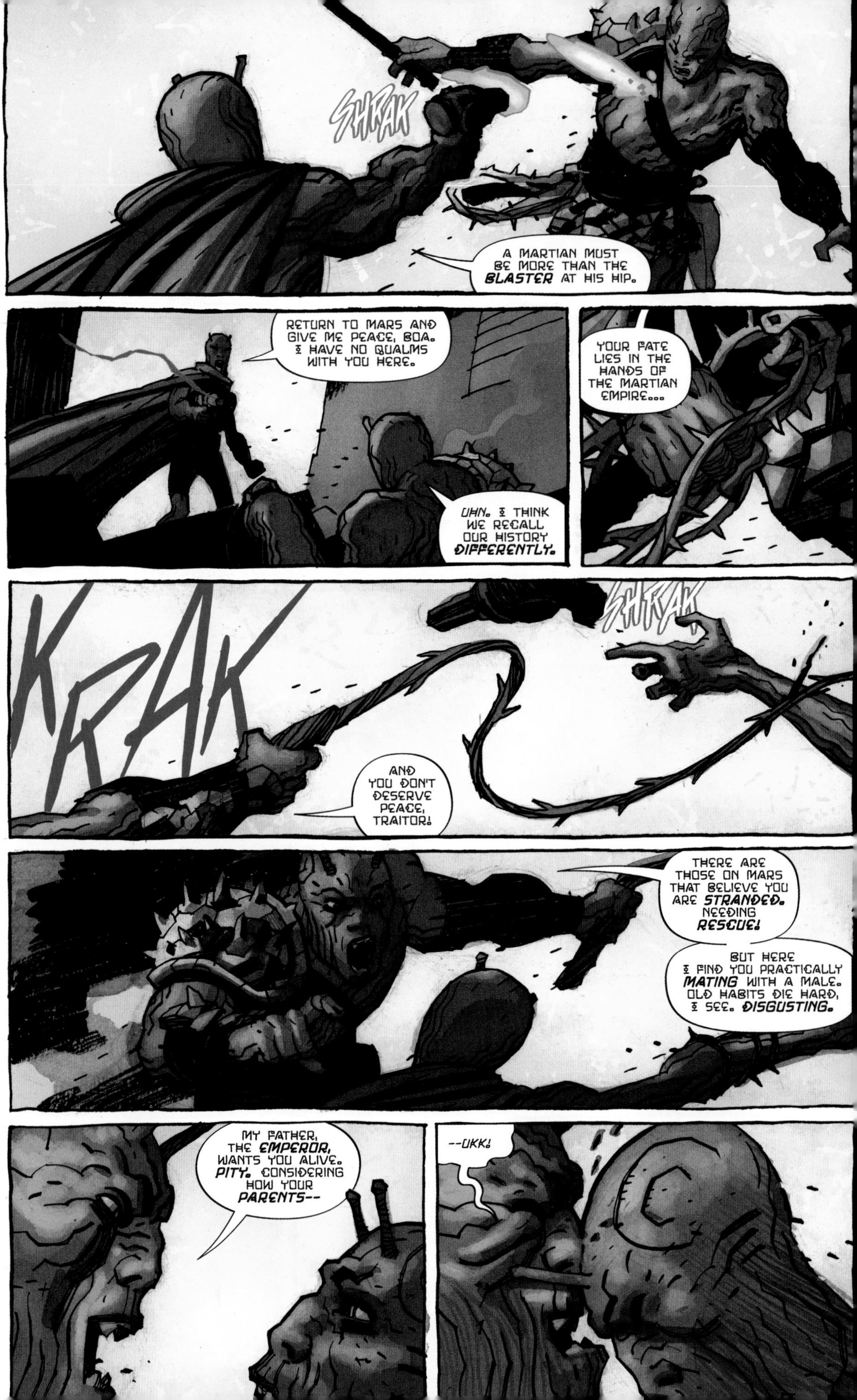

SHRAK
A MARTIAN MUST BE MORE THAN THE BLASTER AT HIS HIP.
RETURN TO MARS AND GIVE ME PEACE, BOA. I HAVE NO QUALMS WITH YOU HERE.
UHN. I THINK WE RECALL OUR HISTORY DIFFERENTLY.
YOUR FATE LIES IN THE HANDS OF THE MARTIAN EMPIRE...
KRAK
SHRAK
AND YOU DON'T DESERVE PEACE, TRAITOR!
THERE ARE THOSE ON MARS THAT BELIEVE YOU ARE STRANDED. NEEDING RESCUE!
BUT HERE I FIND YOU PRACTICALLY MATING WITH A MALE. OLD HABITS DIE HARD, I SEE. DISGUSTING.
MY FATHER, THE EMPEROR, WANTS YOU ALIVE. PITY. CONSIDERING HOW YOUR PARENTS--
--UKK!

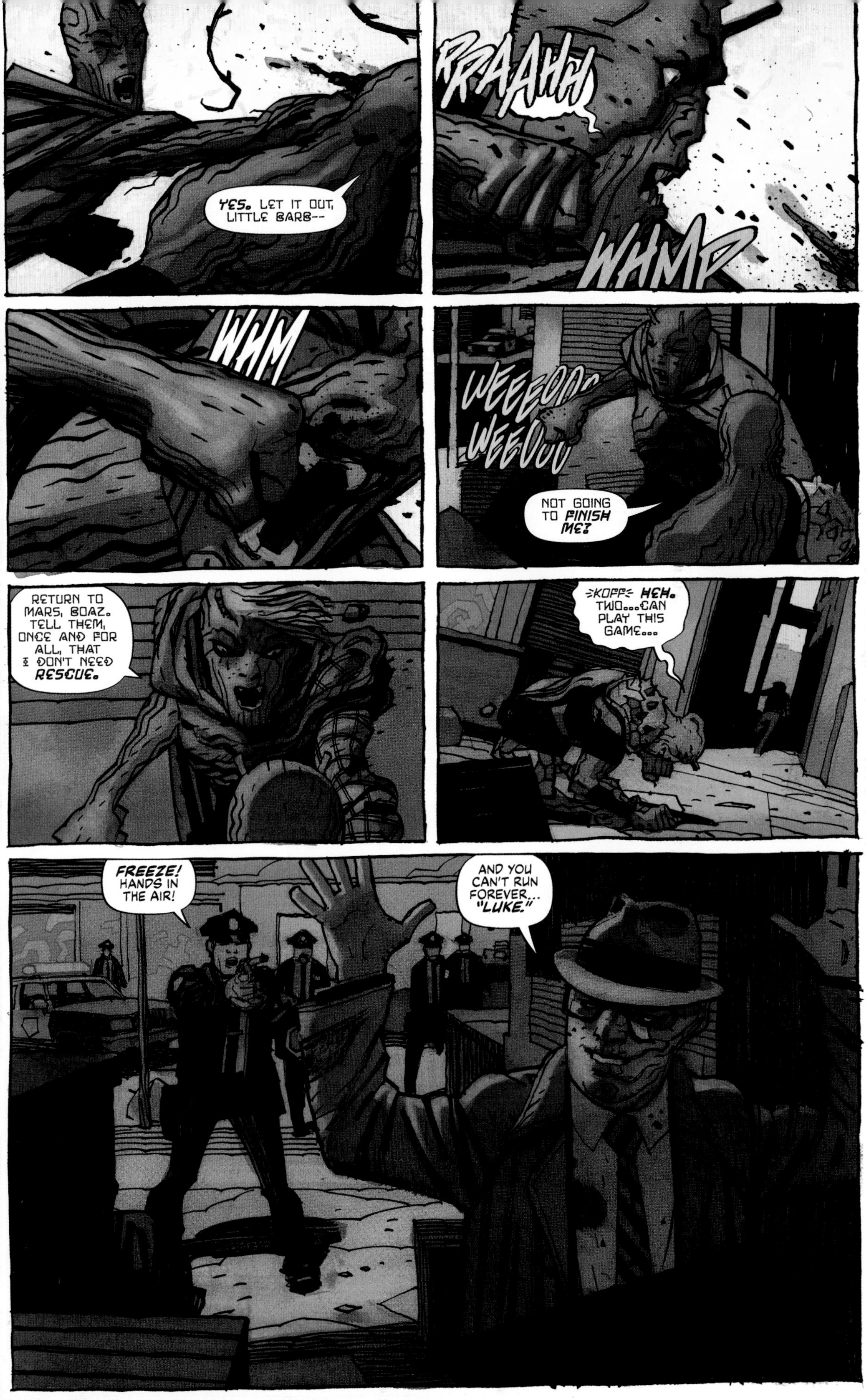
YES. LET IT OUT, LITTLE BARB--
RRAAHH
WHMP
WHM
WEEEOOO WEEOOO
NOT GOING TO FINISH ME?
RETURN TO MARS, BOAZ. TELL THEM, ONCE AND FOR ALL, THAT I DON'T NEED RESCUE.
KOFF HEH. TWO...CAN PLAY THIS GAME...
FREEZE! HANDS IN THE AIR!
AND YOU CAN'T RUN FOREVER... "LUKE."

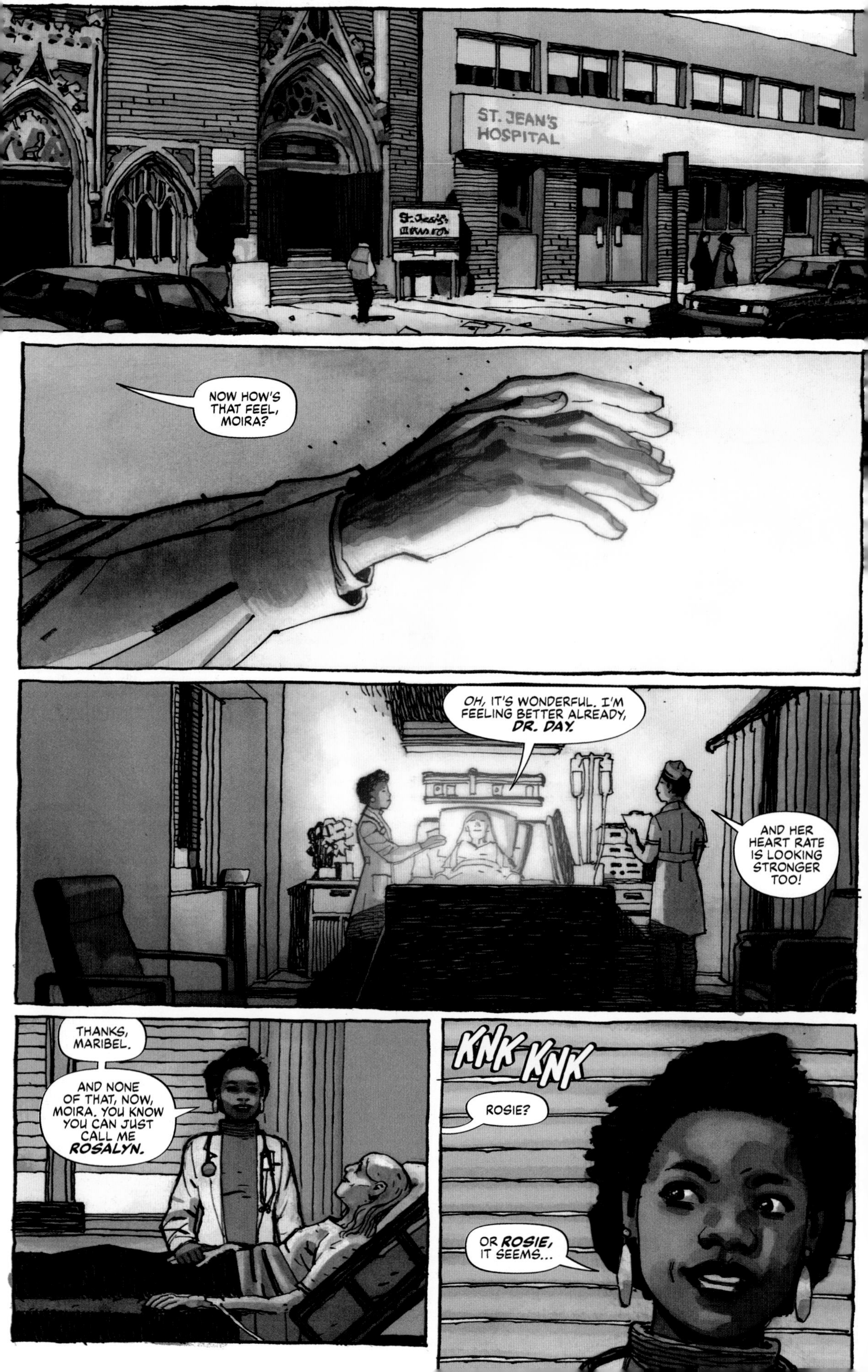
ST. JEAN'S HOSPITAL
NOW HOW'S THAT FEEL, MOIRA?
OH, IT'S WONDERFUL. I'M FEELING BETTER ALREADY, ***DR. DAY.***
AND HER HEART RATE IS LOOKING STRONGER TOO!
THANKS, MARIBEL.
AND NONE OF THAT, NOW, MOIRA. YOU KNOW YOU CAN JUST CALL ME ***ROSALYN.***
KNK KNK
ROSIE?
OR ***ROSIE,*** IT SEEMS...

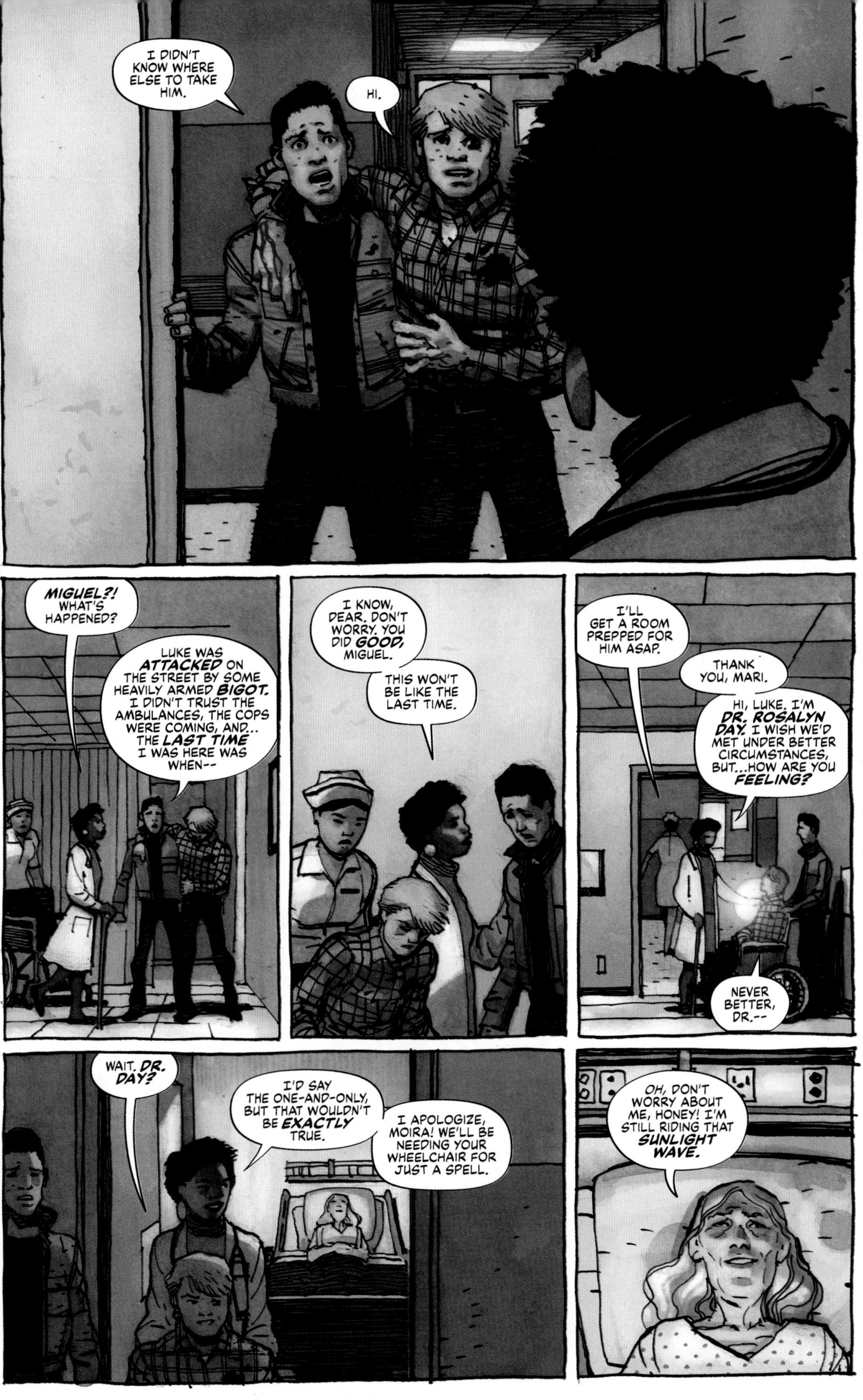
I DIDN'T KNOW WHERE ELSE TO TAKE HIM.
HI.
MIGUEL?! WHAT'S HAPPENED?
LUKE WAS ATTACKED ON THE STREET BY SOME HEAVILY ARMED BIGOT. I DIDN'T TRUST THE AMBULANCES, THE COPS WERE COMING, AND... THE LAST TIME I WAS HERE WAS WHEN--
I KNOW, DEAR. DON'T WORRY. YOU DID GOOD, MIGUEL.
THIS WON'T BE LIKE THE LAST TIME.
I'LL GET A ROOM PREPPED FOR HIM ASAP.
THANK YOU, MARI.
HI, LUKE. I'M DR. ROSALYN DAY. I WISH WE'D MET UNDER BETTER CIRCUMSTANCES, BUT...HOW ARE YOU FEELING?
NEVER BETTER, DR.--
WAIT. DR. DAY?
I'D SAY THE ONE-AND-ONLY, BUT THAT WOULDN'T BE EXACTLY TRUE.
I APOLOGIZE, MOIRA! WE'LL BE NEEDING YOUR WHEELCHAIR FOR JUST A SPELL.
OH, DON'T WORRY ABOUT ME, HONEY! I'M STILL RIDING THAT SUNLIGHT WAVE.

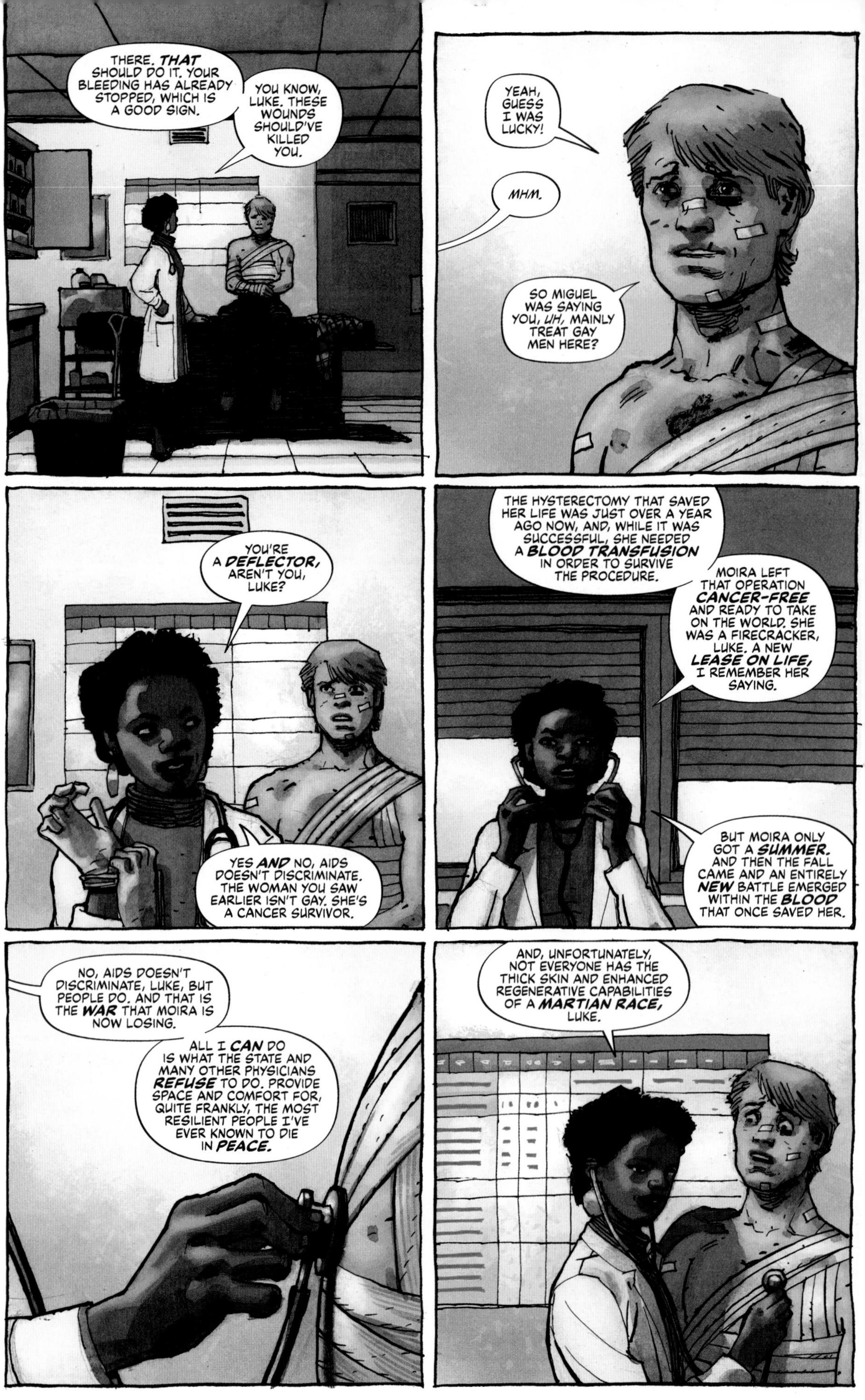
THERE. THAT SHOULD DO IT. YOUR BLEEDING HAS ALREADY STOPPED, WHICH IS A GOOD SIGN.
YOU KNOW, LUKE. THESE WOUNDS SHOULD'VE KILLED YOU.
YEAH, GUESS I WAS LUCKY!
MHM.
SO MIGUEL WAS SAYING YOU, UH, MAINLY TREAT GAY MEN HERE?
YOU'RE A DEFLECTOR, AREN'T YOU, LUKE?
YES AND NO, AIDS DOESN'T DISCRIMINATE. THE WOMAN YOU SAW EARLIER ISN'T GAY. SHE'S A CANCER SURVIVOR.
THE HYSTERECTOMY THAT SAVED HER LIFE WAS JUST OVER A YEAR AGO NOW, AND, WHILE IT WAS SUCCESSFUL, SHE NEEDED A BLOOD TRANSFUSION IN ORDER TO SURVIVE THE PROCEDURE.
MOIRA LEFT THAT OPERATION CANCER-FREE AND READY TO TAKE ON THE WORLD. SHE WAS A FIRECRACKER, LUKE. A NEW LEASE ON LIFE, I REMEMBER HER SAYING.
BUT MOIRA ONLY GOT A SUMMER. AND THEN THE FALL CAME AND AN ENTIRELY NEW BATTLE EMERGED WITHIN THE BLOOD THAT ONCE SAVED HER.
NO, AIDS DOESN'T DISCRIMINATE, LUKE, BUT PEOPLE DO. AND THAT IS THE WAR THAT MOIRA IS NOW LOSING.
ALL I CAN DO IS WHAT THE STATE AND MANY OTHER PHYSICIANS REFUSE TO DO. PROVIDE SPACE AND COMFORT FOR, QUITE FRANKLY, THE MOST RESILIENT PEOPLE I'VE EVER KNOWN TO DIE IN PEACE.
AND, UNFORTUNATELY, NOT EVERYONE HAS THE THICK SKIN AND ENHANCED REGENERATIVE CAPABILITIES OF A MARTIAN RACE, LUKE.

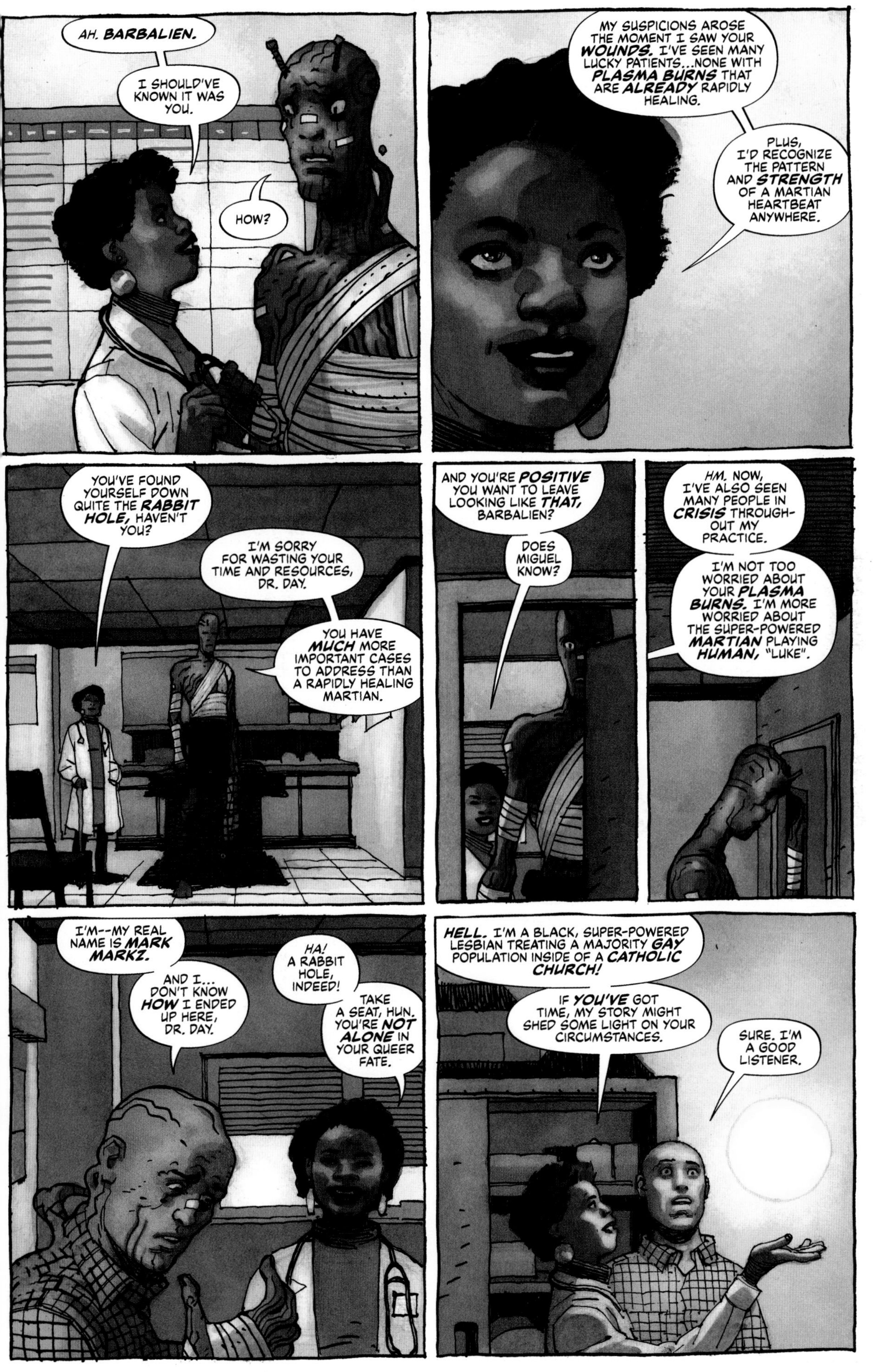
AH. BARBALIEN.
I SHOULD'VE KNOWN IT WAS YOU.
HOW?
MY SUSPICIONS AROSE THE MOMENT I SAW YOUR WOUNDS. I'VE SEEN MANY LUCKY PATIENTS...NONE WITH PLASMA BURNS THAT ARE ALREADY RAPIDLY HEALING.
PLUS, I'D RECOGNIZE THE PATTERN AND STRENGTH OF A MARTIAN HEARTBEAT ANYWHERE.
YOU'VE FOUND YOURSELF DOWN QUITE THE RABBIT HOLE, HAVEN'T YOU?
I'M SORRY FOR WASTING YOUR TIME AND RESOURCES, DR. DAY.
YOU HAVE MUCH MORE IMPORTANT CASES TO ADDRESS THAN A RAPIDLY HEALING MARTIAN.
AND YOU'RE POSITIVE YOU WANT TO LEAVE LOOKING LIKE THAT, BARBALIEN?
DOES MIGUEL KNOW?
HM. NOW, I'VE ALSO SEEN MANY PEOPLE IN CRISIS THROUGH-OUT MY PRACTICE.
I'M NOT TOO WORRIED ABOUT YOUR PLASMA BURNS. I'M MORE WORRIED ABOUT THE SUPER-POWERED MARTIAN PLAYING HUMAN, "LUKE".
I'M--MY REAL NAME IS MARK MARKZ.
AND I... DON'T KNOW HOW I ENDED UP HERE, DR. DAY.
HA! A RABBIT HOLE, INDEED!
TAKE A SEAT, HUN. YOU'RE NOT ALONE IN YOUR QUEER FATE.
HELL. I'M A BLACK, SUPER-POWERED LESBIAN TREATING A MAJORITY GAY POPULATION INSIDE OF A CATHOLIC CHURCH!
IF YOU'VE GOT TIME, MY STORY MIGHT SHED SOME LIGHT ON YOUR CIRCUMSTANCES.
SURE. I'M A GOOD LISTENER.

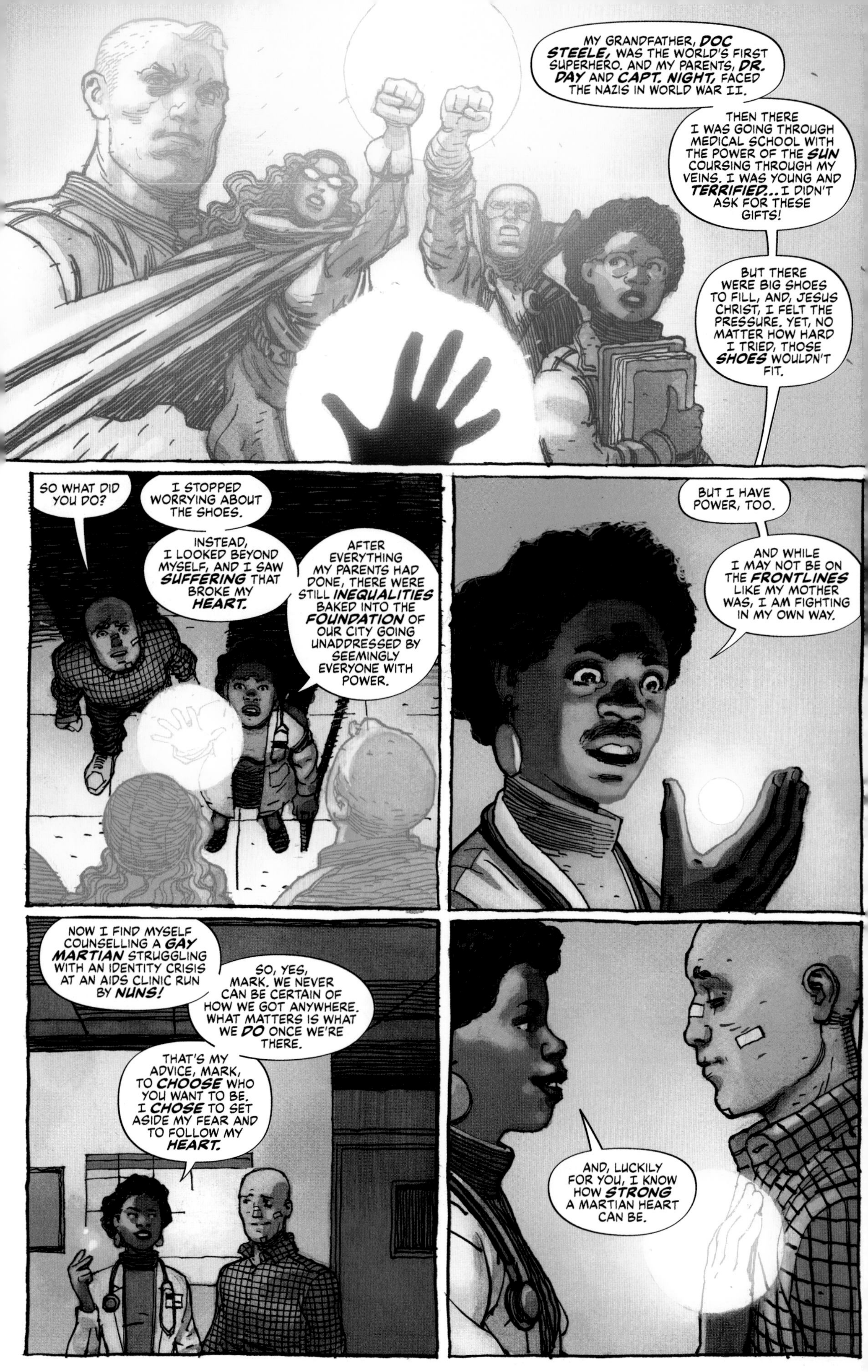
MY GRANDFATHER, DOC STEELE, WAS THE WORLD'S FIRST SUPERHERO. AND MY PARENTS, DR. DAY AND CAPT. NIGHT, FACED THE NAZIS IN WORLD WAR II.
THEN THERE I WAS GOING THROUGH MEDICAL SCHOOL WITH THE POWER OF THE SUN COURSING THROUGH MY VEINS. I WAS YOUNG AND TERRIFIED... I DIDN'T ASK FOR THESE GIFTS!
BUT THERE WERE BIG SHOES TO FILL, AND, JESUS CHRIST, I FELT THE PRESSURE. YET, NO MATTER HOW HARD I TRIED, THOSE SHOES WOULDN'T FIT.
SO WHAT DID YOU DO?
I STOPPED WORRYING ABOUT THE SHOES.
INSTEAD, I LOOKED BEYOND MYSELF, AND I SAW SUFFERING THAT BROKE MY HEART.
AFTER EVERYTHING MY PARENTS HAD DONE, THERE WERE STILL INEQUALITIES BAKED INTO THE FOUNDATION OF OUR CITY GOING UNADDRESSED BY SEEMINGLY EVERYONE WITH POWER.
BUT I HAVE POWER, TOO.
AND WHILE I MAY NOT BE ON THE FRONTLINES LIKE MY MOTHER WAS, I AM FIGHTING IN MY OWN WAY.
NOW I FIND MYSELF COUNSELLING A GAY MARTIAN STRUGGLING WITH AN IDENTITY CRISIS AT AN AIDS CLINIC RUN BY NUNS!
SO, YES, MARK. WE NEVER CAN BE CERTAIN OF HOW WE GOT ANYWHERE. WHAT MATTERS IS WHAT WE DO ONCE WE'RE THERE.
THAT'S MY ADVICE, MARK, TO CHOOSE WHO YOU WANT TO BE. I CHOSE TO SET ASIDE MY FEAR AND TO FOLLOW MY HEART.
AND, LUCKILY FOR YOU, I KNOW HOW STRONG A MARTIAN HEART CAN BE.

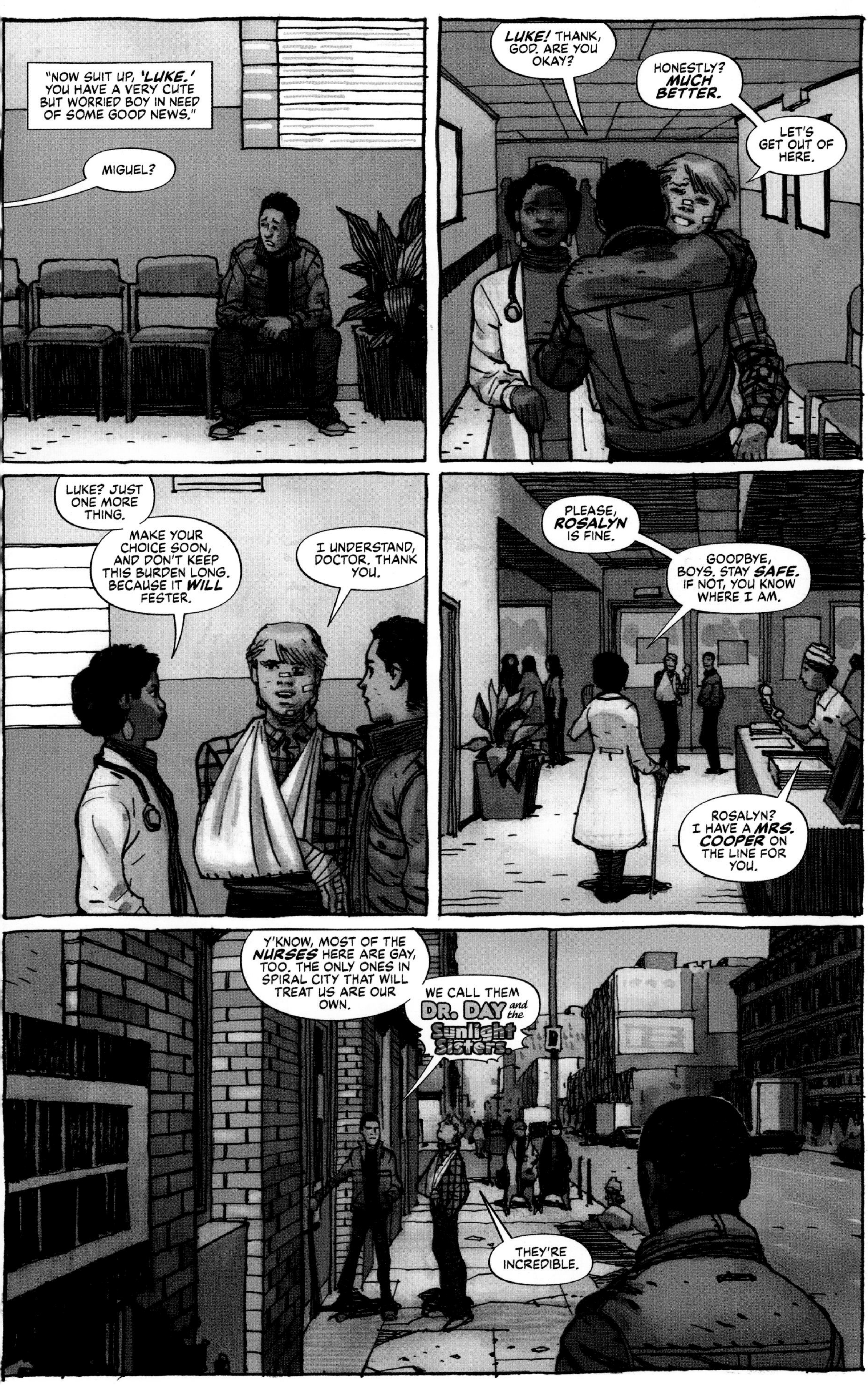"NOW SUIT UP, 'LUKE.' YOU HAVE A VERY CUTE BUT WORRIED BOY IN NEED OF SOME GOOD NEWS."
MIGUEL?
LUKE! THANK, GOD. ARE YOU OKAY?
HONESTLY? MUCH BETTER.
LET'S GET OUT OF HERE.
LUKE? JUST ONE MORE THING.
MAKE YOUR CHOICE SOON, AND DON'T KEEP THIS BURDEN LONG. BECAUSE IT WILL FESTER.
I UNDERSTAND, DOCTOR. THANK YOU.
PLEASE, ROSALYN IS FINE.
GOODBYE, BOYS. STAY SAFE. IF NOT, YOU KNOW WHERE I AM.
ROSALYN? I HAVE A MRS. COOPER ON THE LINE FOR YOU.
Y'KNOW, MOST OF THE NURSES HERE ARE GAY, TOO. THE ONLY ONES IN SPIRAL CITY THAT WILL TREAT US ARE OUR OWN.
WE CALL THEM DR. DAY and the Sunlight Sisters.
THEY'RE INCREDIBLE.

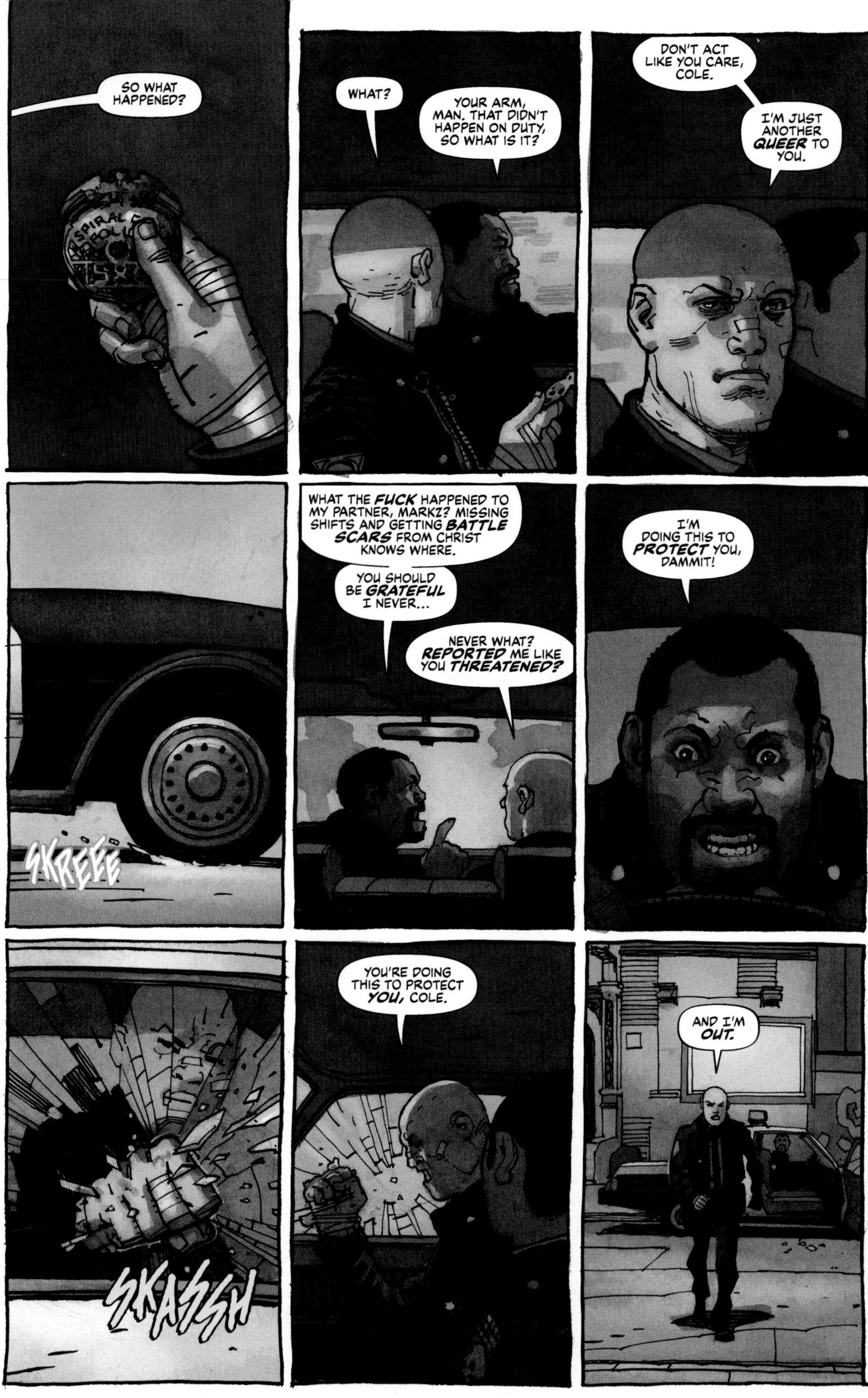
SO WHAT HAPPENED?
WHAT?
YOUR ARM, MAN. THAT DIDN'T HAPPEN ON DUTY, SO WHAT IS IT?
DON'T ACT LIKE YOU CARE, COLE.
I'M JUST ANOTHER QUEER TO YOU.
SKREEE
WHAT THE FUCK HAPPENED TO MY PARTNER, MARKZ? MISSING SHIFTS AND GETTING BATTLE SCARS FROM CHRIST KNOWS WHERE.
YOU SHOULD BE GRATEFUL I NEVER...
NEVER WHAT? REPORTED ME LIKE YOU THREATENED?
I'M DOING THIS TO PROTECT YOU, DAMMIT!
SKASSH
YOU'RE DOING THIS TO PROTECT YOU, COLE.
AND I'M OUT.

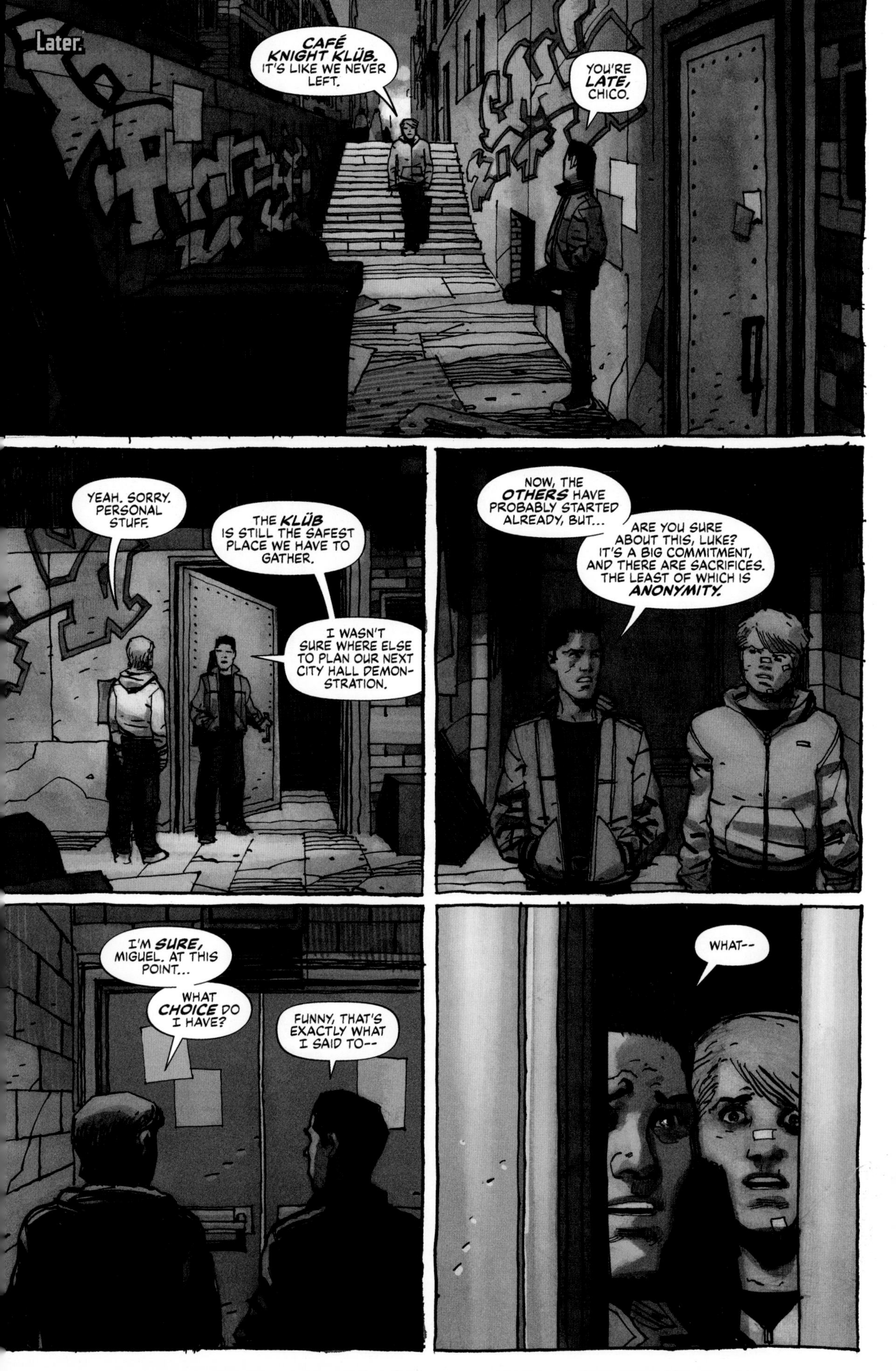
Later.
CAFÉ KNIGHT KLÜB. IT'S LIKE WE NEVER LEFT.
YOU'RE LATE, CHICO.
YEAH. SORRY. PERSONAL STUFF.
THE KLÜB IS STILL THE SAFEST PLACE WE HAVE TO GATHER.
I WASN'T SURE WHERE ELSE TO PLAN OUR NEXT CITY HALL DEMON-STRATION.
NOW, THE OTHERS HAVE PROBABLY STARTED ALREADY, BUT...
ARE YOU SURE ABOUT THIS, LUKE? IT'S A BIG COMMITMENT, AND THERE ARE SACRIFICES. THE LEAST OF WHICH IS ANONYMITY.
I'M SURE, MIGUEL. AT THIS POINT...
WHAT CHOICE DO I HAVE?
FUNNY, THAT'S EXACTLY WHAT I SAID TO--
WHAT--

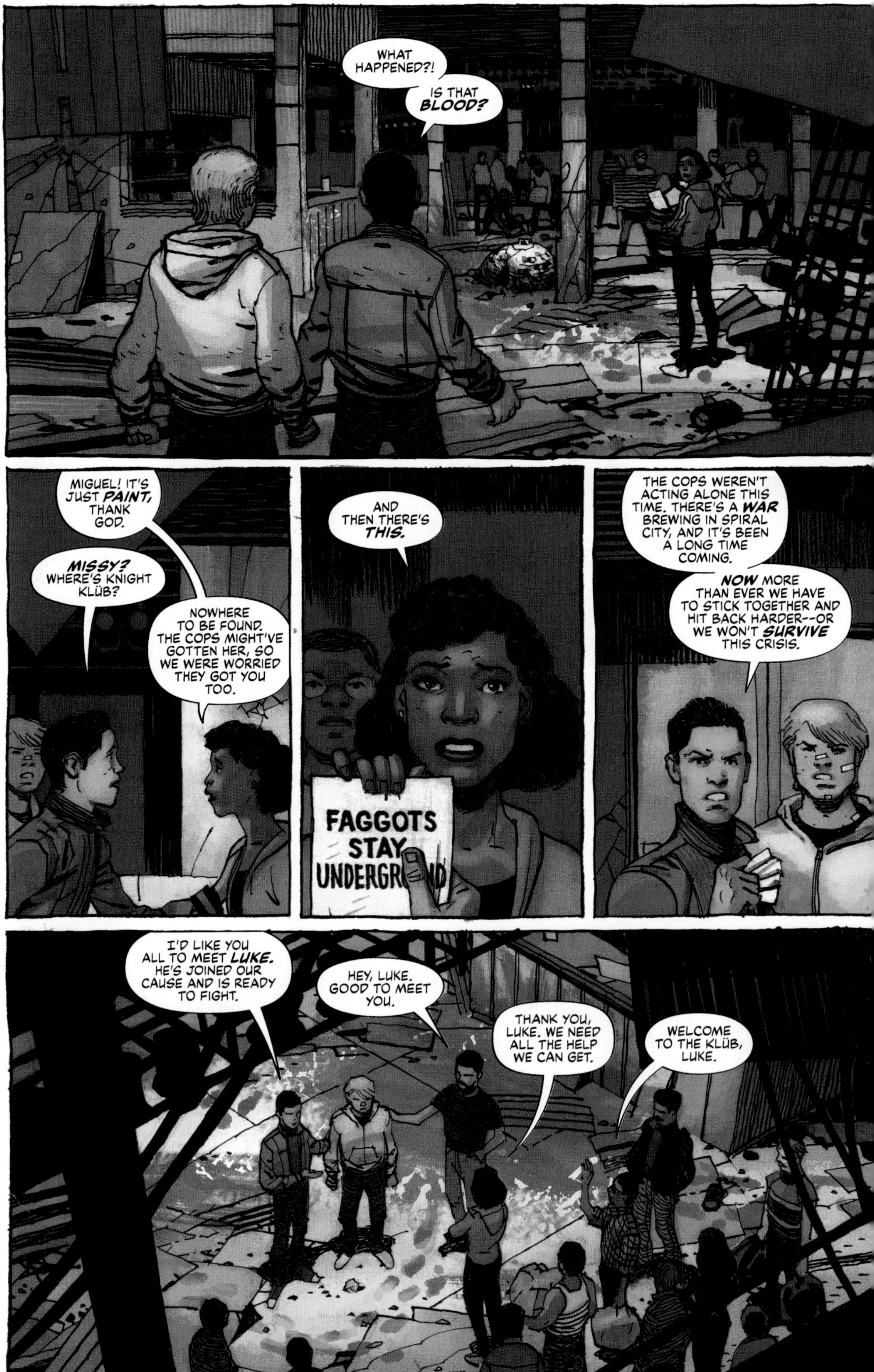

WHAT HAPPENED?!
IS THAT *BLOOD?*
MIGUEL! IT'S JUST *PAINT,* THANK GOD.
MISSY? WHERE'S KNIGHT KLÜB?
NOWHERE TO BE FOUND. THE COPS MIGHT'VE GOTTEN HER, SO WE WERE WORRIED THEY GOT YOU TOO.
AND THEN THERE'S *THIS.*
FAGGOTS STAY UNDERGR
THE COPS WEREN'T ACTING ALONE THIS TIME. THERE'S A *WAR* BREWING IN SPIRAL CITY, AND IT'S BEEN A LONG TIME COMING.
NOW MORE THAN EVER WE HAVE TO STICK TOGETHER AND HIT BACK HARDER--OR WE WON'T *SURVIVE* THIS CRISIS.
I'D LIKE YOU ALL TO MEET *LUKE.* HE'S JOINED OUR CAUSE AND IS READY TO FIGHT.
HEY, LUKE. GOOD TO MEET YOU.
THANK YOU, LUKE. WE NEED ALL THE HELP WE CAN GET.
WELCOME TO THE KLÜB, LUKE.

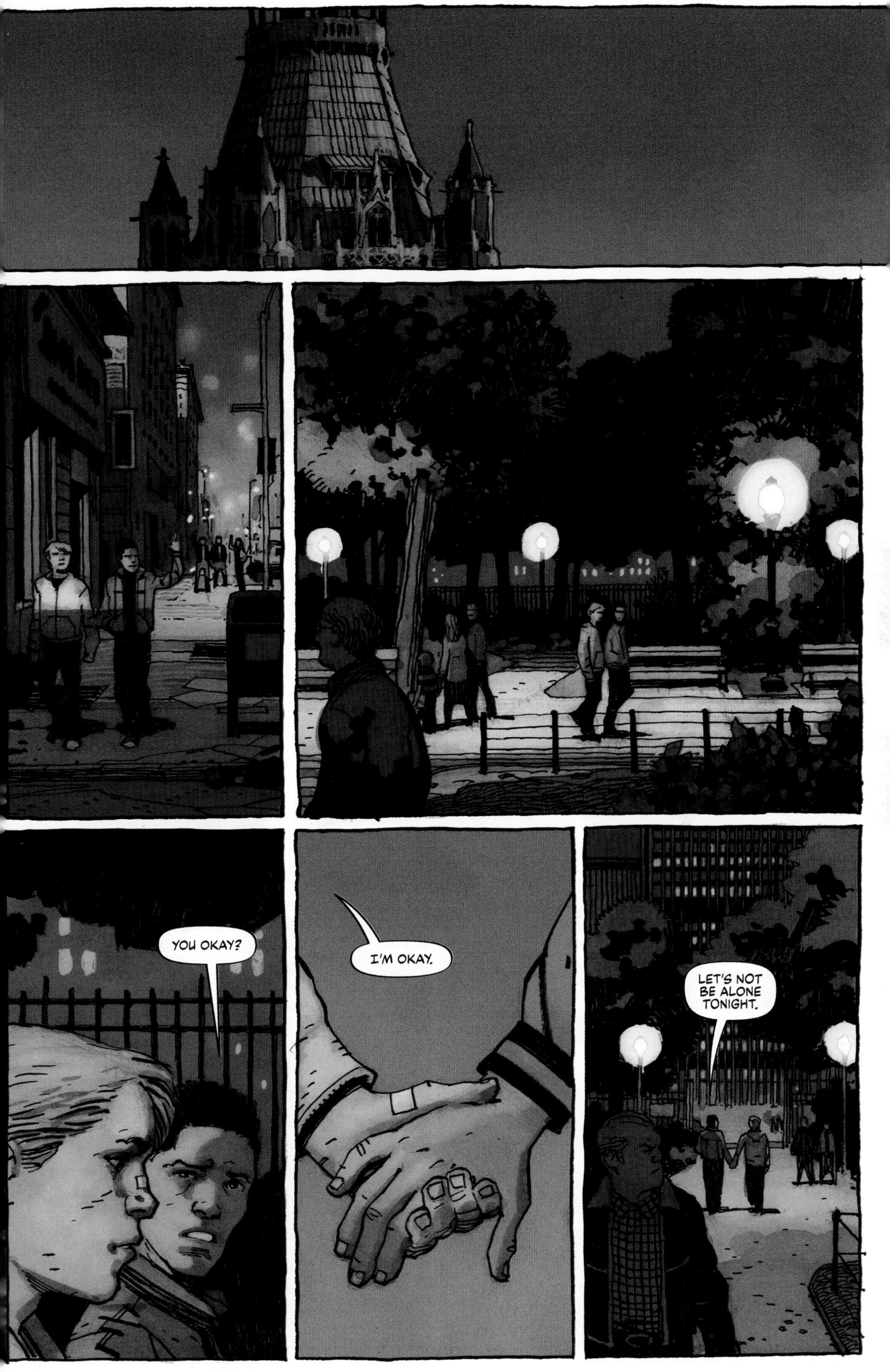
YOU OKAY?
I'M OKAY.
LET'S NOT BE ALONE TONIGHT.

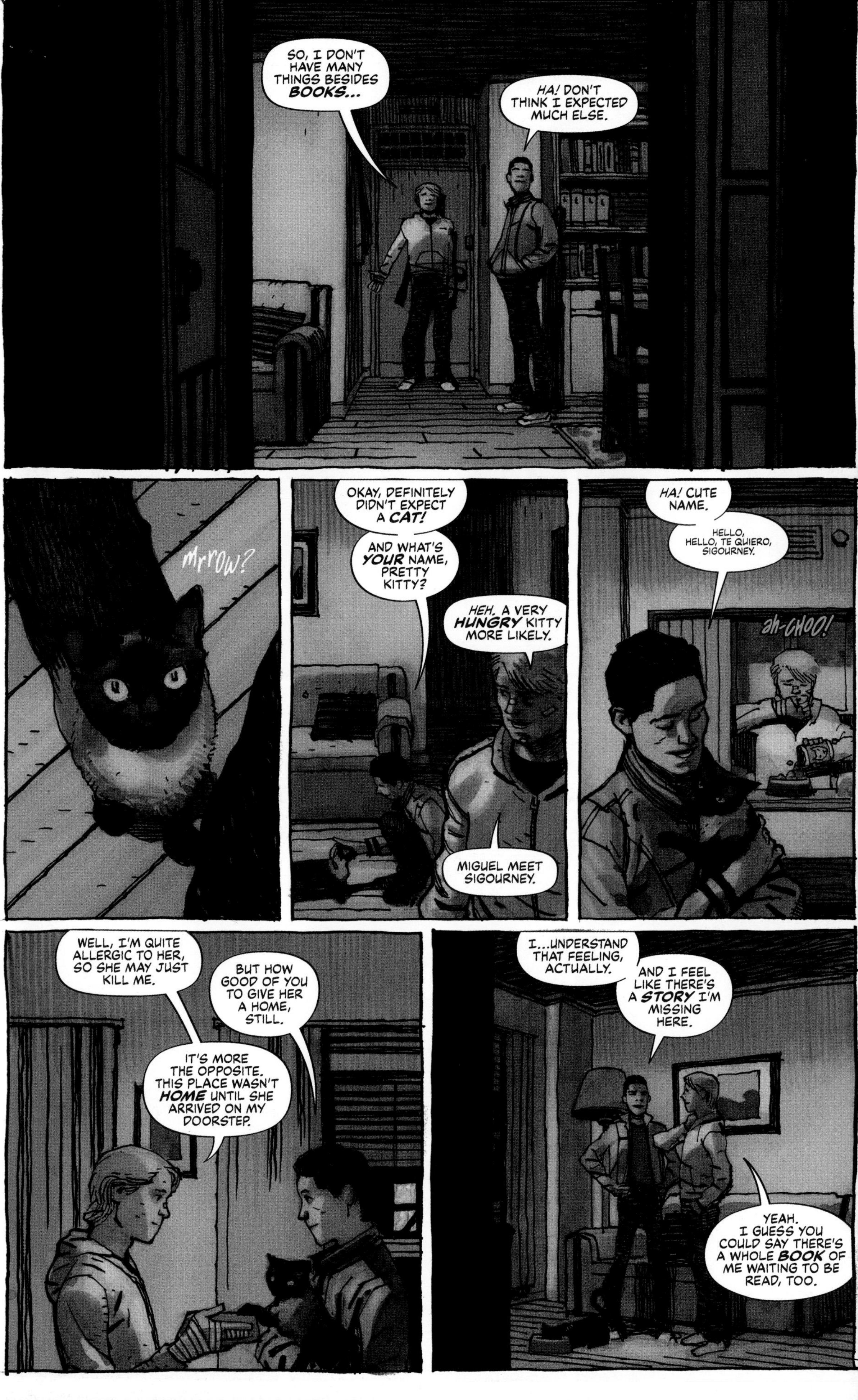

SO, I DON'T HAVE MANY THINGS BESIDES BOOKS...
HA! DON'T THINK I EXPECTED MUCH ELSE.
MRROW?
OKAY, DEFINITELY DIDN'T EXPECT A CAT!
AND WHAT'S YOUR NAME, PRETTY KITTY?
HEH. A VERY HUNGRY KITTY MORE LIKELY.
MIGUEL MEET SIGOURNEY.
HA! CUTE NAME.
HELLO, HELLO, TE QUIERO, SIGOURNEY.
AH-CHOO!
WELL, I'M QUITE ALLERGIC TO HER, SO SHE MAY JUST KILL ME.
BUT HOW GOOD OF YOU TO GIVE HER A HOME, STILL.
IT'S MORE THE OPPOSITE. THIS PLACE WASN'T HOME UNTIL SHE ARRIVED ON MY DOORSTEP.
I...UNDERSTAND THAT FEELING, ACTUALLY.
AND I FEEL LIKE THERE'S A STORY I'M MISSING HERE.
YEAH. I GUESS YOU COULD SAY THERE'S A WHOLE BOOK OF ME WAITING TO BE READ, TOO.

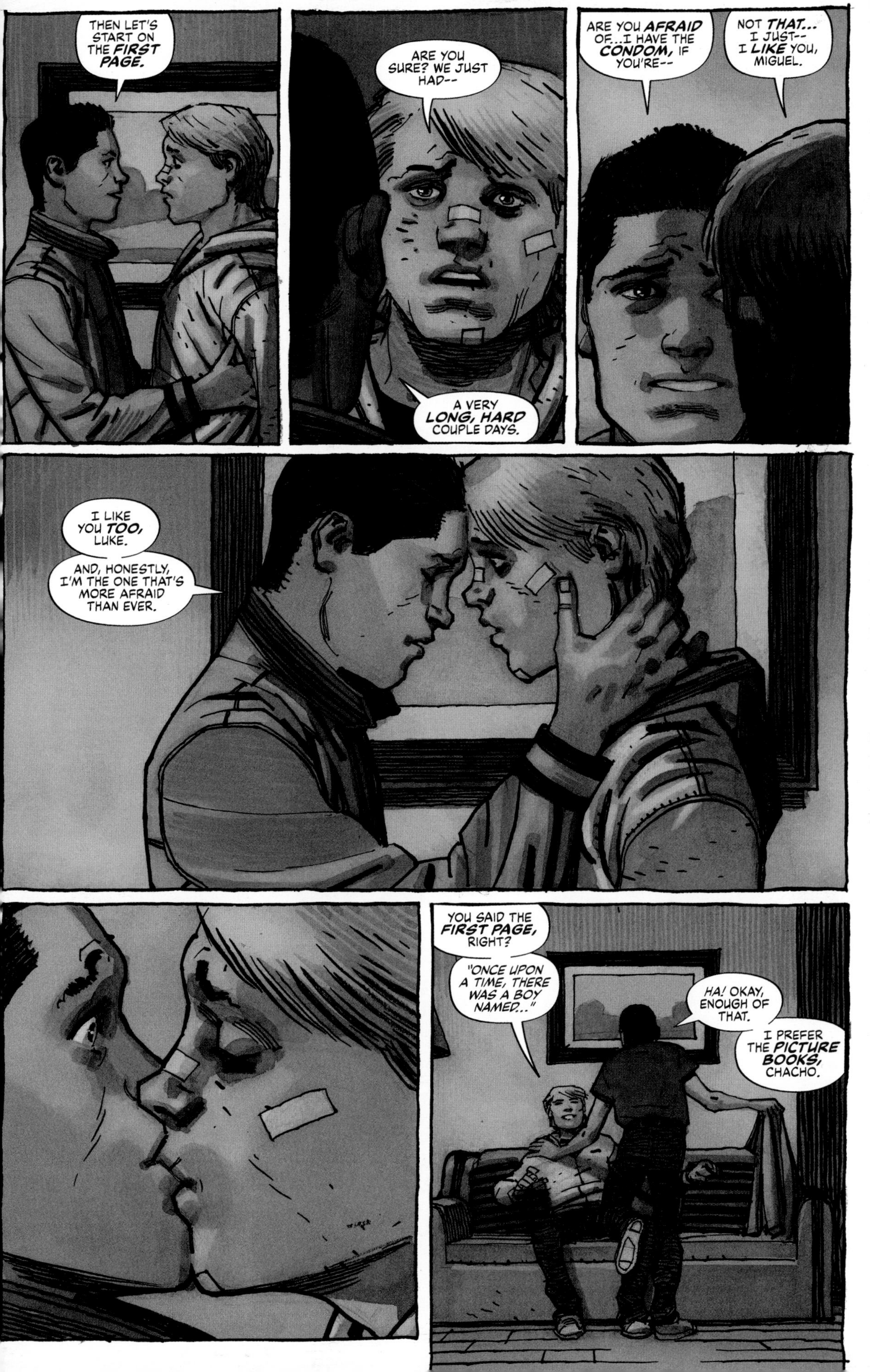
THEN LET'S START ON THE *FIRST PAGE.*
ARE YOU SURE? WE JUST HAD--
A VERY *LONG, HARD* COUPLE DAYS.
ARE YOU *AFRAID* OF...I HAVE THE *CONDOM,* IF YOU'RE--
NOT *THAT...* I JUST-- I *LIKE* YOU, MIGUEL.
I LIKE YOU *TOO,* LUKE.
AND, HONESTLY, I'M THE ONE THAT'S MORE AFRAID THAN EVER.
YOU SAID THE *FIRST PAGE,* RIGHT?
"ONCE UPON A TIME, THERE WAS A BOY NAMED..."
HA! OKAY, ENOUGH OF THAT.
I PREFER THE *PICTURE BOOKS,* CHACHO.

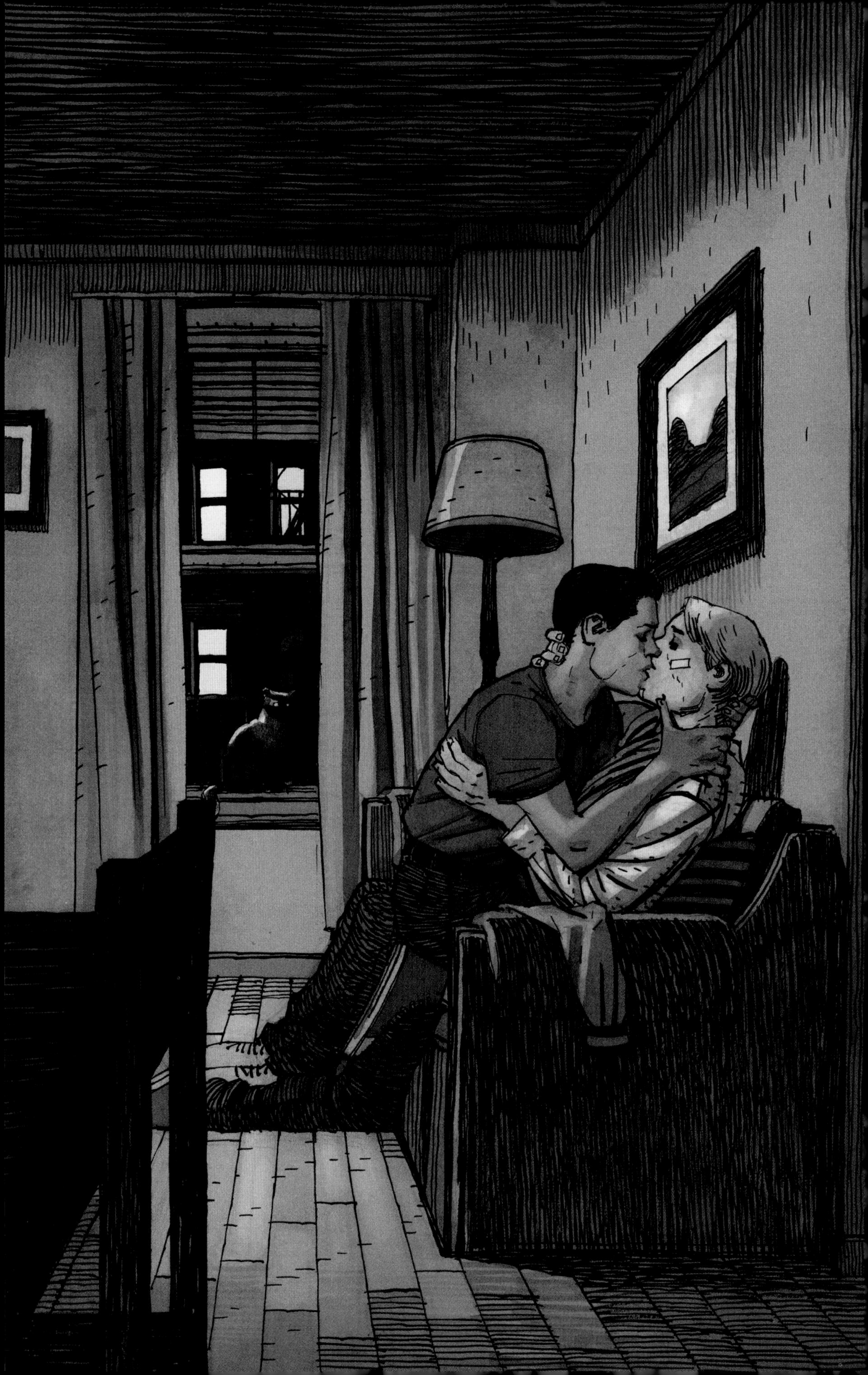

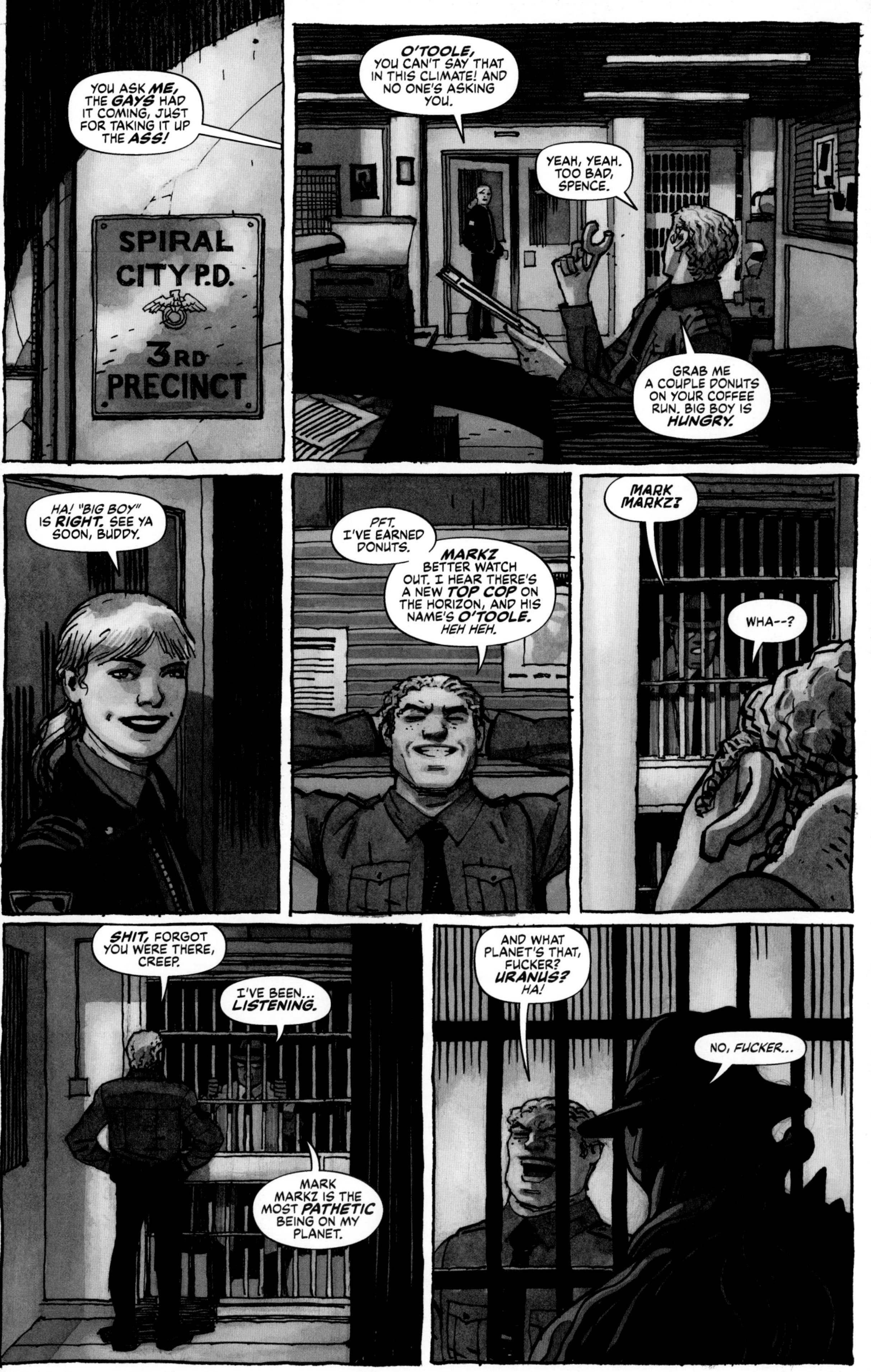
YOU ASK ME, THE GAYS HAD IT COMING, JUST FOR TAKING IT UP THE ASS!
SPIRAL CITY P.D.
3RD PRECINCT
O'TOOLE, YOU CAN'T SAY THAT IN THIS CLIMATE! AND NO ONE'S ASKING YOU.
YEAH, YEAH. TOO BAD, SPENCE.
GRAB ME A COUPLE DONUTS ON YOUR COFFEE RUN. BIG BOY IS HUNGRY.
HA! "BIG BOY" IS RIGHT. SEE YA SOON, BUDDY.
PFT. I'VE EARNED DONUTS.
MARKZ BETTER WATCH OUT. I HEAR THERE'S A NEW TOP COP ON THE HORIZON, AND HIS NAME'S O'TOOLE. HEH HEH.
MARK MARKZ?
WHA--?
SHIT, FORGOT YOU WERE THERE, CREEP.
I'VE BEEN... LISTENING.
MARK MARKZ IS THE MOST PATHETIC BEING ON MY PLANET.
AND WHAT PLANET'S THAT, FUCKER? URANUS? HA!
NO, FUCKER...

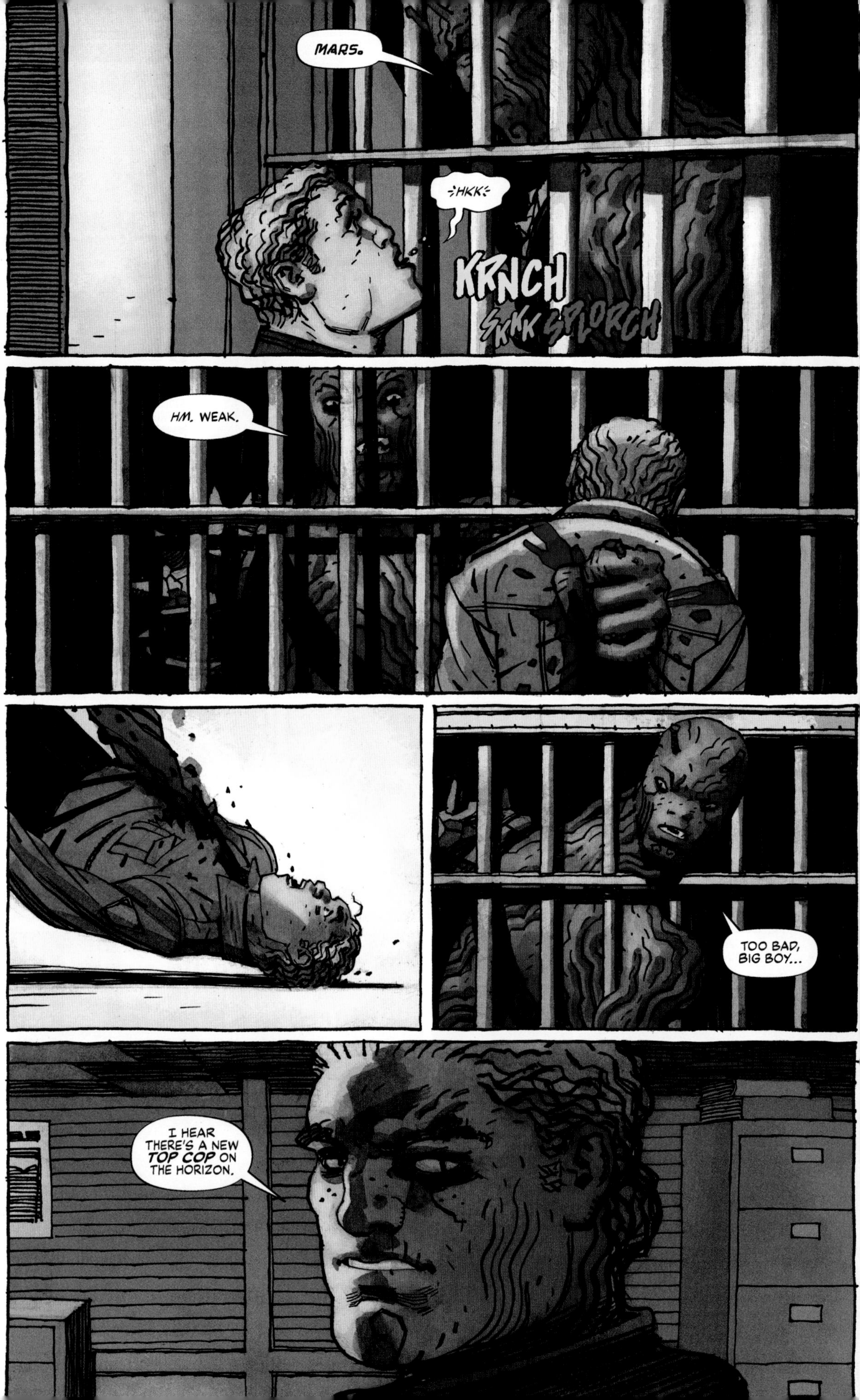
MARS.
HKK
KRNCH
SKKK SPLORCH
HM. WEAK.
TOO BAD, BIG BOY...
I HEAR THERE'S A NEW TOP COP ON THE HORIZON.

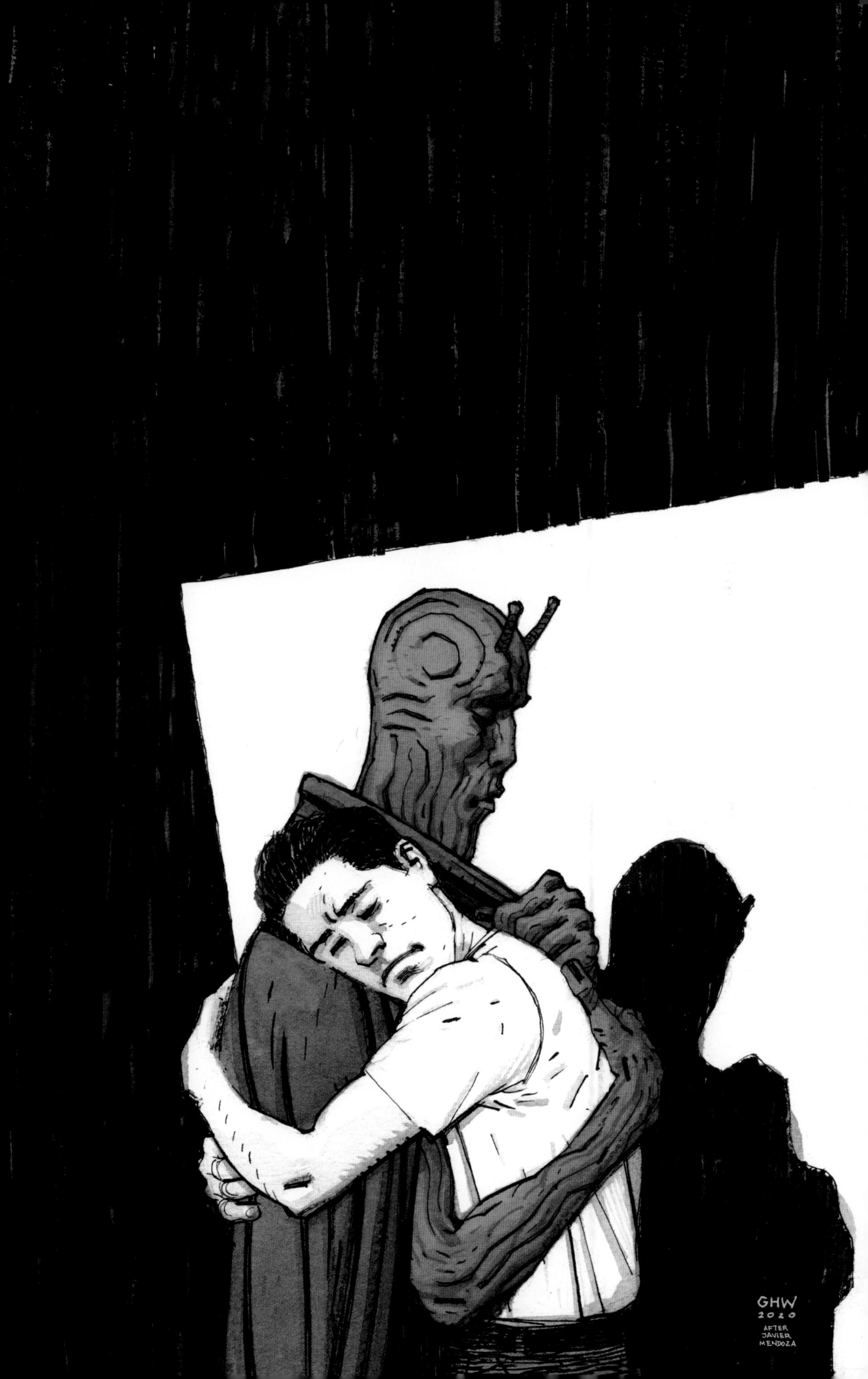
GHW
2020
AFTER
JAVIER
MENDOZA

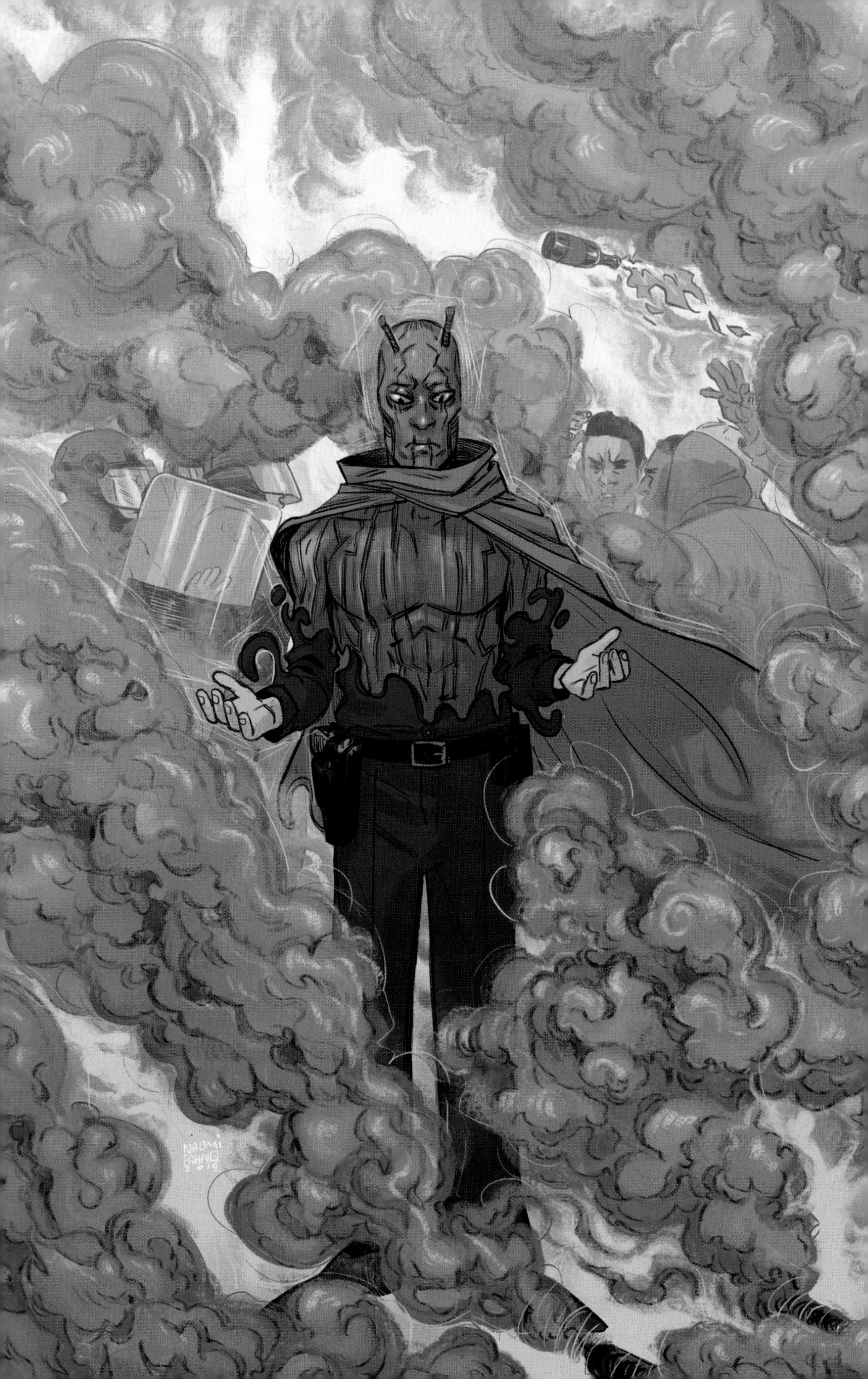
NAOMI FRANQ 2019

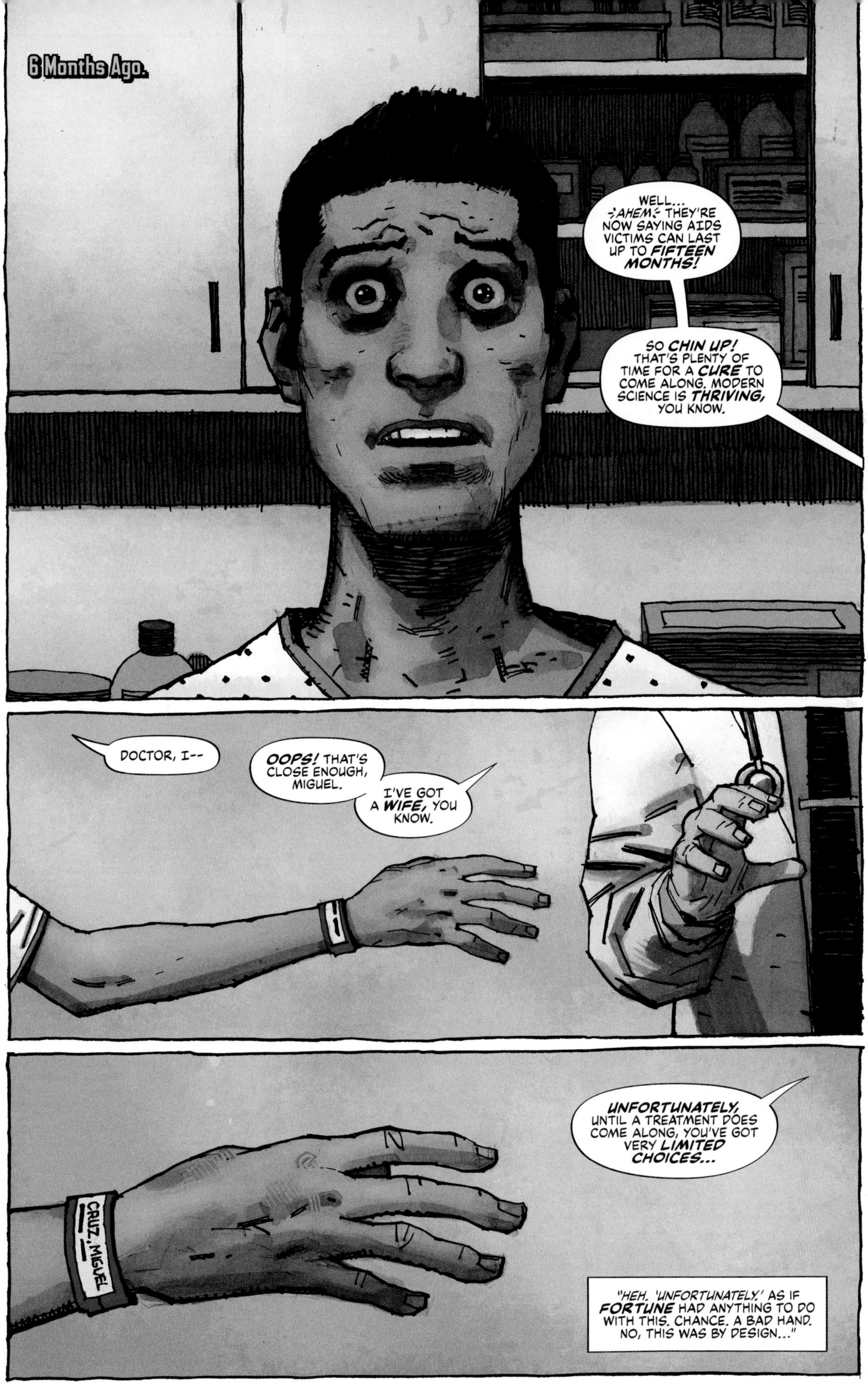
6 Months Ago.
WELL... -AHEM- THEY'RE NOW SAYING AIDS VICTIMS CAN LAST UP TO FIFTEEN MONTHS!
SO CHIN UP! THAT'S PLENTY OF TIME FOR A CURE TO COME ALONG. MODERN SCIENCE IS THRIVING, YOU KNOW.
DOCTOR, I--
OOPS! THAT'S CLOSE ENOUGH, MIGUEL.
I'VE GOT A WIFE, YOU KNOW.
UNFORTUNATELY, UNTIL A TREATMENT DOES COME ALONG, YOU'VE GOT VERY LIMITED CHOICES...
CRUZ, MIGUEL
"HEH. 'UNFORTUNATELY.' AS IF FORTUNE HAD ANYTHING TO DO WITH THIS. CHANCE. A BAD HAND. NO, THIS WAS BY DESIGN..."

"...AND I LEARNED *THAT* AT A YOUNG AGE."

VAMOS, NENE!

MADRES CONTRA LA CONSCRIPCIÓN

RESISTE EL SERVICIO

MADRES

"NO *CHOICE* IN THE MATTER.

7777

"NO *WAITING* FOR THE WORLD TO DEAL ME A BETTER HAND.

"BECAUSE THE WORLD ONLY WANTED TO PUT ME *DOWN.*

"AND WHO ELSE WOULD FIGHT FOR ME...

"...BUT *ME?*"

VAMOS, NENE.

"SO I KEPT FIGHTING.

GENTRIFICATION IS RACISM

¡Nunca es tarde! ¡LUCHA!

HANDS OFF SPIRAL EAST SIDE

NUESTRO BARRIO NO ES TUYO!

"AND *FIGHTING...*

"...AND *FIGHTING.* EVEN IF THE *FIGHT* WAS JUST HOLDING A HAND IN PUBLIC."

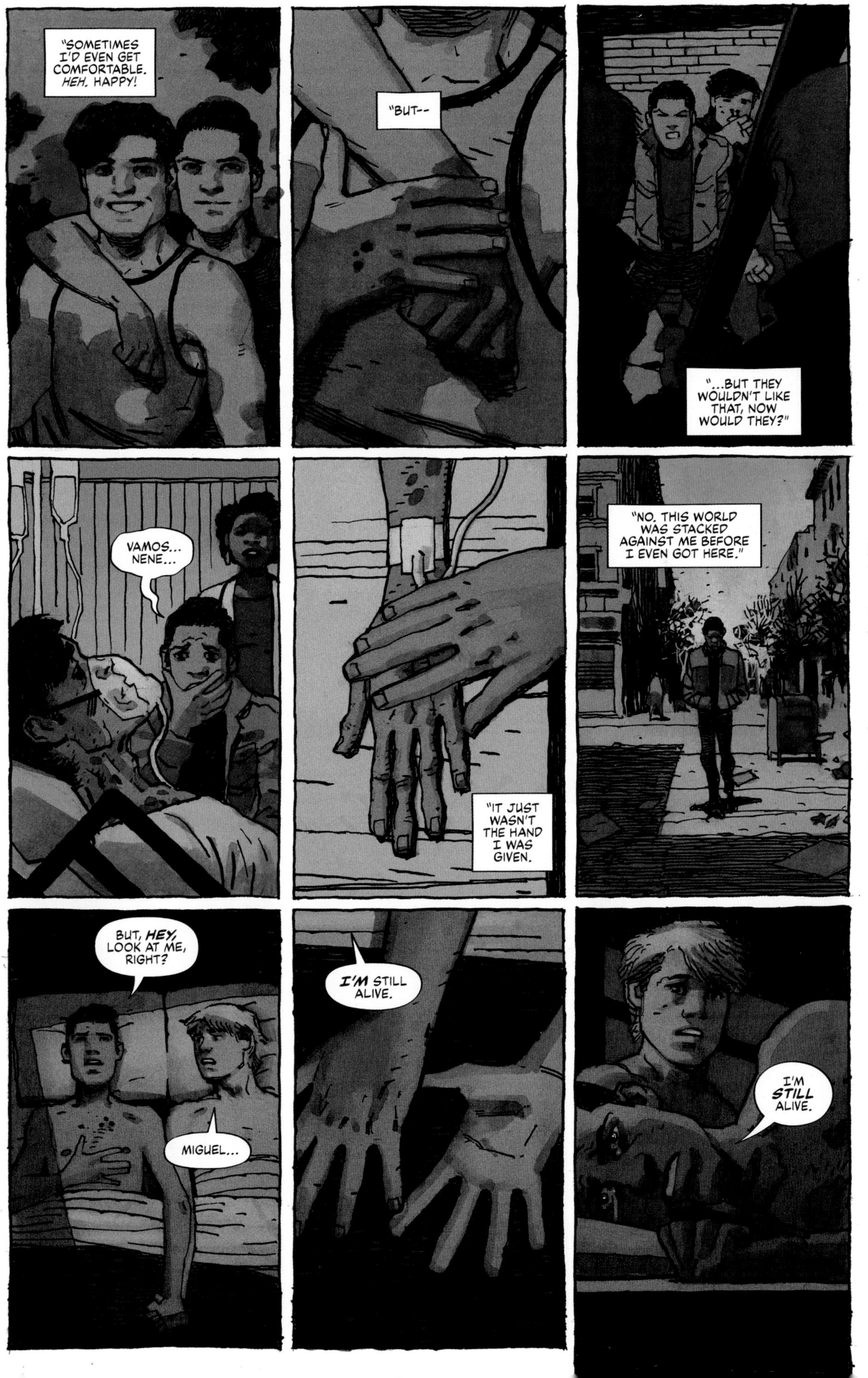
"SOMETIMES I'D EVEN GET COMFORTABLE. *HEH.* HAPPY!
"BUT--
"...BUT THEY WOULDN'T LIKE THAT, NOW WOULD THEY?"
VAMOS... NENE...
"IT JUST WASN'T THE HAND I WAS GIVEN.
"NO. THIS WORLD WAS STACKED AGAINST ME BEFORE I EVEN GOT HERE."
BUT, ***HEY,*** LOOK AT ME, RIGHT?
MIGUEL...
I'M STILL ALIVE.
I'M ***STILL*** ALIVE.

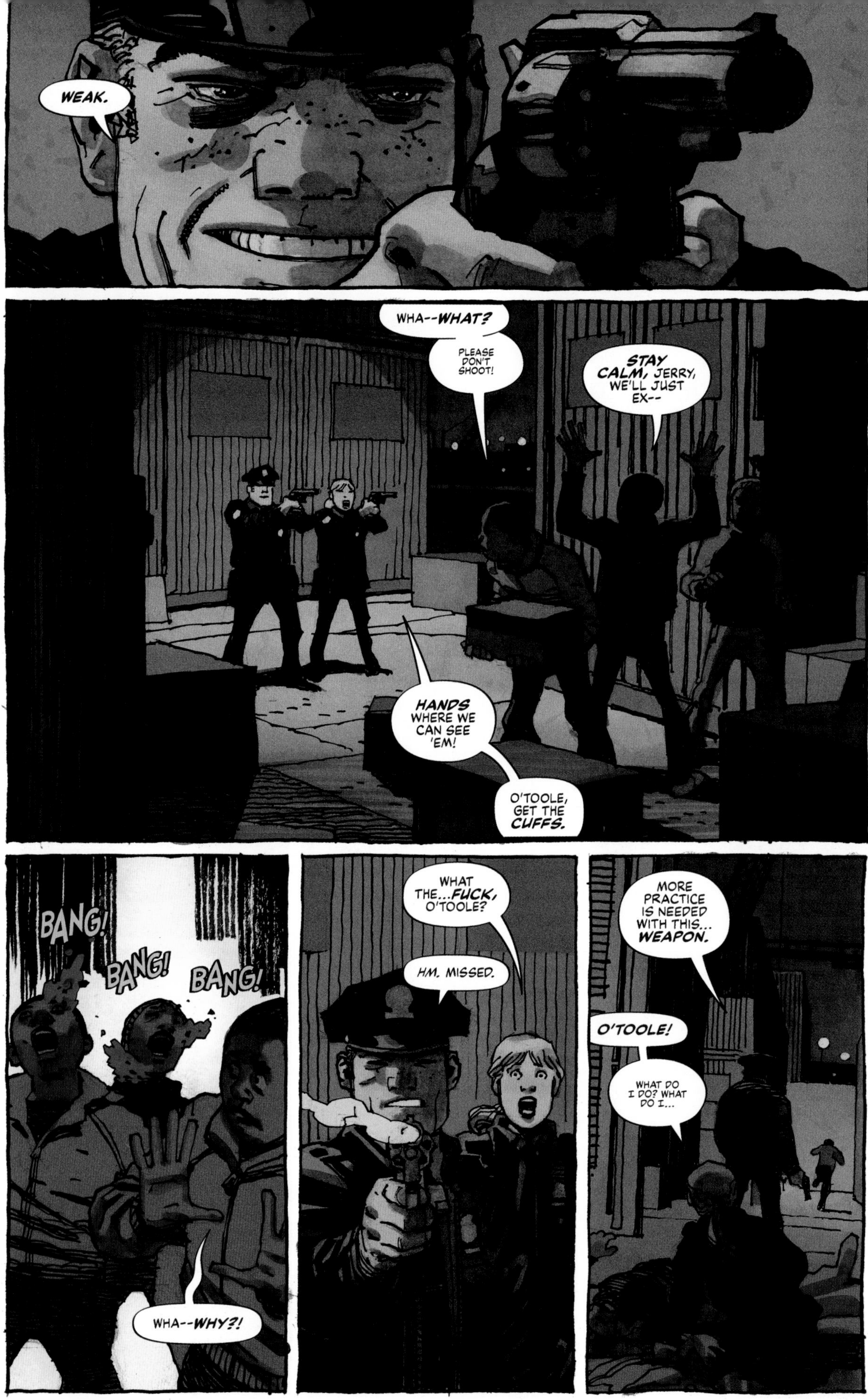
WEAK.
WHA--WHAT?
PLEASE DON'T SHOOT!
STAY CALM, JERRY, WE'LL JUST EX--
HANDS WHERE WE CAN SEE 'EM!
O'TOOLE, GET THE CUFFS.
BANG!
BANG!
BANG!
WHA--WHY?!
WHAT THE...FUCK, O'TOOLE?
HM. MISSED.
MORE PRACTICE IS NEEDED WITH THIS... WEAPON.
O'TOOLE!
WHAT DO I DO? WHAT DO I...

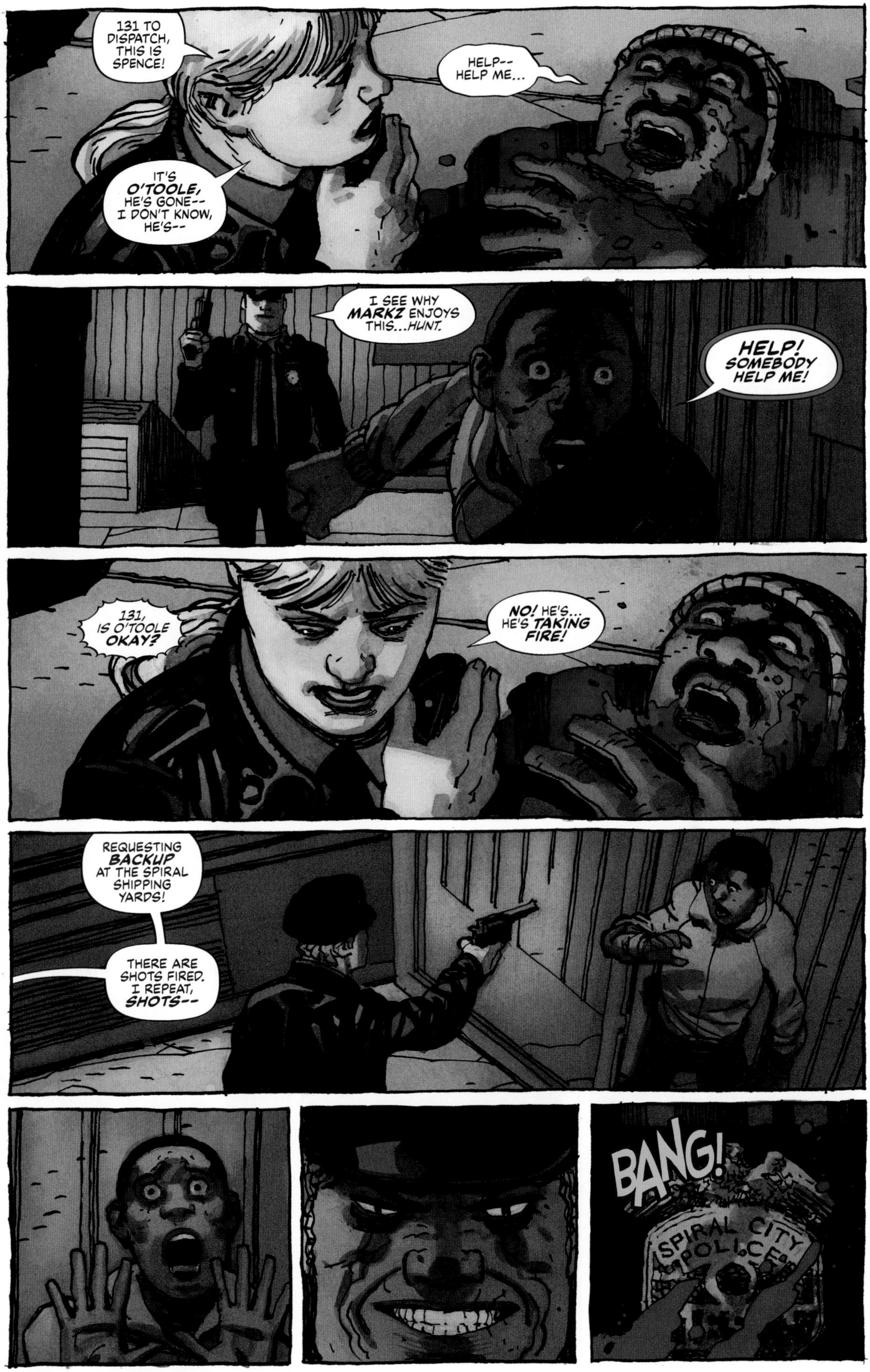
131 TO DISPATCH, THIS IS SPENCE!
HELP-- HELP ME...
IT'S O'TOOLE, HE'S GONE-- I DON'T KNOW, HE'S--
I SEE WHY MARKZ ENJOYS THIS...HUNT.
HELP! SOMEBODY HELP ME!
131, IS O'TOOLE OKAY?
NO! HE'S... HE'S TAKING FIRE!
REQUESTING BACKUP AT THE SPIRAL SHIPPING YARDS!
THERE ARE SHOTS FIRED. I REPEAT, SHOTS--
BANG!
SPIRAL CITY POLICE

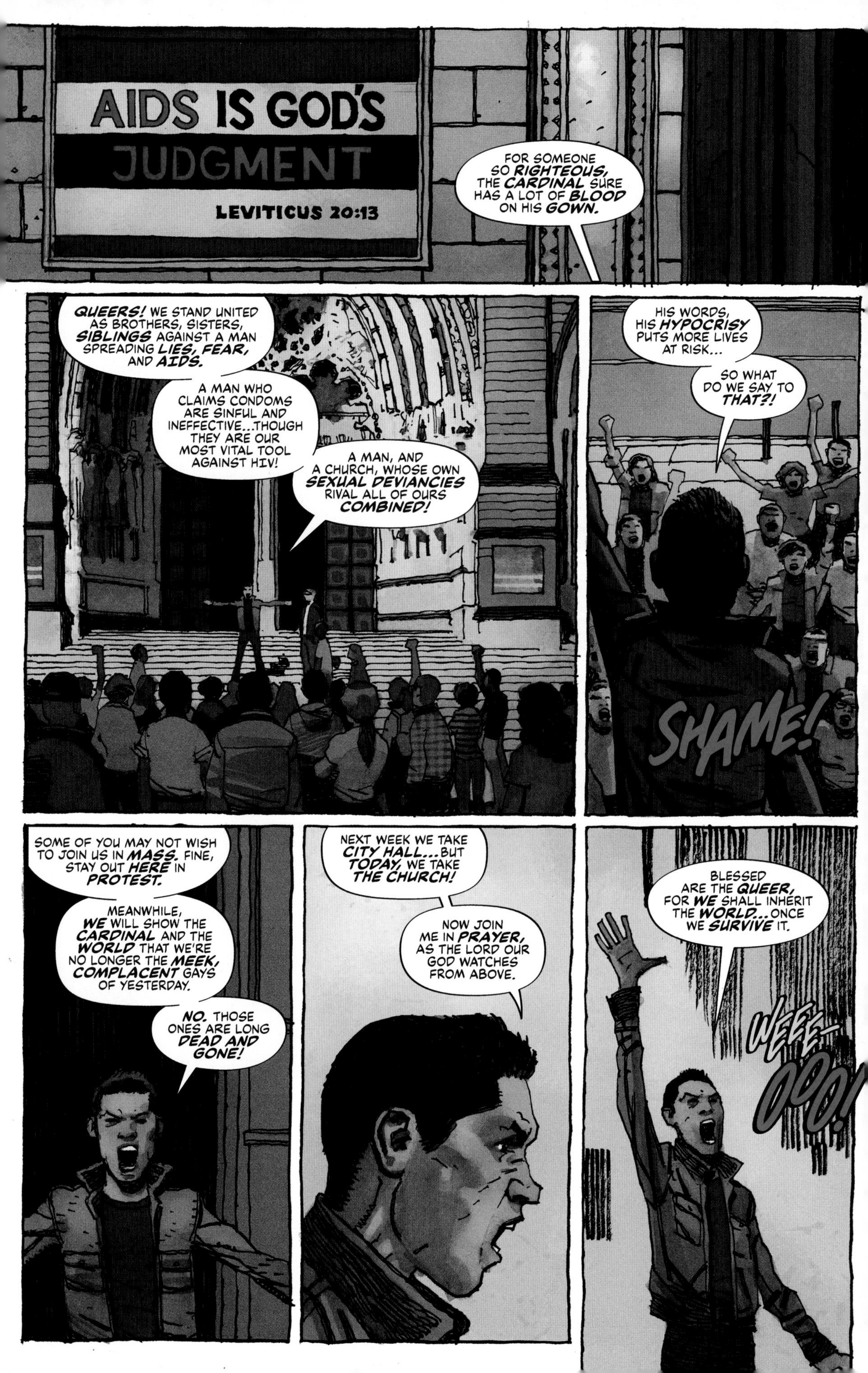
AIDS IS GOD'S JUDGMENT
LEVITICUS 20:13
FOR SOMEONE SO RIGHTEOUS, THE CARDINAL SURE HAS A LOT OF BLOOD ON HIS GOWN.
QUEERS! WE STAND UNITED AS BROTHERS, SISTERS, SIBLINGS AGAINST A MAN SPREADING LIES, FEAR, AND AIDS.
A MAN WHO CLAIMS CONDOMS ARE SINFUL AND INEFFECTIVE...THOUGH THEY ARE OUR MOST VITAL TOOL AGAINST HIV!
A MAN, AND A CHURCH, WHOSE OWN SEXUAL DEVIANCIES RIVAL ALL OF OURS COMBINED!
HIS WORDS, HIS HYPOCRISY PUTS MORE LIVES AT RISK...
SO WHAT DO WE SAY TO THAT?!
SHAME!
SOME OF YOU MAY NOT WISH TO JOIN US IN MASS. FINE, STAY OUT HERE IN PROTEST.
MEANWHILE, WE WILL SHOW THE CARDINAL AND THE WORLD THAT WE'RE NO LONGER THE MEEK, COMPLACENT GAYS OF YESTERDAY.
NO. THOSE ONES ARE LONG DEAD AND GONE!
NEXT WEEK WE TAKE CITY HALL... BUT TODAY, WE TAKE THE CHURCH!
NOW JOIN ME IN PRAYER, AS THE LORD OUR GOD WATCHES FROM ABOVE.
BLESSED ARE THE QUEER, FOR WE SHALL INHERIT THE WORLD... ONCE WE SURVIVE IT.
WEEE-OOO!

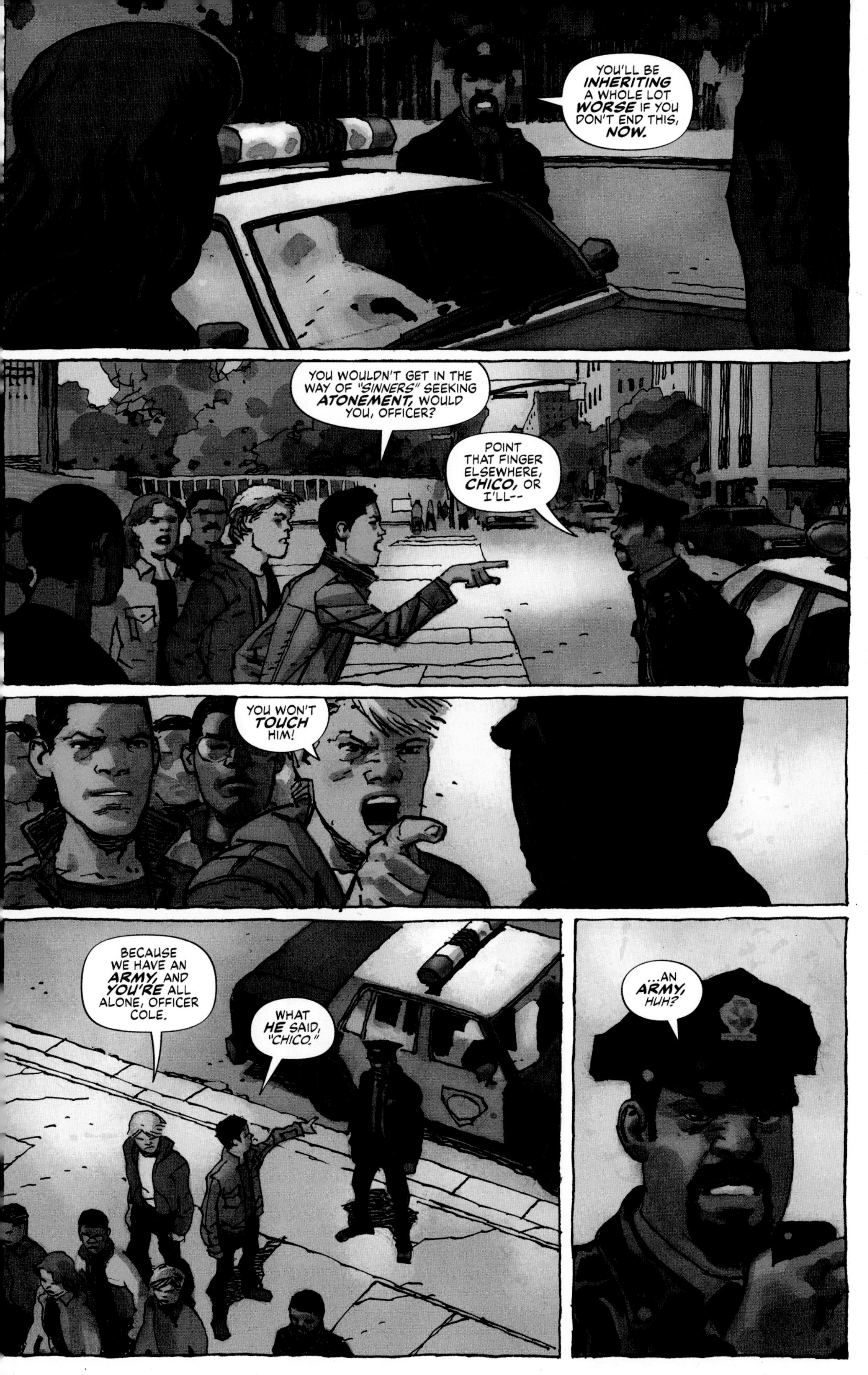
YOU'LL BE INHERITING A WHOLE LOT WORSE IF YOU DON'T END THIS, NOW.
YOU WOULDN'T GET IN THE WAY OF "SINNERS" SEEKING ATONEMENT, WOULD YOU, OFFICER?
POINT THAT FINGER ELSEWHERE, CHICO, OR I'LL--
YOU WON'T TOUCH HIM!
BECAUSE WE HAVE AN ARMY, AND YOU'RE ALL ALONE, OFFICER COLE.
WHAT HE SAID, "CHICO."
...AN ARMY, HUH?

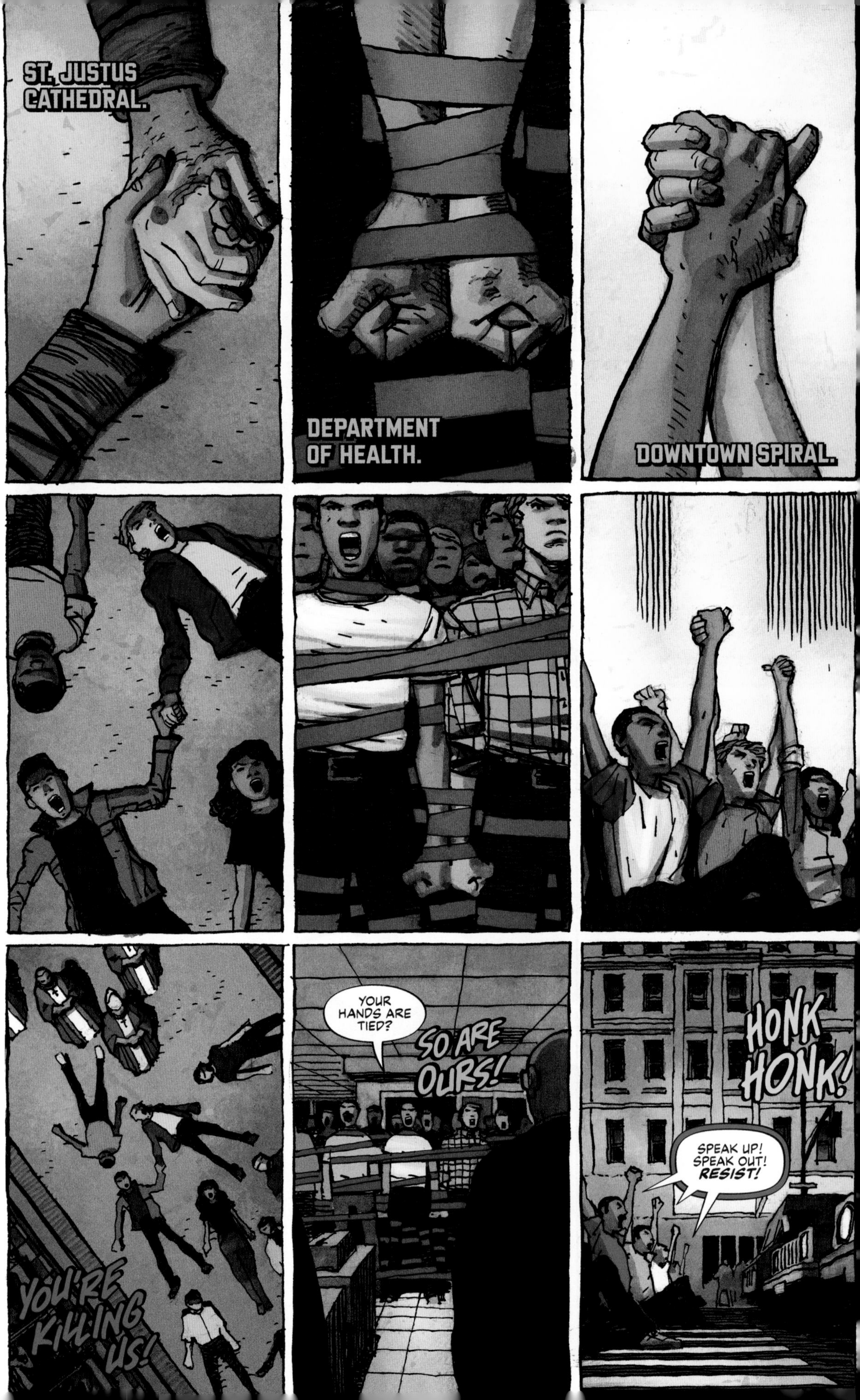
ST. JUSTUS CATHEDRAL.
DEPARTMENT OF HEALTH.
DOWNTOWN SPIRAL.
YOU'RE KILLING US!
YOUR HANDS ARE TIED?
SO ARE OURS!
HONK HONK!
SPEAK UP! SPEAK OUT! RESIST!

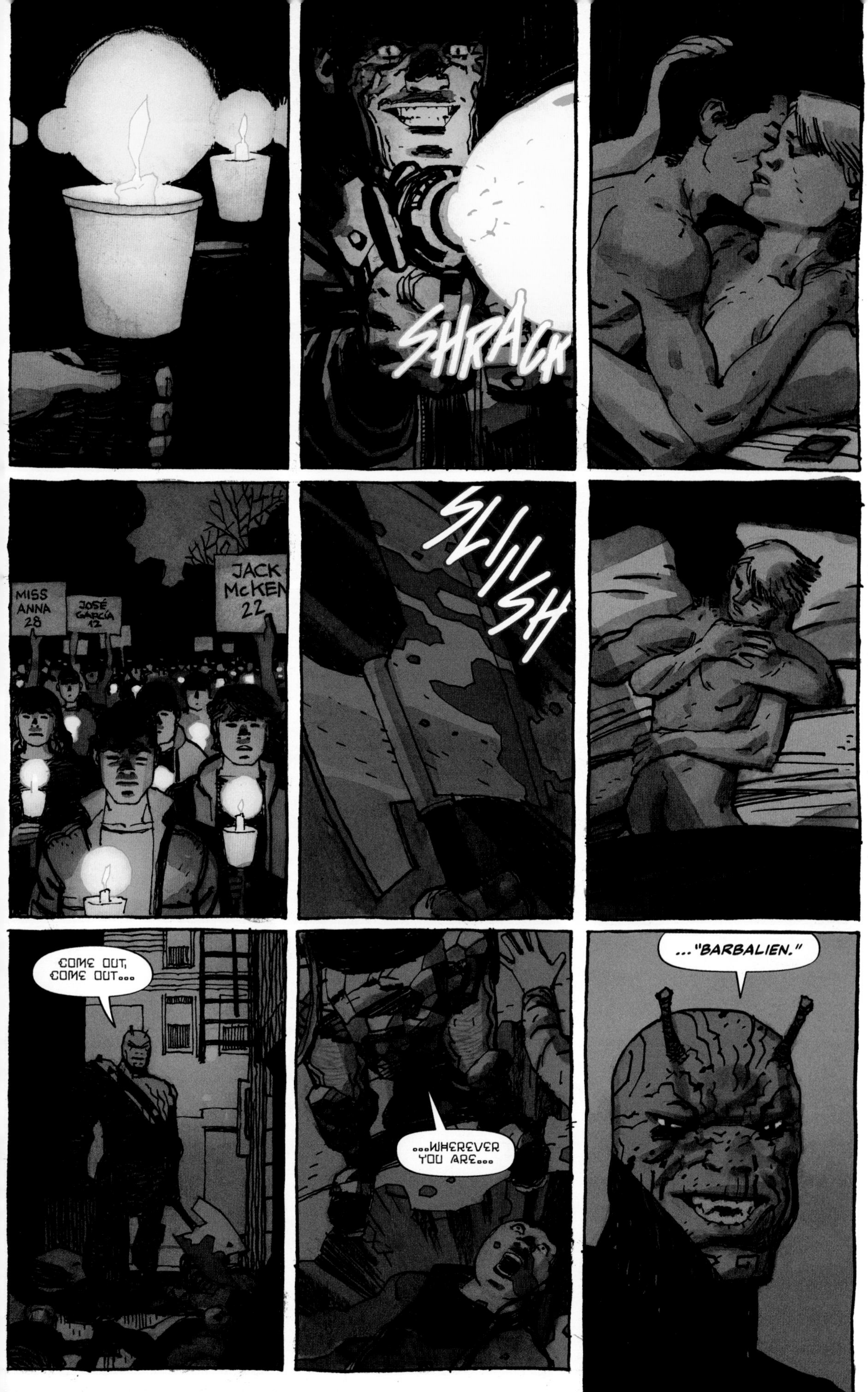
SHRACK
MISS ANNA 28
JOSÉ GARCÍA 12
JACK McKEN 22
SLIIISH
COME OUT, COME OUT...
...WHEREVER YOU ARE...
..."BARBALIEN."

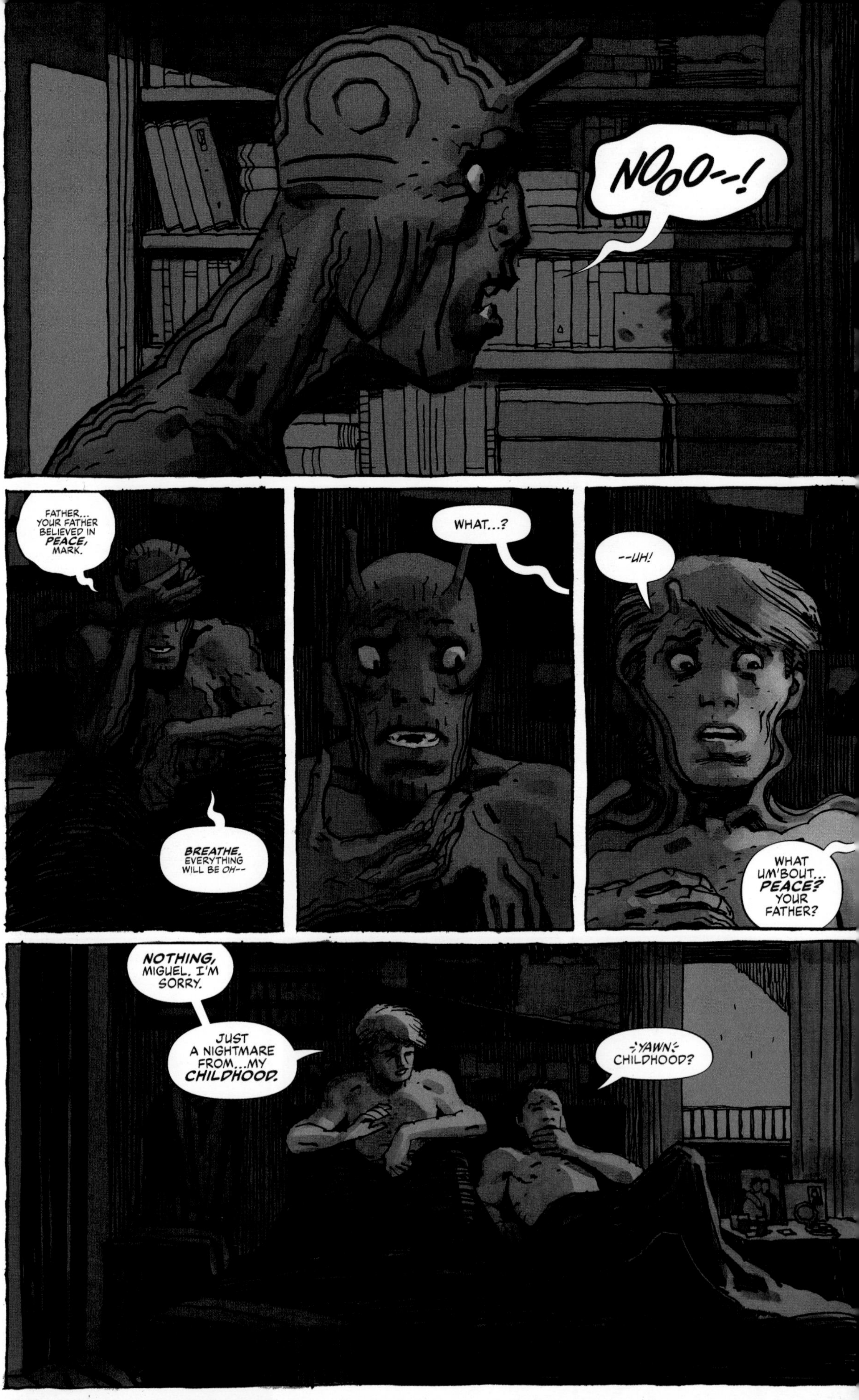
NOOO--!
FATHER... YOUR FATHER BELIEVED IN PEACE, MARK.
BREATHE. EVERYTHING WILL BE OH--
WHAT...?
--UH!
WHAT UM'BOUT... PEACE? YOUR FATHER?
NOTHING, MIGUEL. I'M SORRY.
JUST A NIGHTMARE FROM...MY CHILDHOOD.
-YAWN- CHILDHOOD?

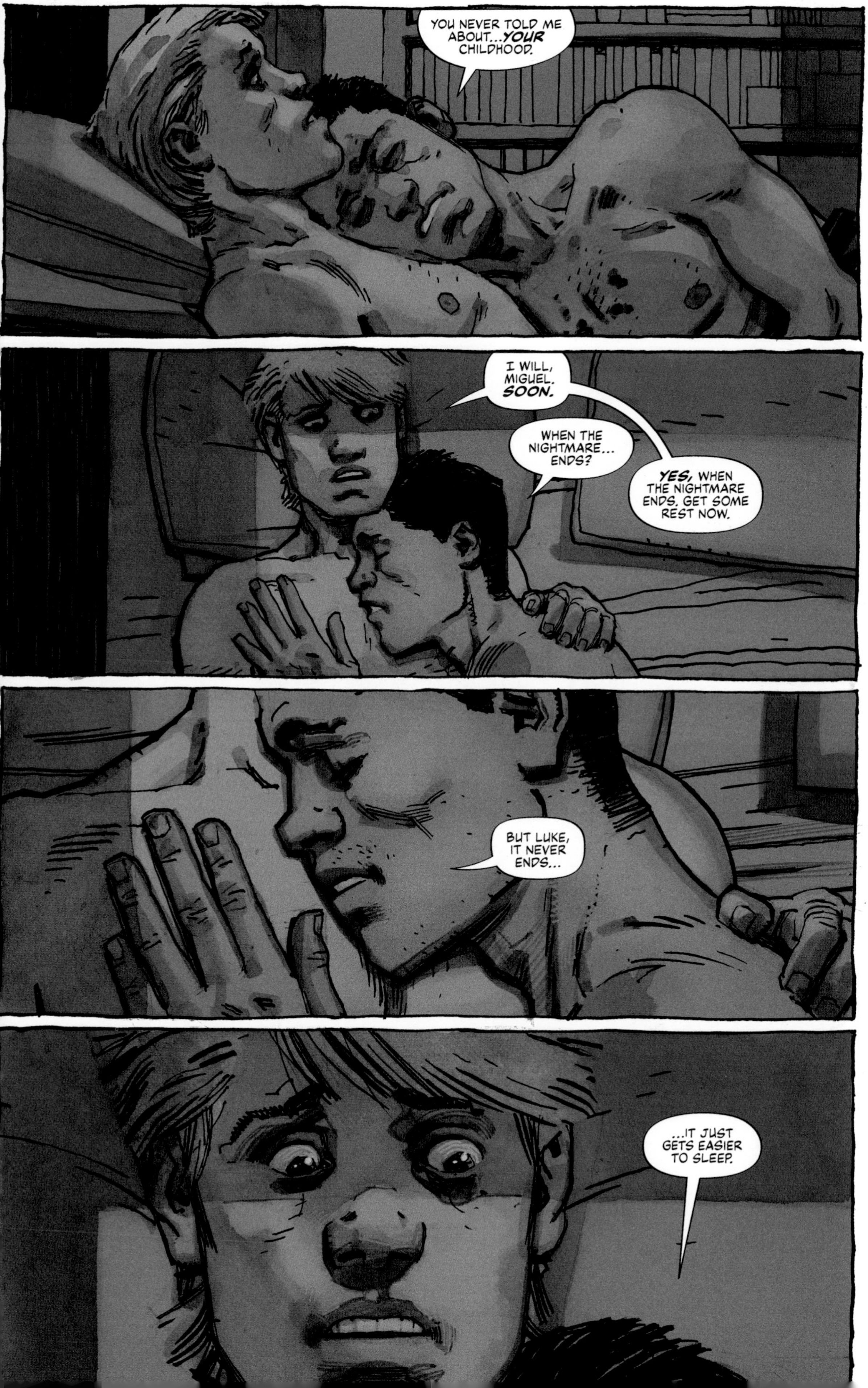
YOU NEVER TOLD ME ABOUT... YOUR CHILDHOOD.
I WILL, MIGUEL. SOON.
WHEN THE NIGHTMARE... ENDS?
YES, WHEN THE NIGHTMARE ENDS. GET SOME REST NOW.
BUT LUKE, IT NEVER ENDS...
...IT JUST GETS EASIER TO SLEEP.

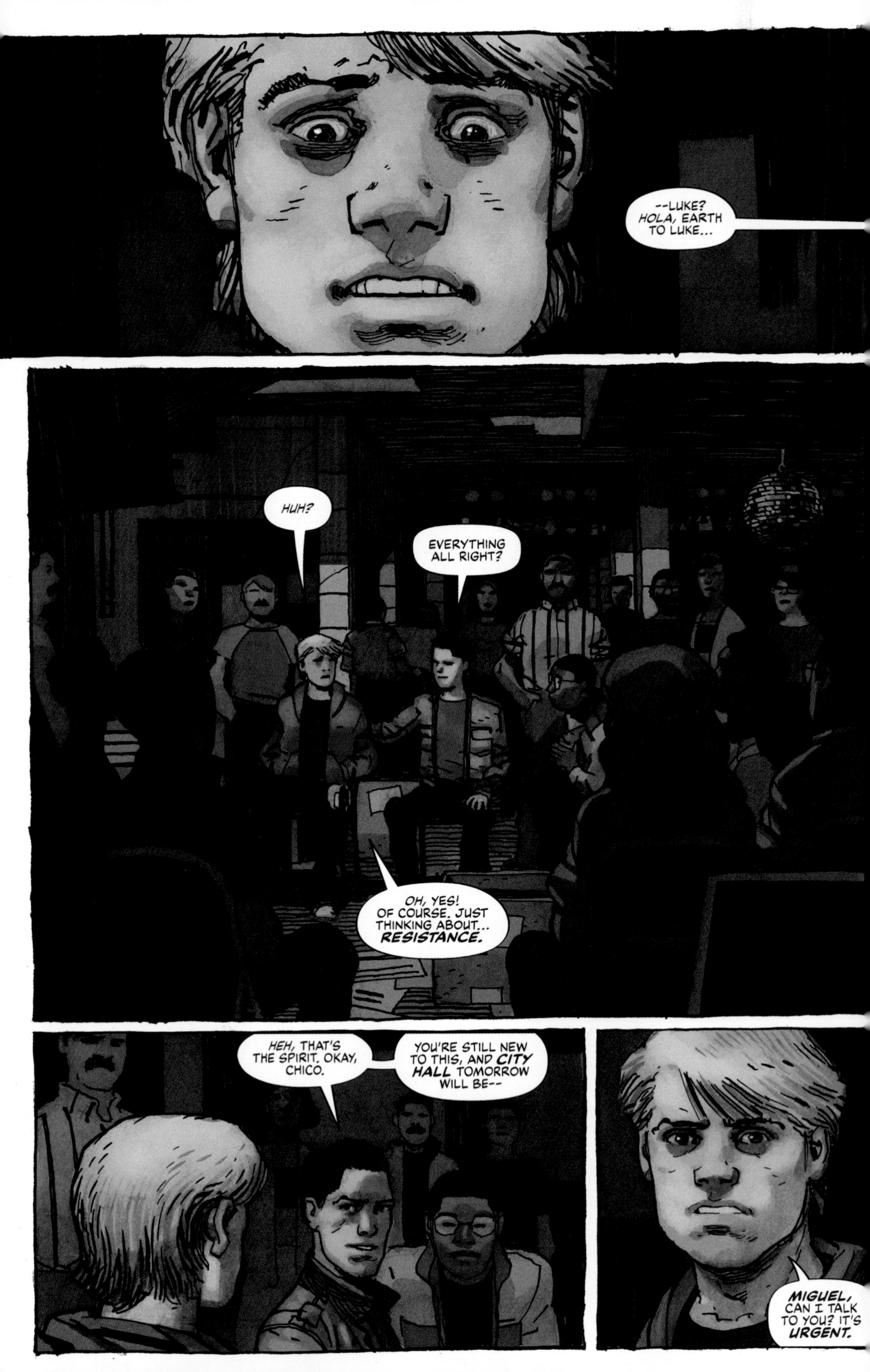
--LUKE? HOLA, EARTH TO LUKE...
HUH?
EVERYTHING ALL RIGHT?
OH, YES! OF COURSE. JUST THINKING ABOUT... RESISTANCE.
HEH, THAT'S THE SPIRIT. OKAY, CHICO.
YOU'RE STILL NEW TO THIS, AND CITY HALL TOMORROW WILL BE--
MIGUEL, CAN I TALK TO YOU? IT'S URGENT.

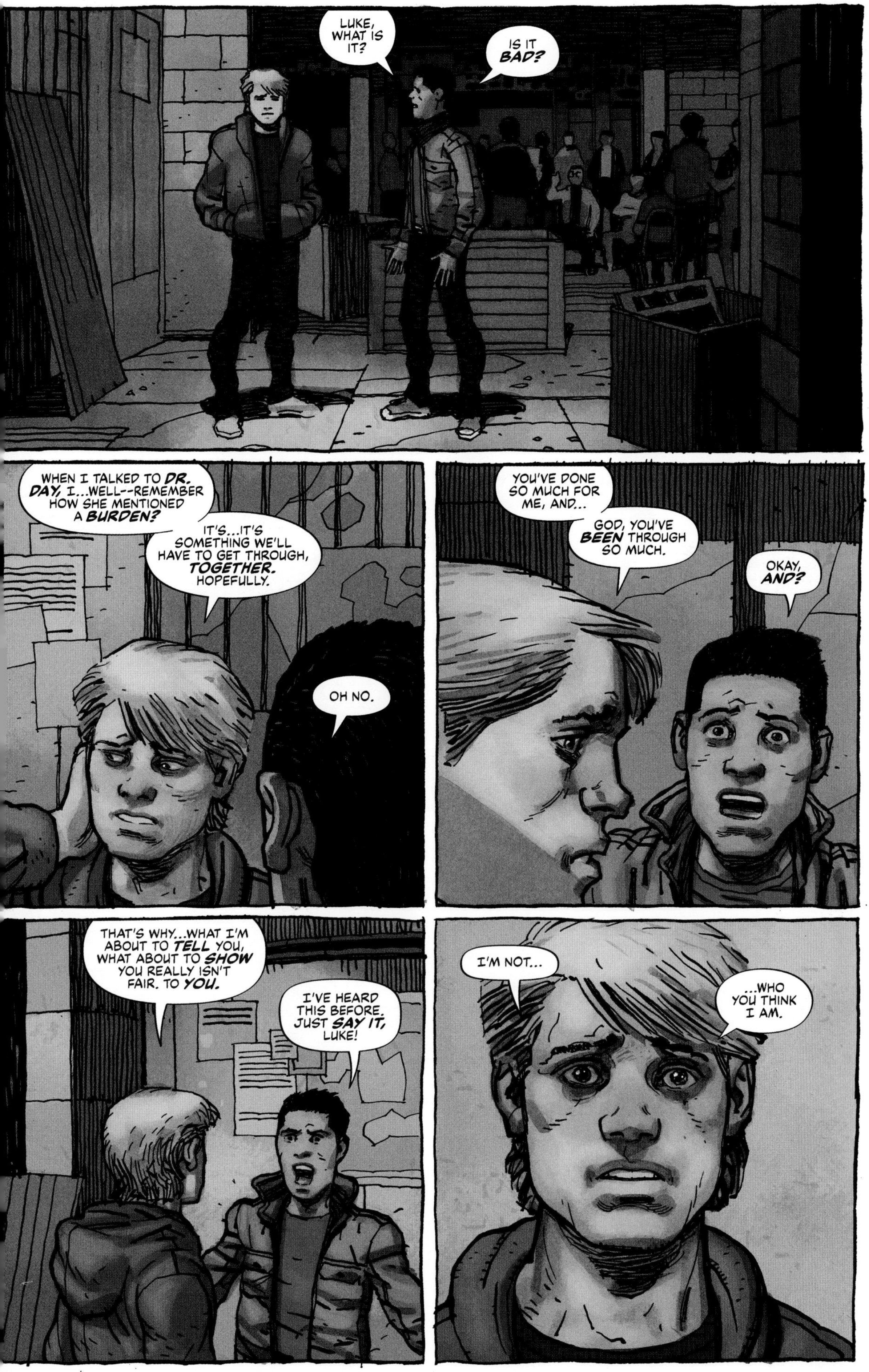
LUKE, WHAT IS IT?
IS IT BAD?
WHEN I TALKED TO DR. DAY, I...WELL--REMEMBER HOW SHE MENTIONED A BURDEN?
IT'S...IT'S SOMETHING WE'LL HAVE TO GET THROUGH, TOGETHER. HOPEFULLY.
OH NO.
YOU'VE DONE SO MUCH FOR ME, AND...
GOD, YOU'VE BEEN THROUGH SO MUCH.
OKAY, AND?
THAT'S WHY...WHAT I'M ABOUT TO TELL YOU, WHAT ABOUT TO SHOW YOU REALLY ISN'T FAIR. TO YOU.
I'VE HEARD THIS BEFORE. JUST SAY IT, LUKE!
I'M NOT...
...WHO YOU THINK I AM.

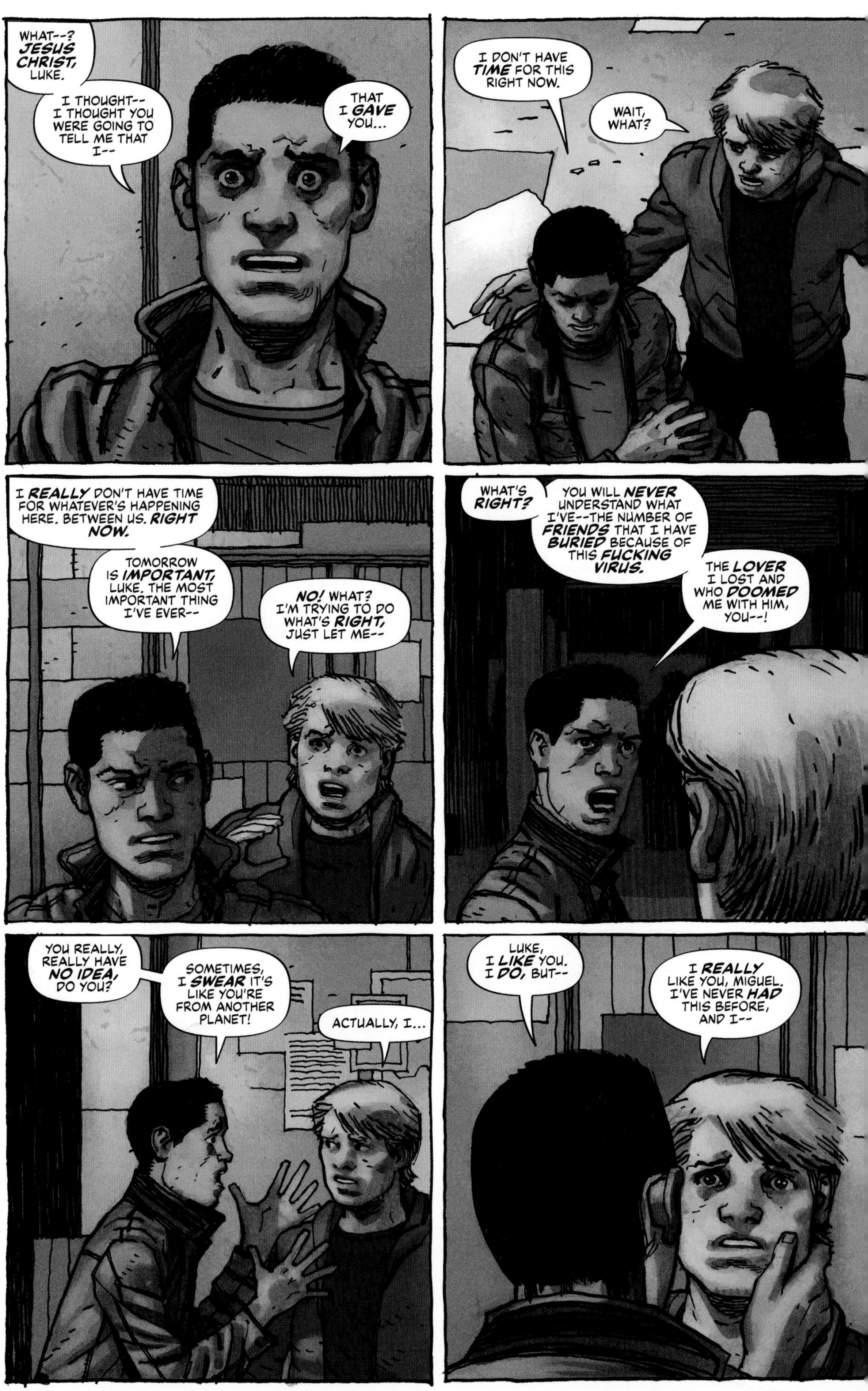
WHAT--? JESUS CHRIST, LUKE.
I THOUGHT-- I THOUGHT YOU WERE GOING TO TELL ME THAT I--
THAT I GAVE YOU...
I DON'T HAVE TIME FOR THIS RIGHT NOW.
WAIT, WHAT?
I REALLY DON'T HAVE TIME FOR WHATEVER'S HAPPENING HERE. BETWEEN US. RIGHT NOW.
TOMORROW IS IMPORTANT, LUKE. THE MOST IMPORTANT THING I'VE EVER--
NO! WHAT? I'M TRYING TO DO WHAT'S RIGHT, JUST LET ME--
WHAT'S RIGHT?
YOU WILL NEVER UNDERSTAND WHAT I'VE--THE NUMBER OF FRIENDS THAT I HAVE BURIED BECAUSE OF THIS FUCKING VIRUS.
THE LOVER I LOST AND WHO DOOMED ME WITH HIM, YOU--!
YOU REALLY, REALLY HAVE NO IDEA, DO YOU?
SOMETIMES, I SWEAR IT'S LIKE YOU'RE FROM ANOTHER PLANET!
ACTUALLY, I...
LUKE, I LIKE YOU. I DO, BUT--
I REALLY LIKE YOU, MIGUEL. I'VE NEVER HAD THIS BEFORE, AND I--

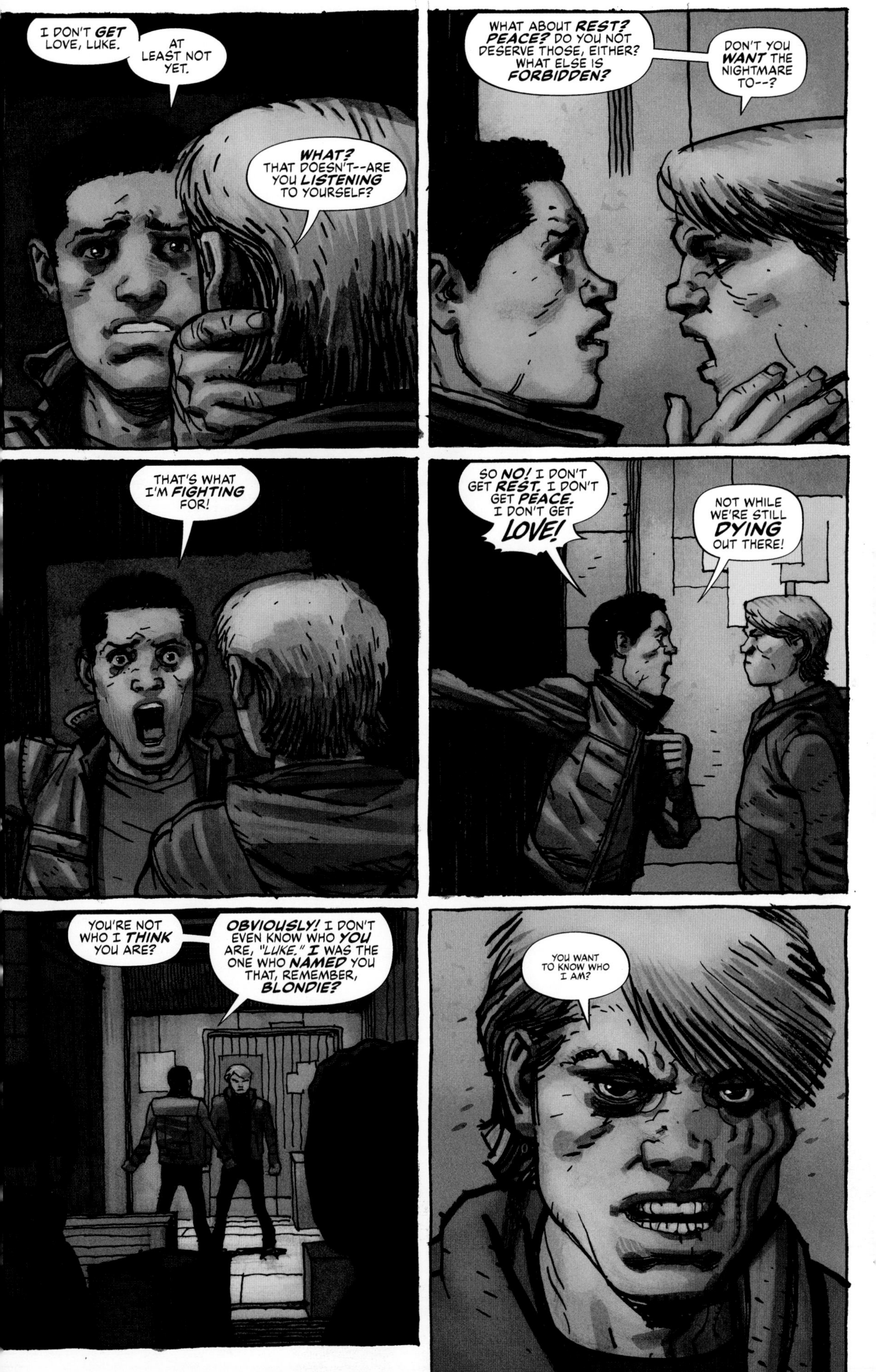
I DON'T GET LOVE, LUKE.
AT LEAST NOT YET.
WHAT? THAT DOESN'T--ARE YOU LISTENING TO YOURSELF?
WHAT ABOUT REST? PEACE? DO YOU NOT DESERVE THOSE, EITHER? WHAT ELSE IS FORBIDDEN?
DON'T YOU WANT THE NIGHTMARE TO--?
THAT'S WHAT I'M FIGHTING FOR!
SO NO! I DON'T GET REST. I DON'T GET PEACE. I DON'T GET LOVE!
NOT WHILE WE'RE STILL DYING OUT THERE!
YOU'RE NOT WHO I THINK YOU ARE?
OBVIOUSLY! I DON'T EVEN KNOW WHO YOU ARE, "LUKE." I WAS THE ONE WHO NAMED YOU THAT, REMEMBER, BLONDIE?
YOU WANT TO KNOW WHO I AM?

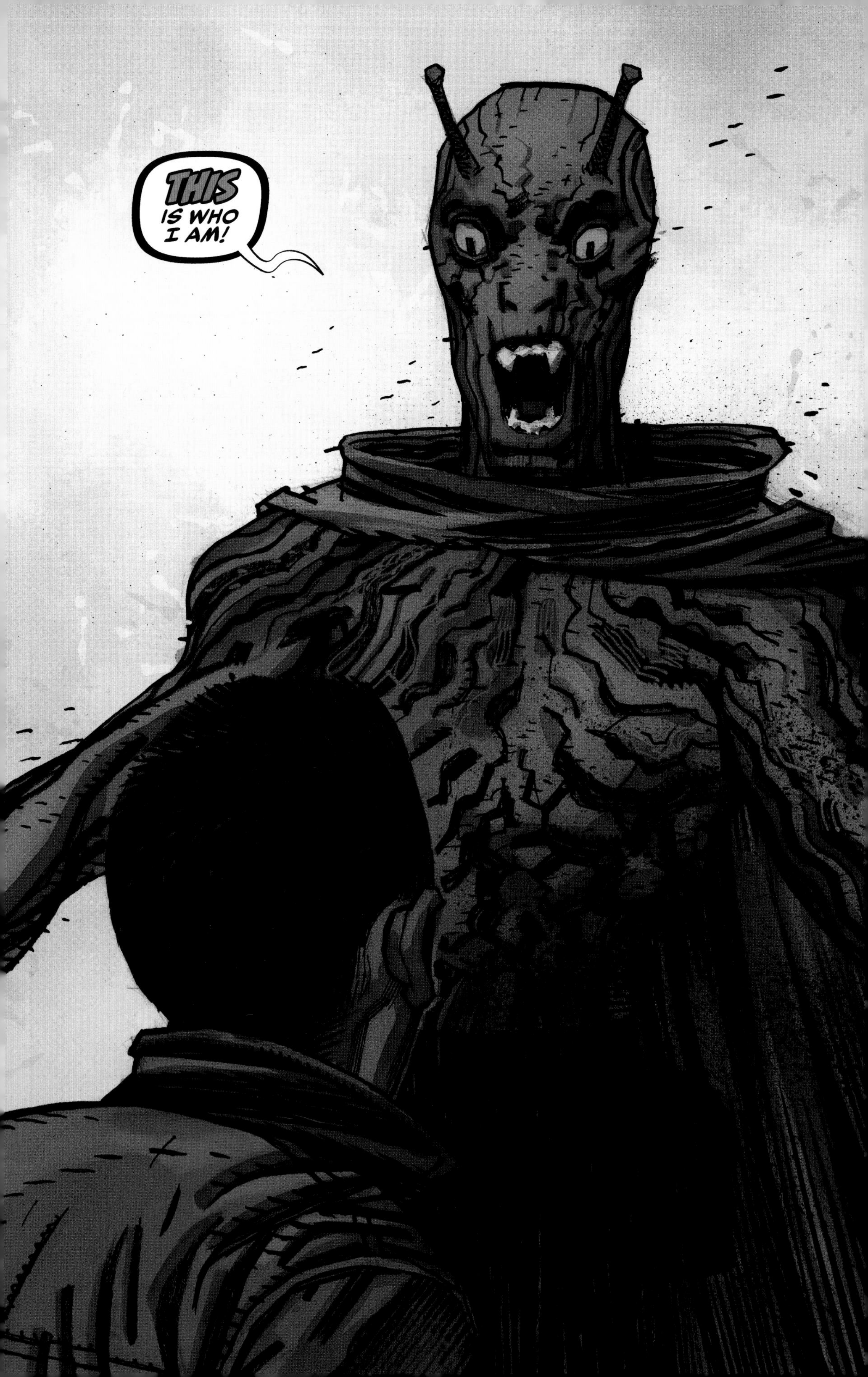
THIS IS WHO I AM!

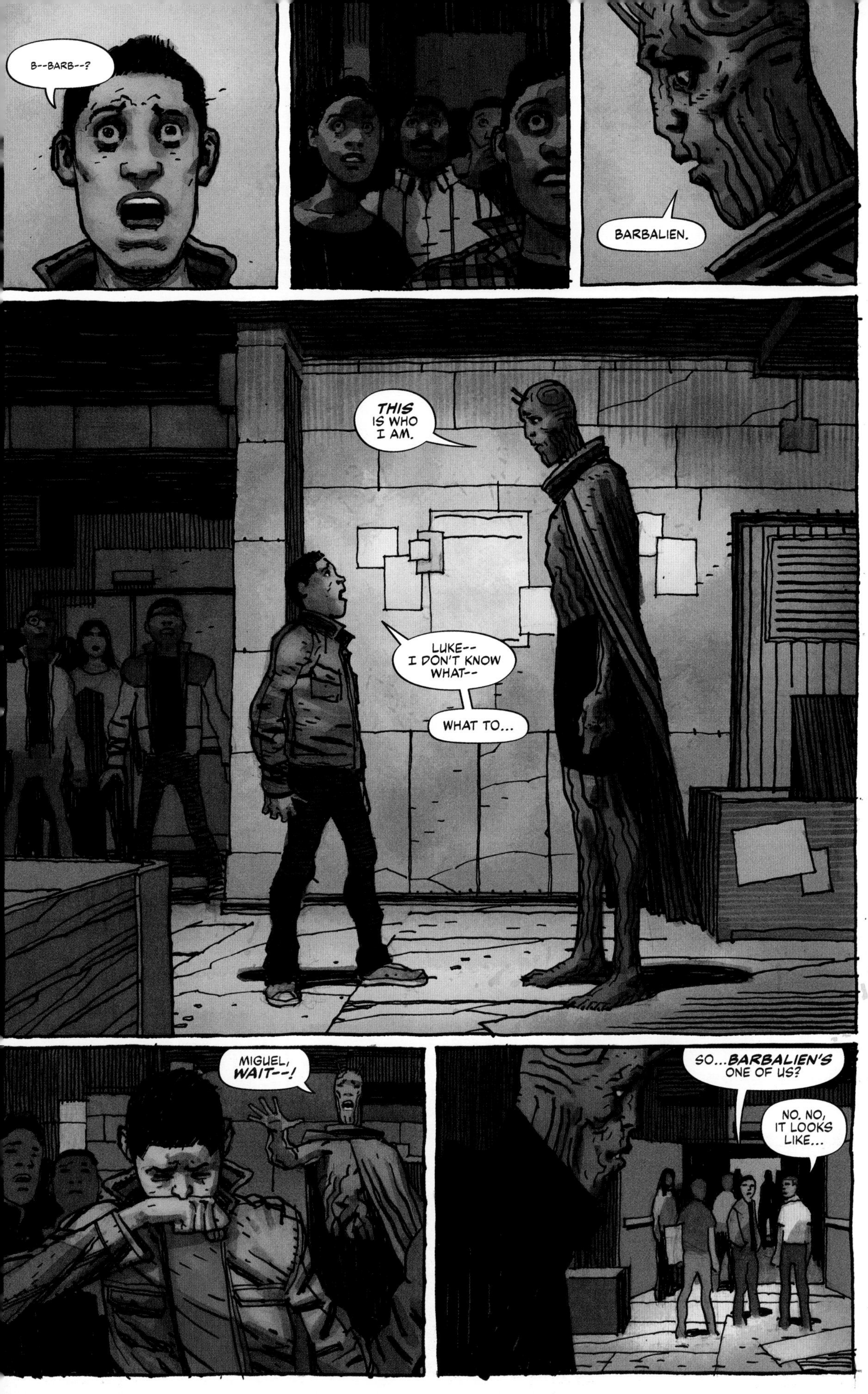
B--BARB--?
BARBALIEN.
THIS IS WHO I AM.
LUKE-- I DON'T KNOW WHAT--
WHAT TO...
MIGUEL, WAIT--!
SO...BARBALIEN'S ONE OF US?
NO. NO, IT LOOKS LIKE...

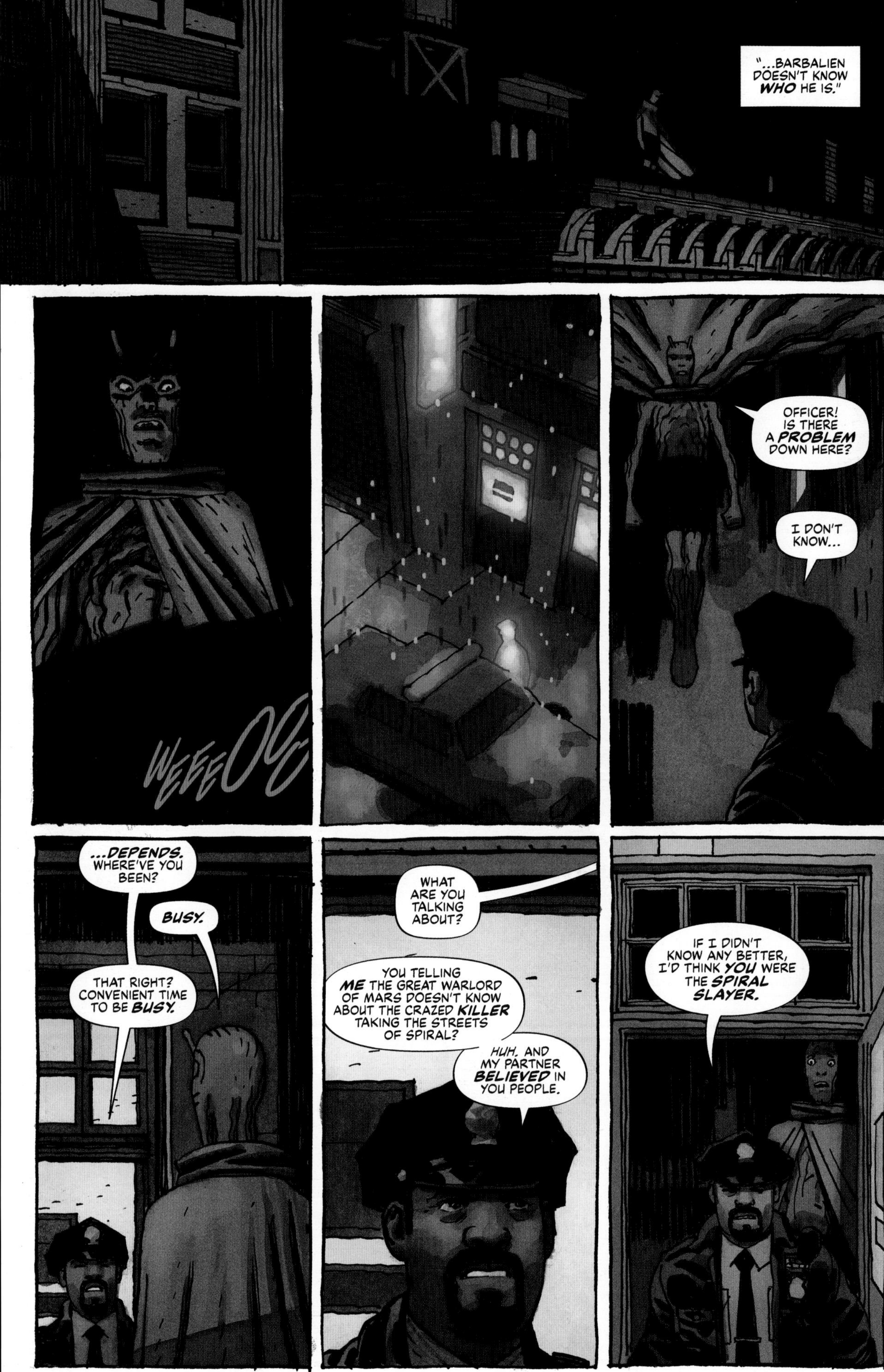
"...BARBALIEN DOESN'T KNOW WHO HE IS."
WEEEOO
OFFICER! IS THERE A PROBLEM DOWN HERE?
I DON'T KNOW...
...DEPENDS. WHERE'VE YOU BEEN?
BUSY.
THAT RIGHT? CONVENIENT TIME TO BE BUSY.
WHAT ARE YOU TALKING ABOUT?
YOU TELLING ME THE GREAT WARLORD OF MARS DOESN'T KNOW ABOUT THE CRAZED KILLER TAKING THE STREETS OF SPIRAL?
HUH. AND MY PARTNER BELIEVED IN YOU PEOPLE.
IF I DIDN'T KNOW ANY BETTER, I'D THINK YOU WERE THE SPIRAL SLAYER.

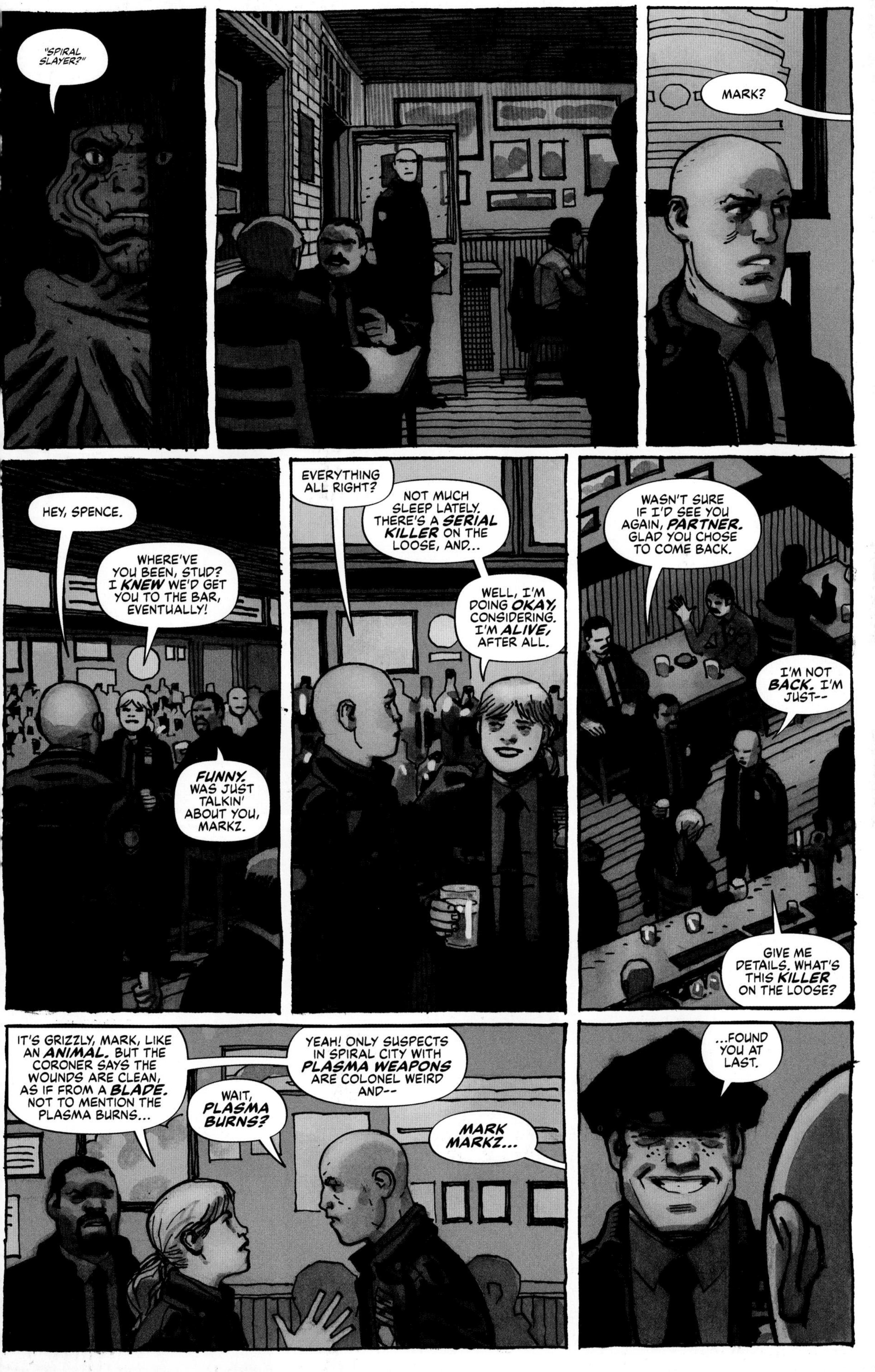
"SPIRAL SLAYER?"
MARK?
HEY, SPENCE.
WHERE'VE YOU BEEN, STUD? I KNEW WE'D GET YOU TO THE BAR, EVENTUALLY!
FUNNY. WAS JUST TALKIN' ABOUT YOU, MARKZ.
EVERYTHING ALL RIGHT?
NOT MUCH SLEEP LATELY. THERE'S A SERIAL KILLER ON THE LOOSE, AND...
WELL, I'M DOING OKAY, CONSIDERING. I'M ALIVE, AFTER ALL.
WASN'T SURE IF I'D SEE YOU AGAIN, PARTNER. GLAD YOU CHOSE TO COME BACK.
I'M NOT BACK. I'M JUST--
GIVE ME DETAILS. WHAT'S THIS KILLER ON THE LOOSE?
IT'S GRIZZLY, MARK, LIKE AN ANIMAL. BUT THE CORONER SAYS THE WOUNDS ARE CLEAN, AS IF FROM A BLADE. NOT TO MENTION THE PLASMA BURNS...
YEAH! ONLY SUSPECTS IN SPIRAL CITY WITH PLASMA WEAPONS ARE COLONEL WEIRD AND--
WAIT, PLASMA BURNS?
MARK MARKZ...
...FOUND YOU AT LAST.

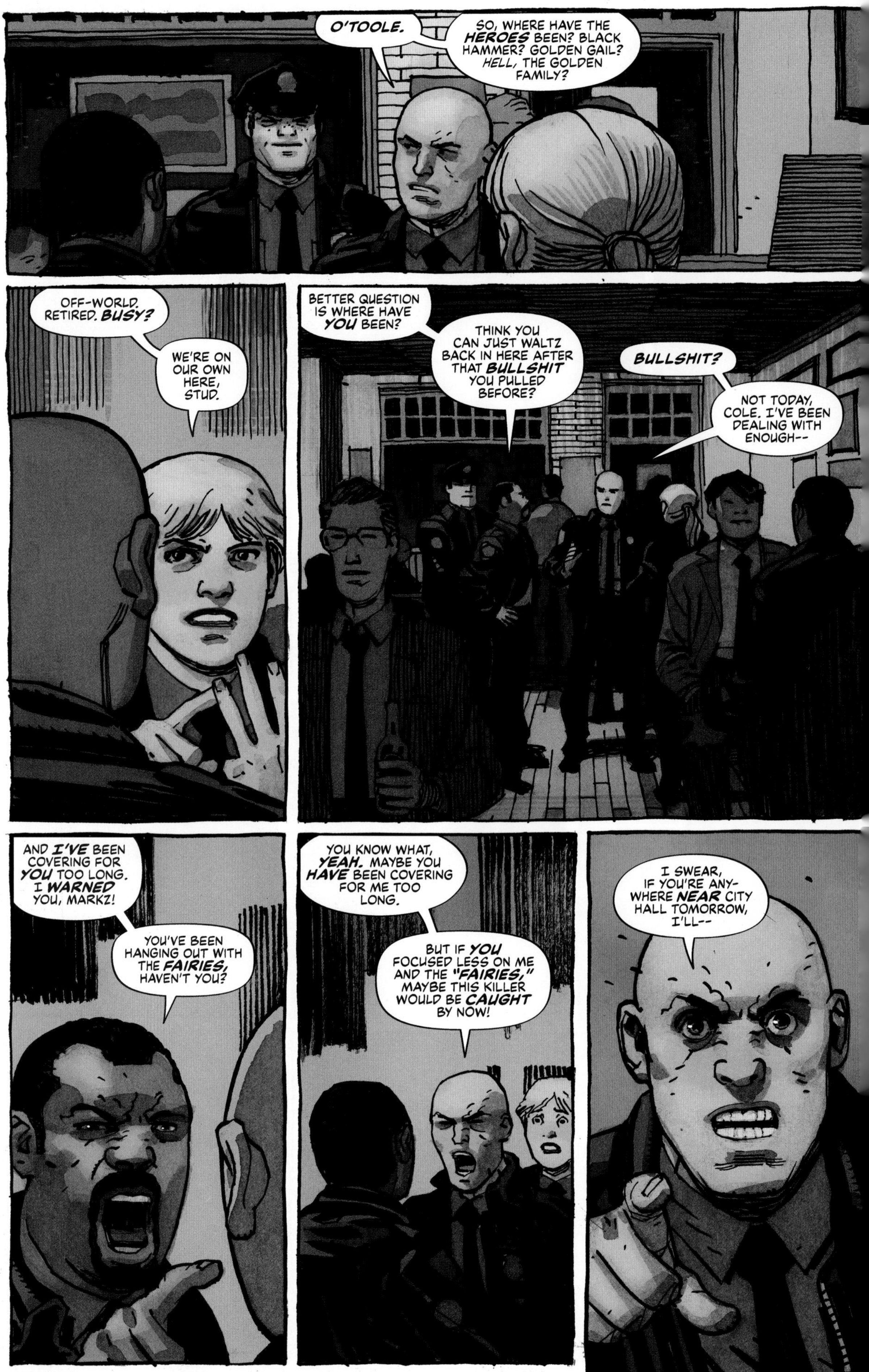
O'TOOLE.
SO, WHERE HAVE THE HEROES BEEN? BLACK HAMMER? GOLDEN GAIL? HELL, THE GOLDEN FAMILY?
OFF-WORLD. RETIRED. BUSY?
WE'RE ON OUR OWN HERE, STUD.
BETTER QUESTION IS WHERE HAVE YOU BEEN?
THINK YOU CAN JUST WALTZ BACK IN HERE AFTER THAT BULLSHIT YOU PULLED BEFORE?
BULLSHIT?
NOT TODAY, COLE. I'VE BEEN DEALING WITH ENOUGH--
AND I'VE BEEN COVERING FOR YOU TOO LONG. I WARNED YOU, MARKZ!
YOU'VE BEEN HANGING OUT WITH THE FAIRIES, HAVEN'T YOU?
YOU KNOW WHAT, YEAH. MAYBE YOU HAVE BEEN COVERING FOR ME TOO LONG.
BUT IF YOU FOCUSED LESS ON ME AND THE "FAIRIES," MAYBE THIS KILLER WOULD BE CAUGHT BY NOW!
I SWEAR, IF YOU'RE ANY-WHERE NEAR CITY HALL TOMORROW, I'LL--

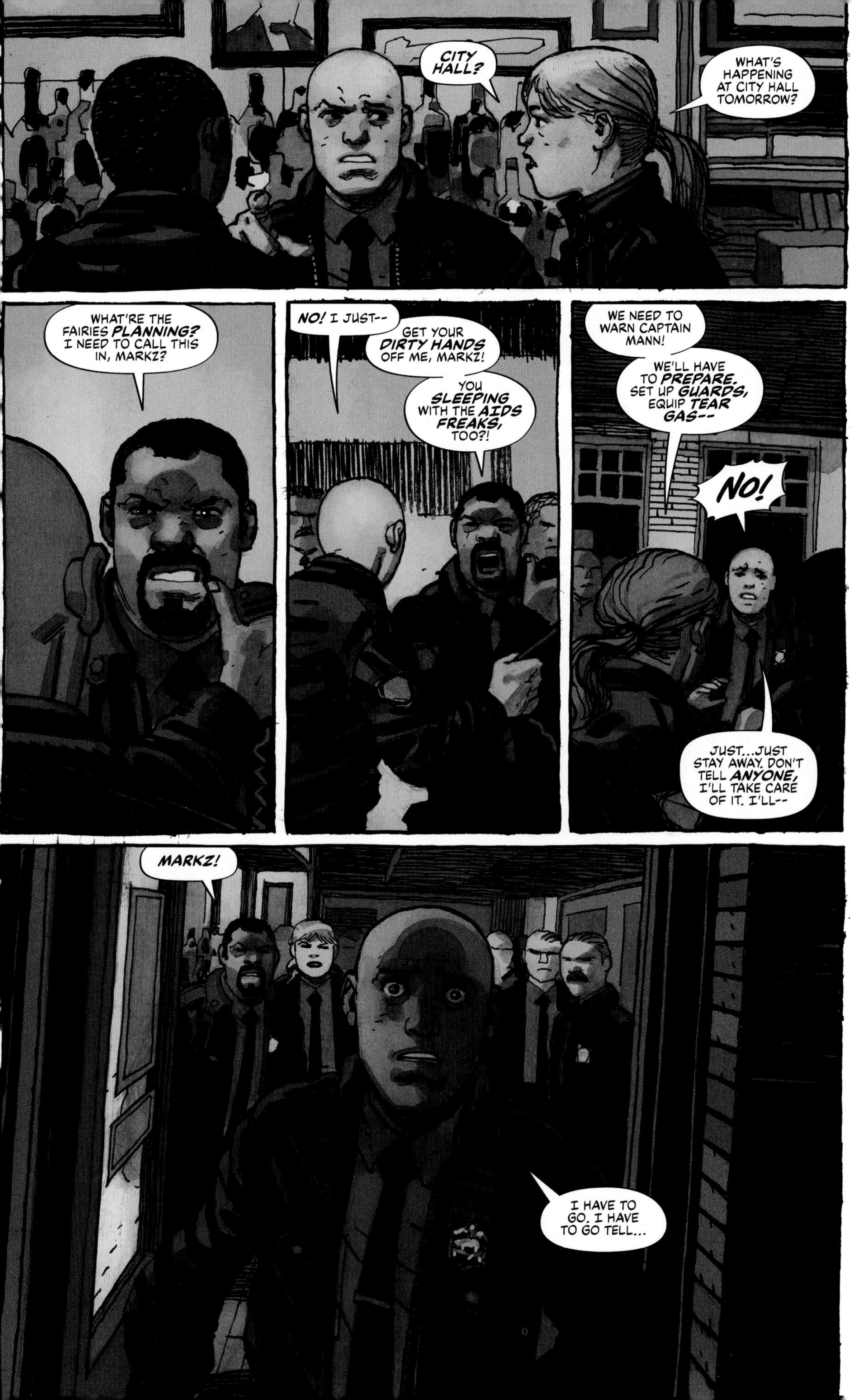
CITY HALL?
WHAT'S HAPPENING AT CITY HALL TOMORROW?
WHAT'RE THE FAIRIES PLANNING? I NEED TO CALL THIS IN, MARKZ?
NO! I JUST--
GET YOUR DIRTY HANDS OFF ME, MARKZ!
YOU SLEEPING WITH THE AIDS FREAKS, TOO?!
WE NEED TO WARN CAPTAIN MANN!
WE'LL HAVE TO PREPARE. SET UP GUARDS, EQUIP TEAR GAS--
NO!
JUST...JUST STAY AWAY. DON'T TELL ANYONE, I'LL TAKE CARE OF IT. I'LL--
MARKZ!
I HAVE TO GO. I HAVE TO GO TELL...

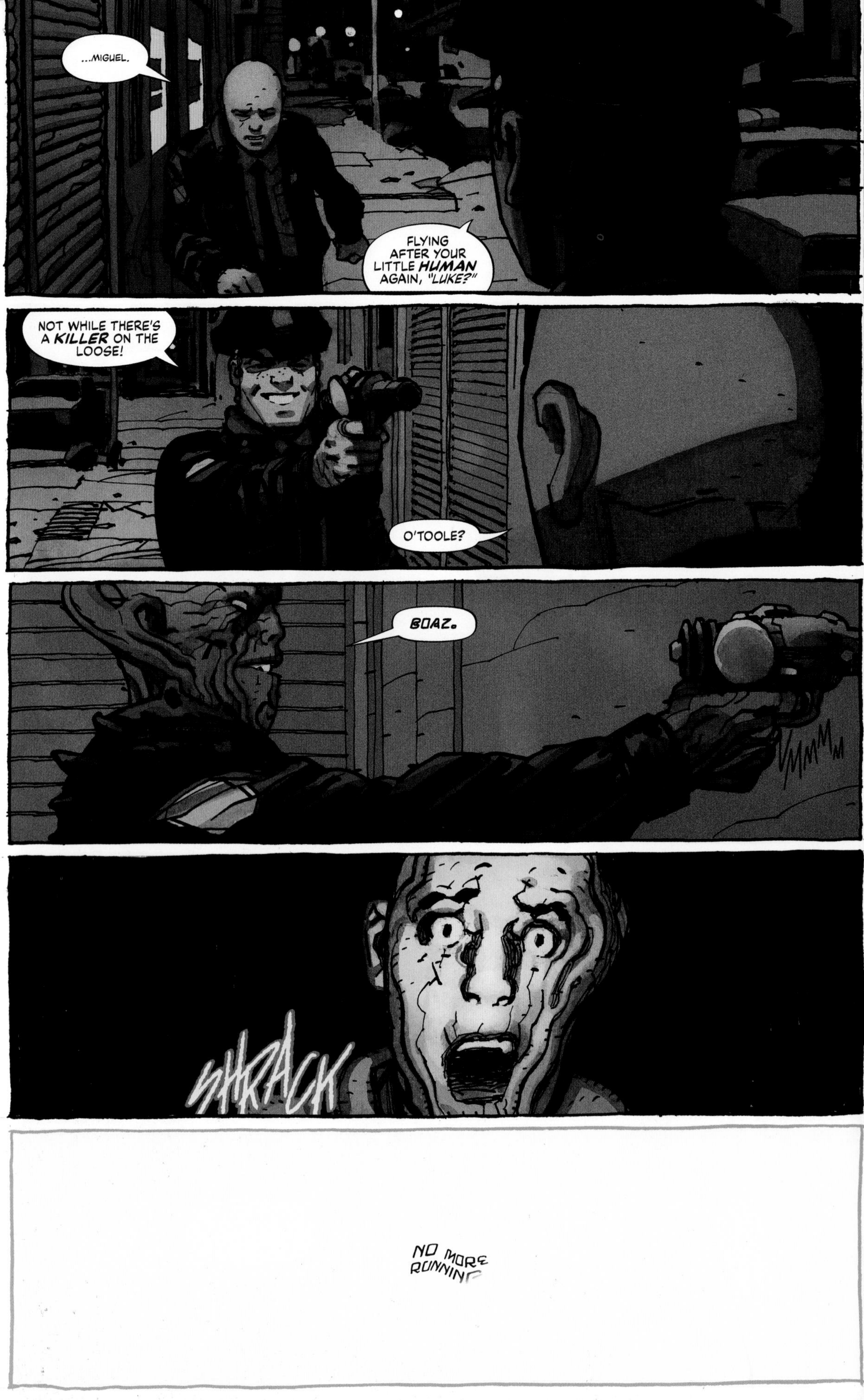
...MIGUEL.
FLYING AFTER YOUR LITTLE HUMAN AGAIN, "LUKE?"
NOT WHILE THERE'S A KILLER ON THE LOOSE!
O'TOOLE?
BOAZ.
VMMMM
SHRACK
NO MORE RUNNIN

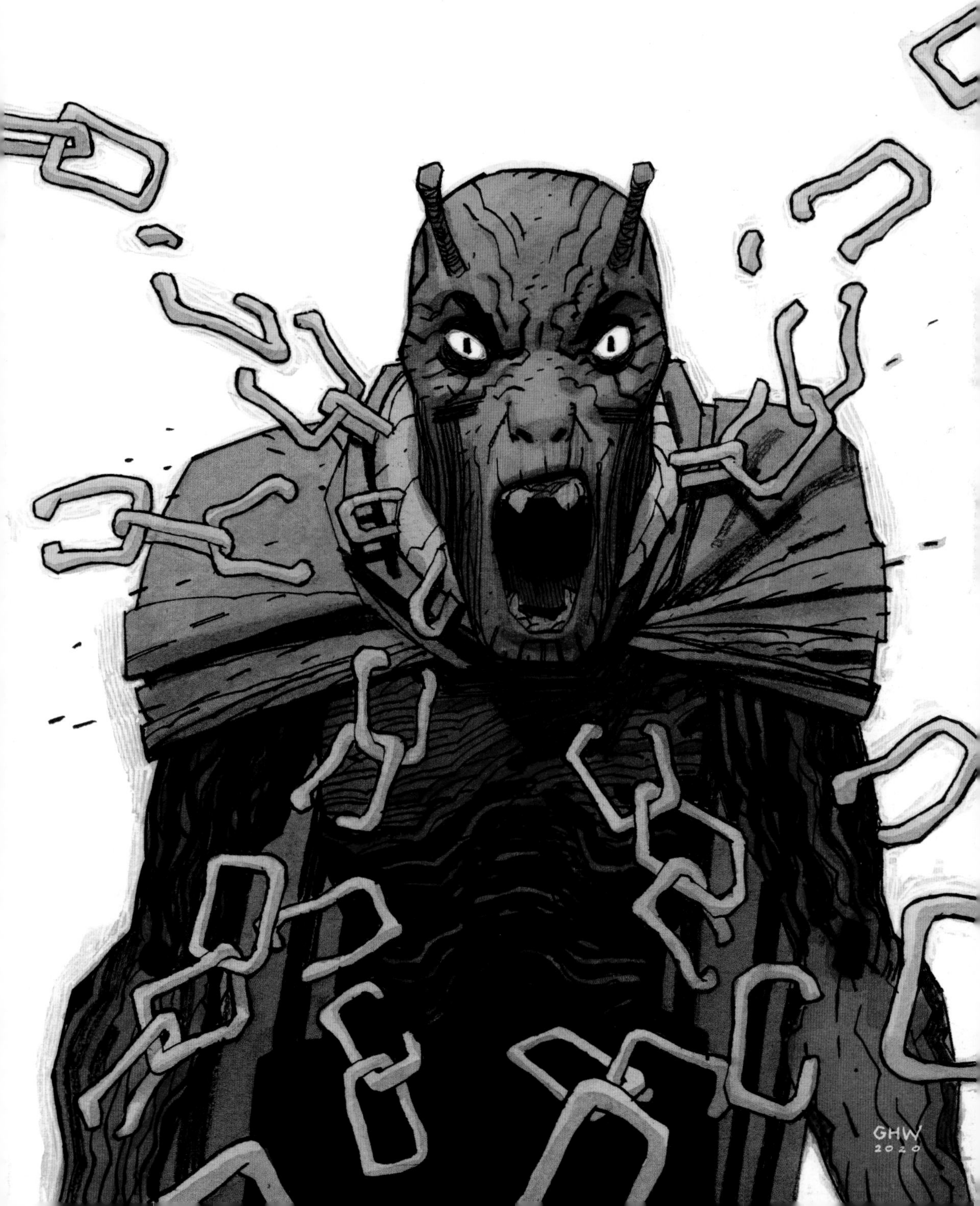
GHW
2020

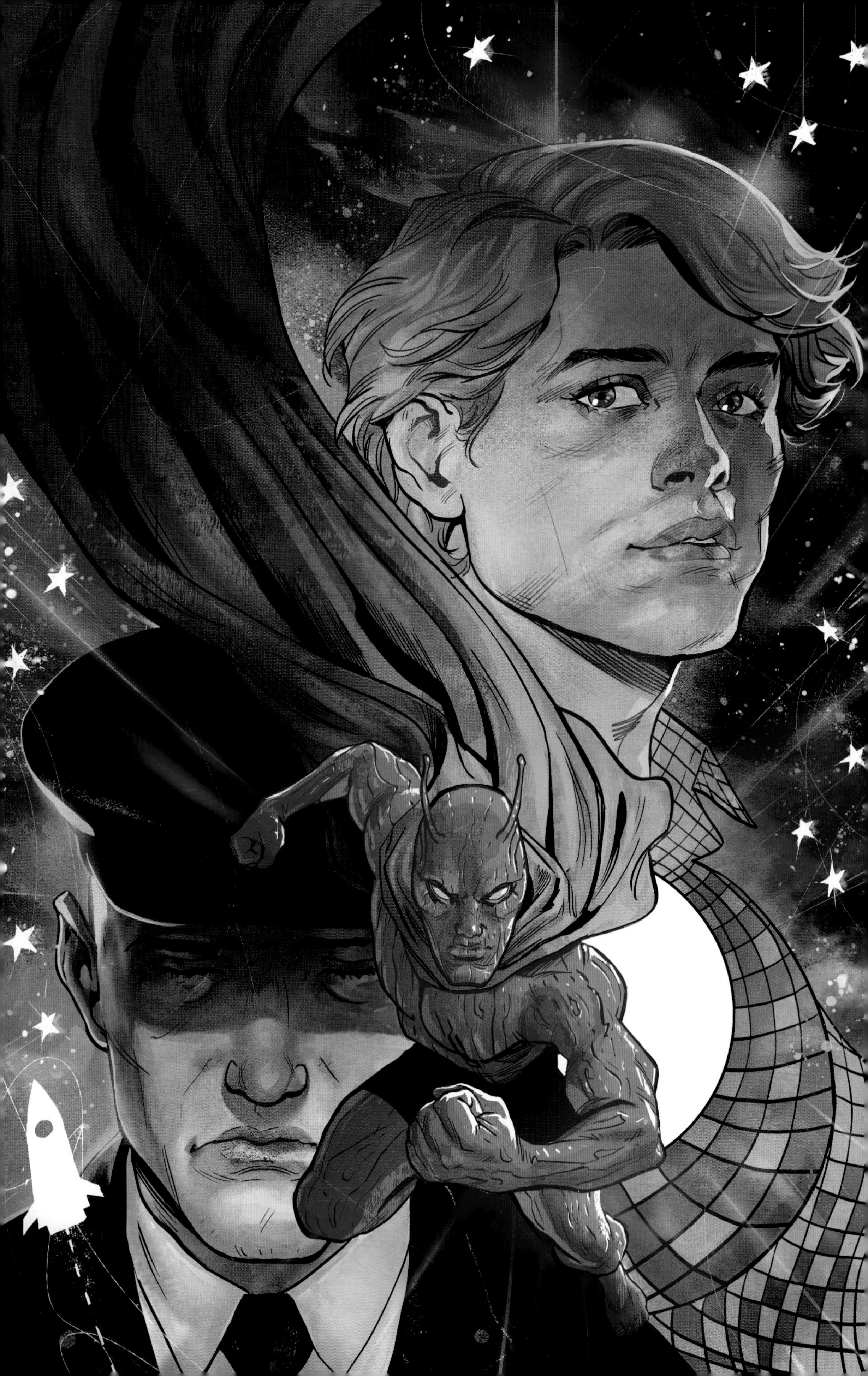

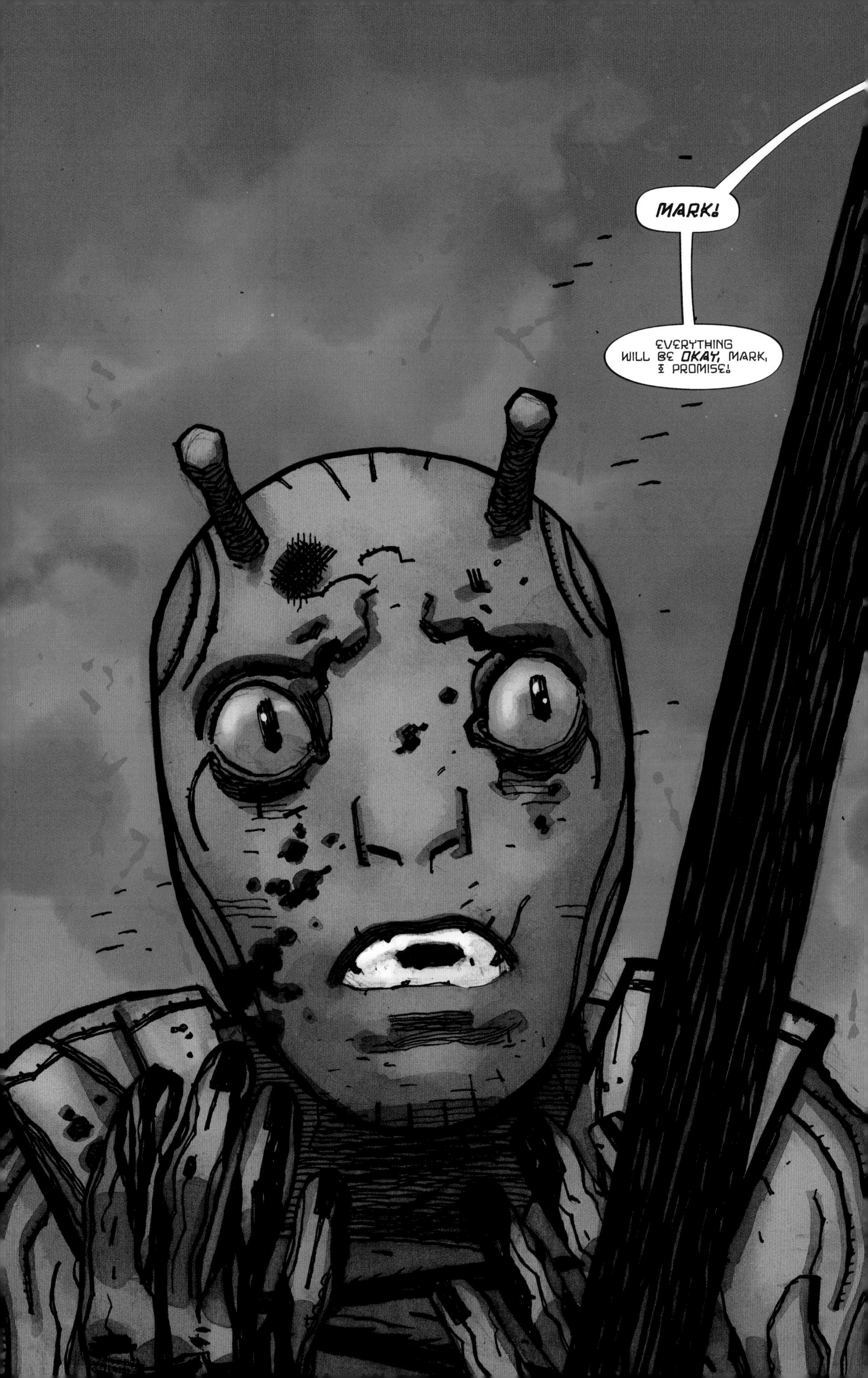
MARK!
EVERYTHING WILL BE OKAY, MARK, I PROMISE!

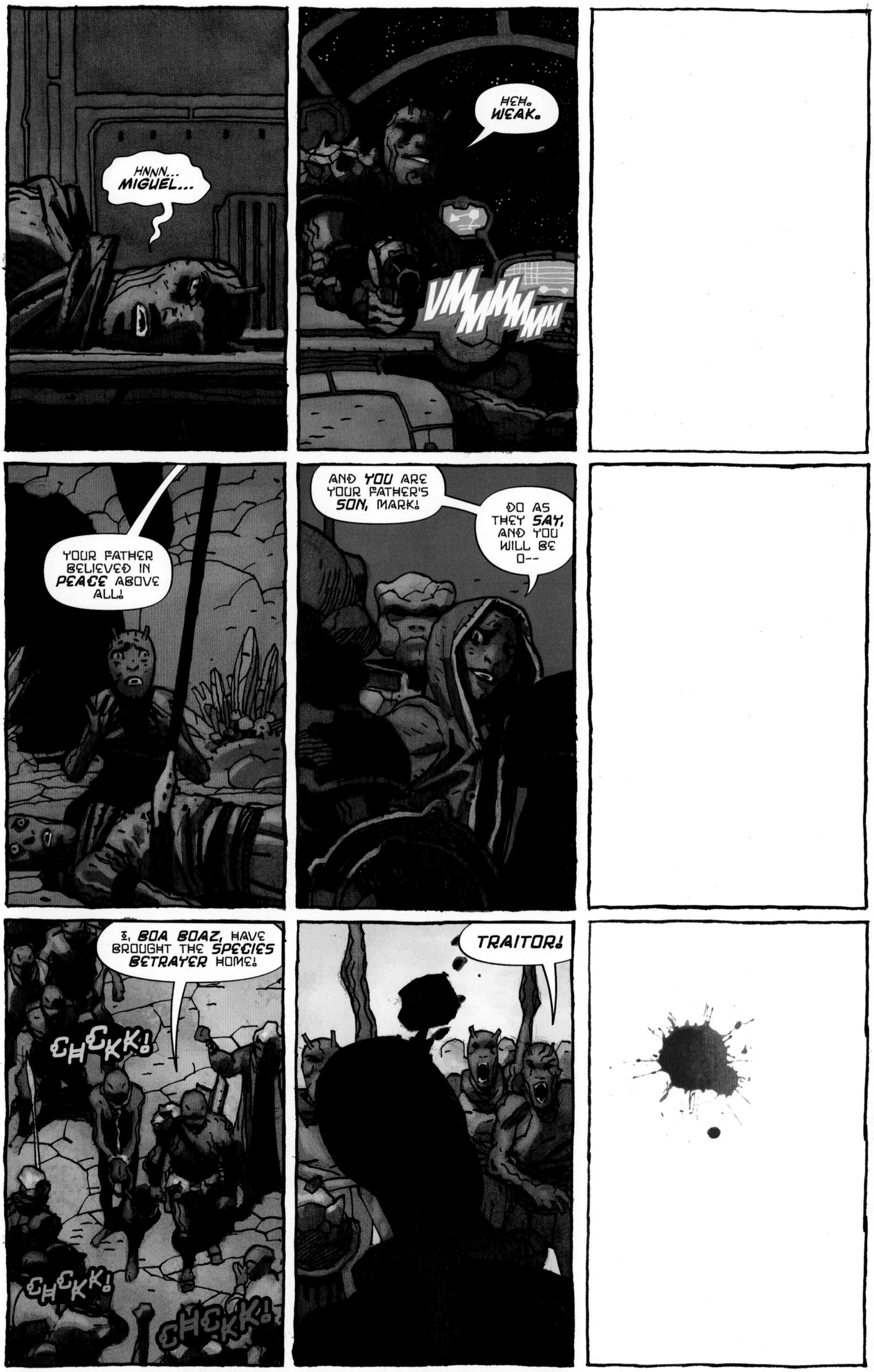
HNNN...
MIGUEL...
HEH.
WEAK.
VMMMMMMM
YOUR FATHER BELIEVED IN PEACE ABOVE ALL!
AND YOU ARE YOUR FATHER'S SON, MARK!
DO AS THEY SAY, AND YOU WILL BE O--
I, BOA BOAZ, HAVE BROUGHT THE SPECIES BETRAYER HOME!
CHEKK!
CHEKK!
CHEKK!
TRAITOR!

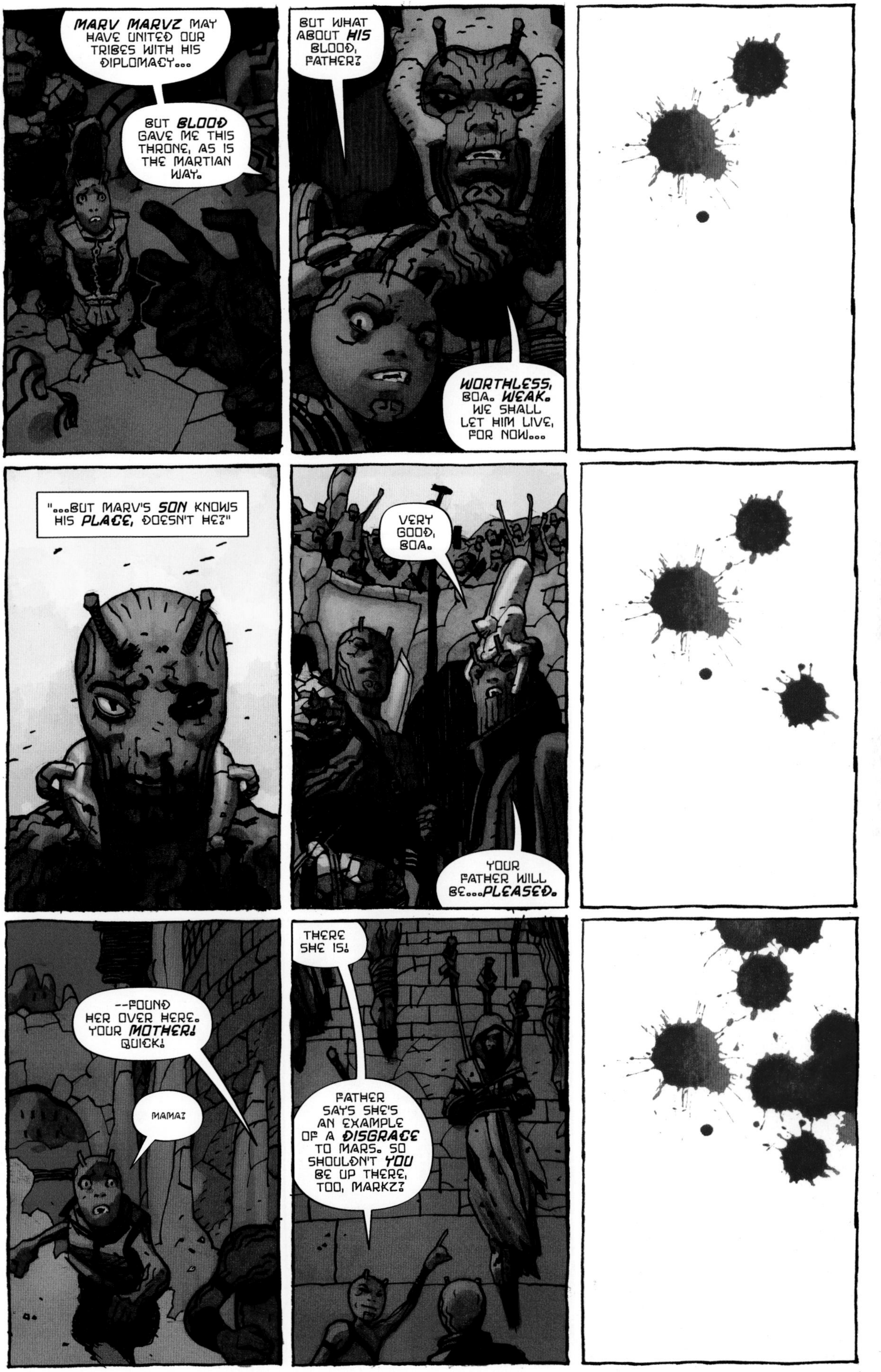
MARV MARVZ MAY HAVE UNITED OUR TRIBES WITH HIS DIPLOMACY...
BUT BLOOD GAVE ME THIS THRONE, AS IS THE MARTIAN WAY.
BUT WHAT ABOUT HIS BLOOD, FATHER?
WORTHLESS, BOA. WEAK. WE SHALL LET HIM LIVE, FOR NOW...
"...BUT MARV'S SON KNOWS HIS PLACE, DOESN'T HE?"
VERY GOOD, BOA.
YOUR FATHER WILL BE...PLEASED.
--FOUND HER OVER HERE. YOUR MOTHER! QUICK!
MAMA?
THERE SHE IS!
FATHER SAYS SHE'S AN EXAMPLE OF A DISGRACE TO MARS. SO SHOULDN'T YOU BE UP THERE, TOO, MARKZ?

"WE ARE THE *VICTIMS* OF A PLAGUE WE COULDN'T SEE COMING.

"OUR GOVERNMENT IGNORES US AS WE DROP LIKE *FLIES*.

...VAMOS, NENE.

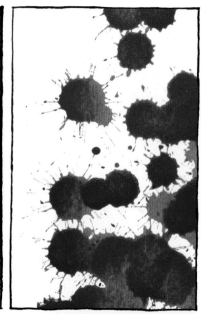

"THE POLICE *BEAT* AND *JAIL* US AS WE CRY OUT FOR HELP.

"THE PUBLIC, OUR *NEIGHBORS* INVADE OUR ONLY REFUGE AND *THREATEN* OUR LIVES."

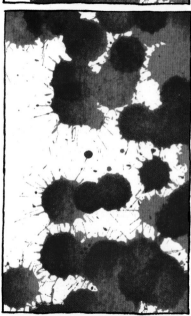

MAKE NO MISTAKE, THIS IS ALL BY DESIGN. *THEY* ARE ANGRY THAT *WE* WON'T DIE QUIETLY.

SO WE WILL *SCREAM* FROM THE VERY *TOP* OF *SPIRAL CITY*...

NO MORE BLOOD!

AND THEY WON'T SEE US COMING.

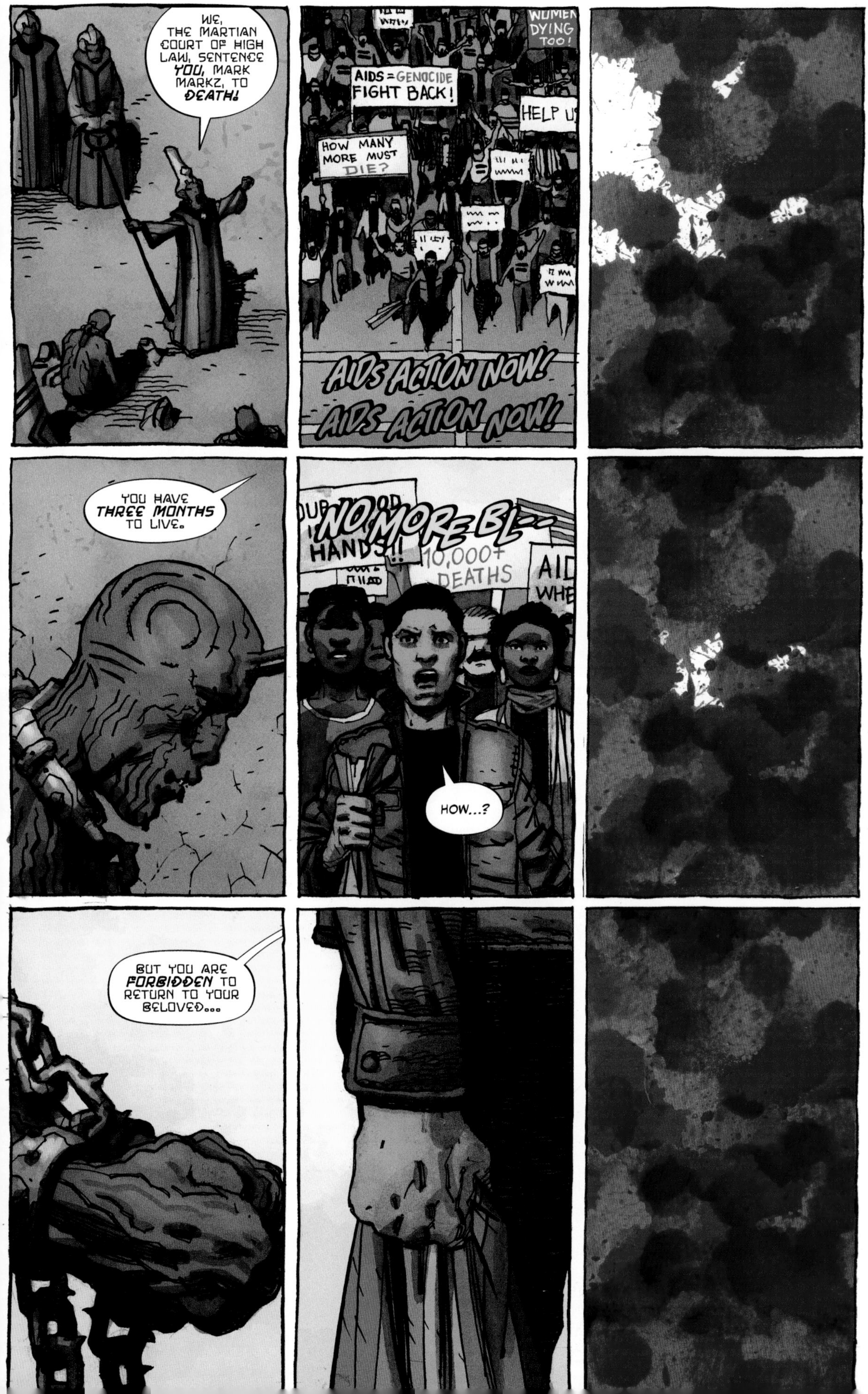
WE, THE MARTIAN COURT OF HIGH LAW, SENTENCE YOU, MARK MARKZ, TO DEATH!
WOMEN DYING TOO!
AIDS = GENOCIDE FIGHT BACK!
HELP US
HOW MANY MORE MUST DIE?
AIDS ACTION NOW!
AIDS ACTION NOW!
YOU HAVE THREE MONTHS TO LIVE.
NO MORE BL--
HANDS!!
10,000+ DEATHS
HOW...?
BUT YOU ARE FORBIDDEN TO RETURN TO YOUR BELOVED...

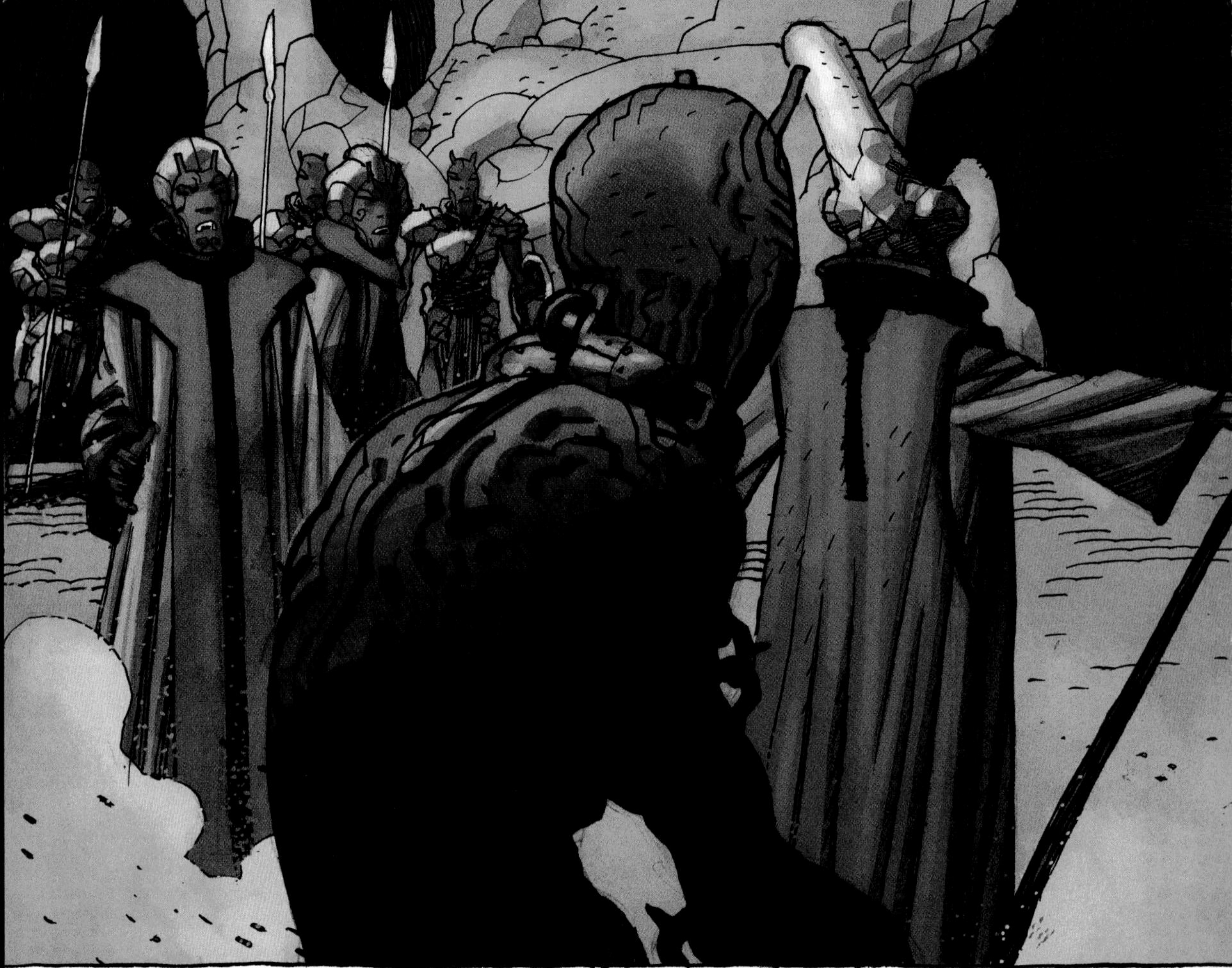

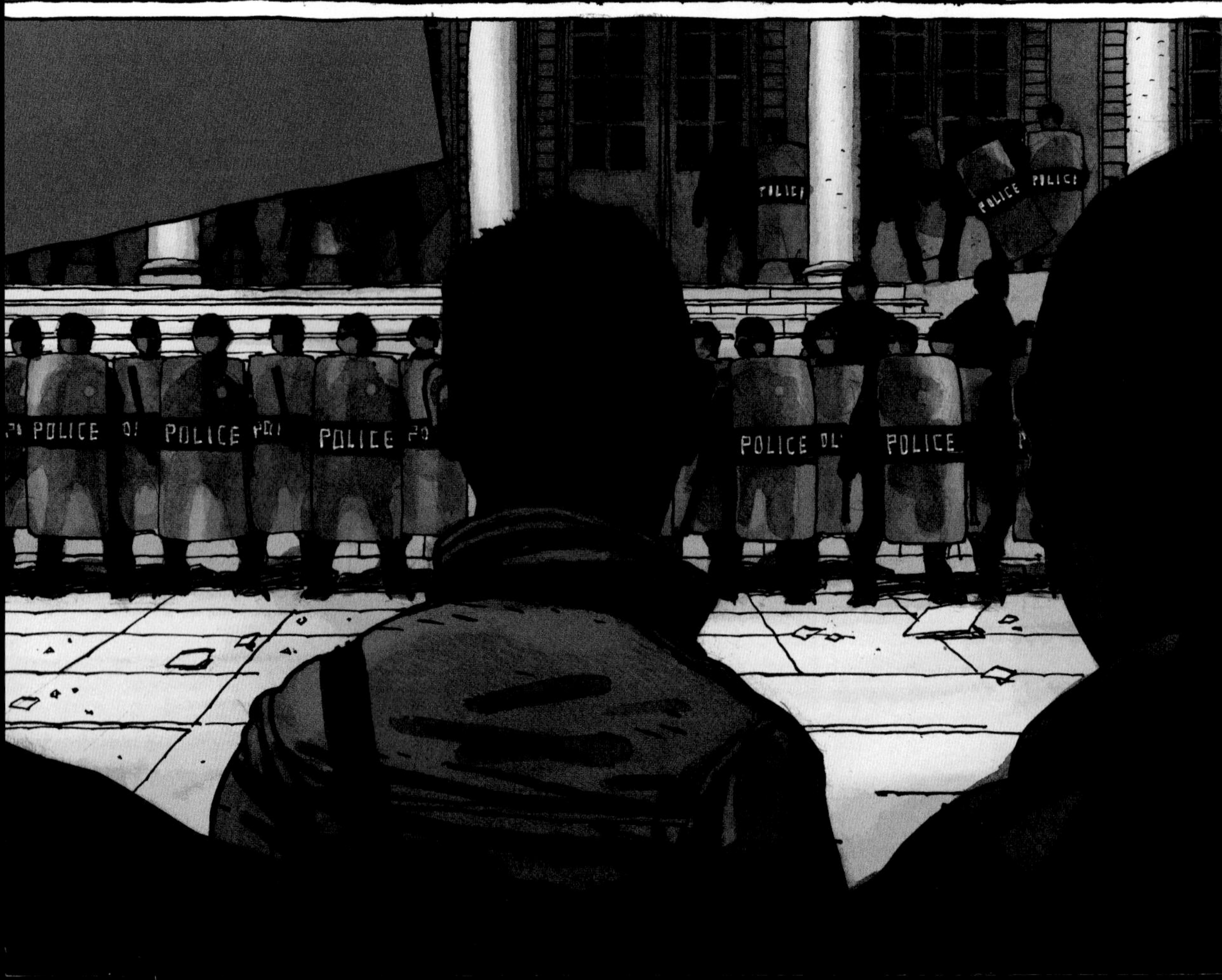
POLICE
POLICE
POLICE
POLICE
POLICE
POLICE
POLICE
POLICE

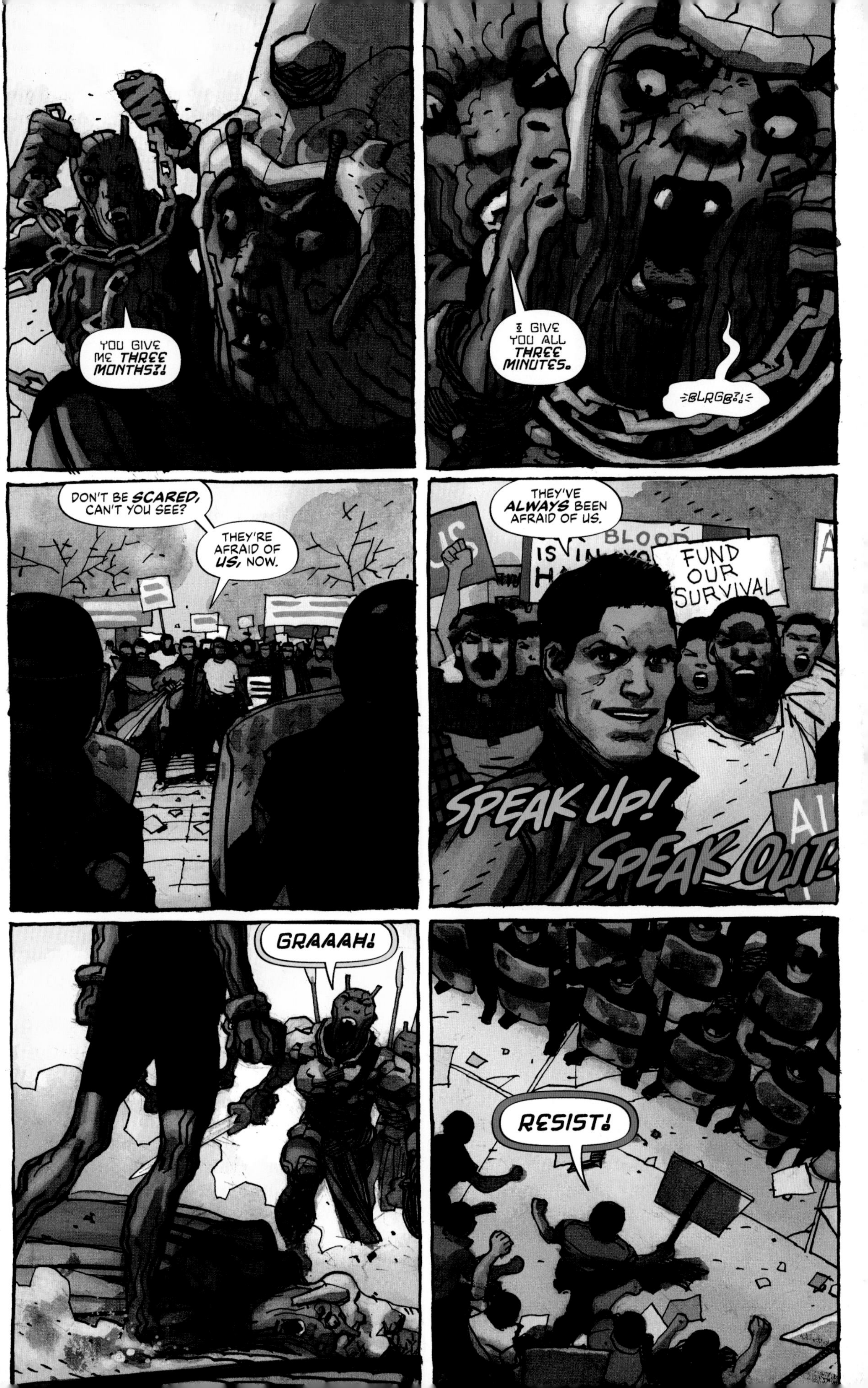
YOU GIVE ME THREE MONTHS?!
I GIVE YOU ALL THREE MINUTES.
BLRGB?!
DON'T BE SCARED, CAN'T YOU SEE?
THEY'RE AFRAID OF US, NOW.
THEY'VE ALWAYS BEEN AFRAID OF US.
FUND OUR SURVIVAL
SPEAK UP!
SPEAK OUT
GRAAAH!
RESIST!

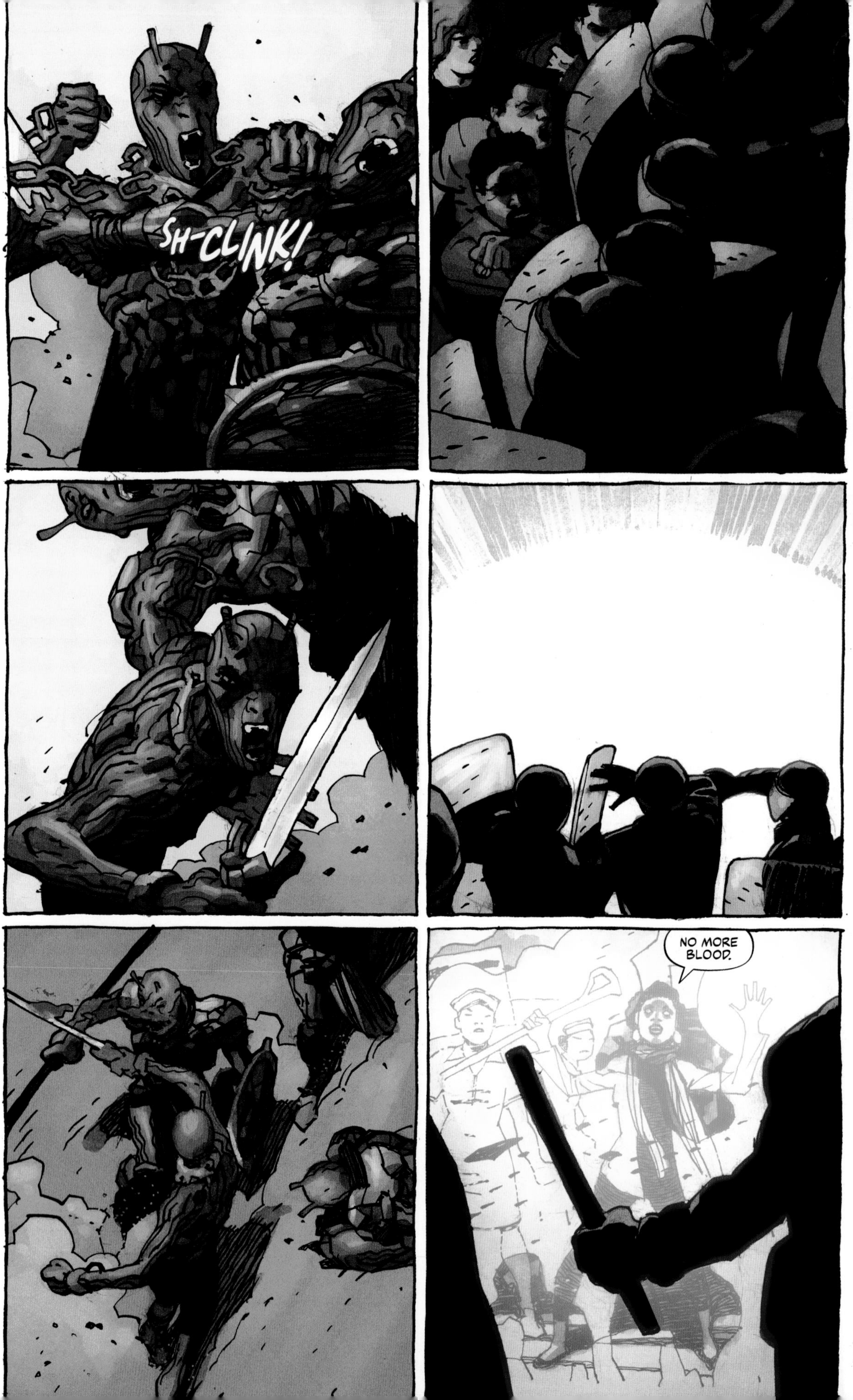
SH-CLINK!
NO MORE BLOOD.

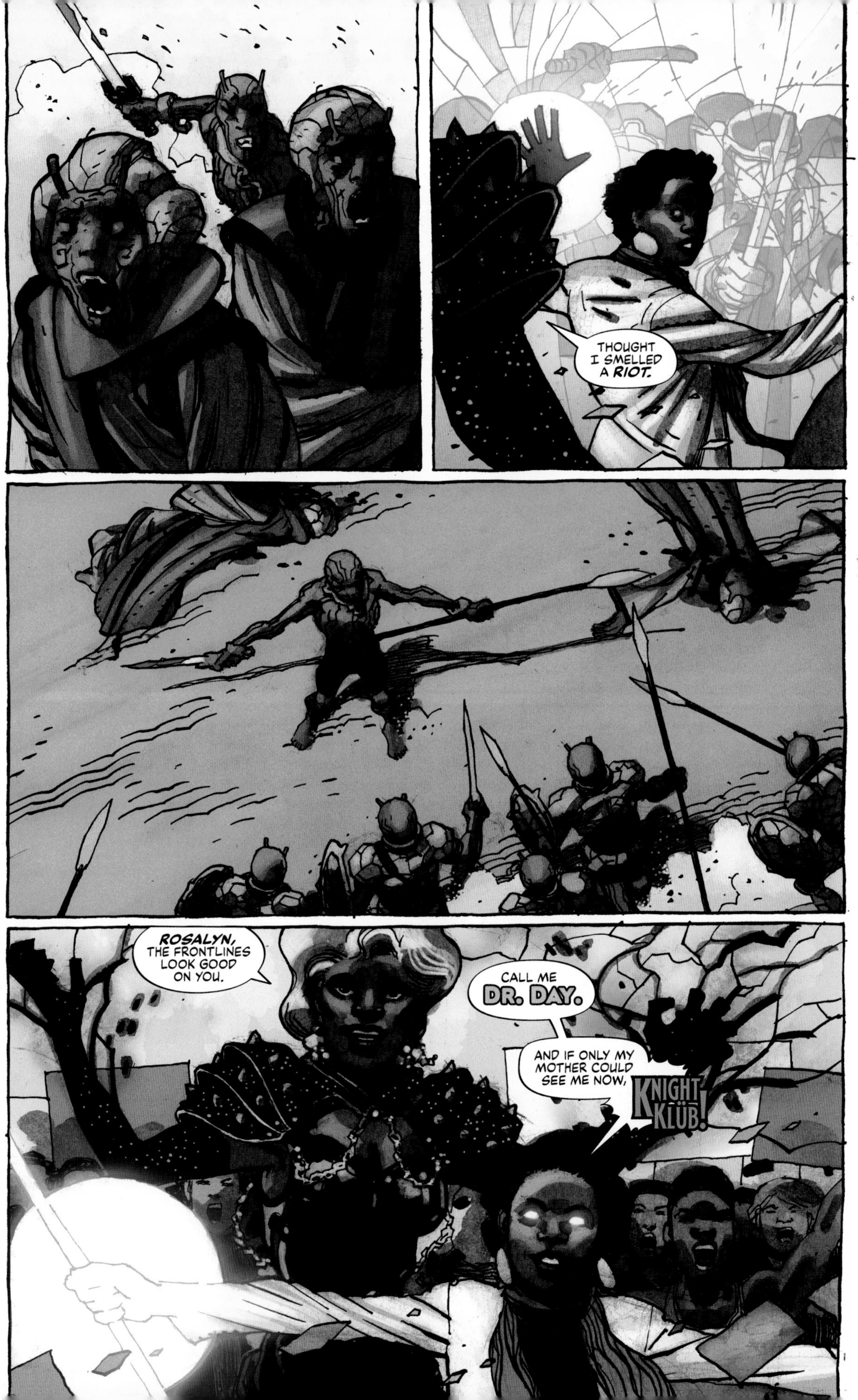
THOUGHT I SMELLED A RIOT.
ROSALYN, THE FRONTLINES LOOK GOOD ON YOU.
CALL ME DR. DAY.
AND IF ONLY MY MOTHER COULD SEE ME NOW, KNIGHT KLÜB!

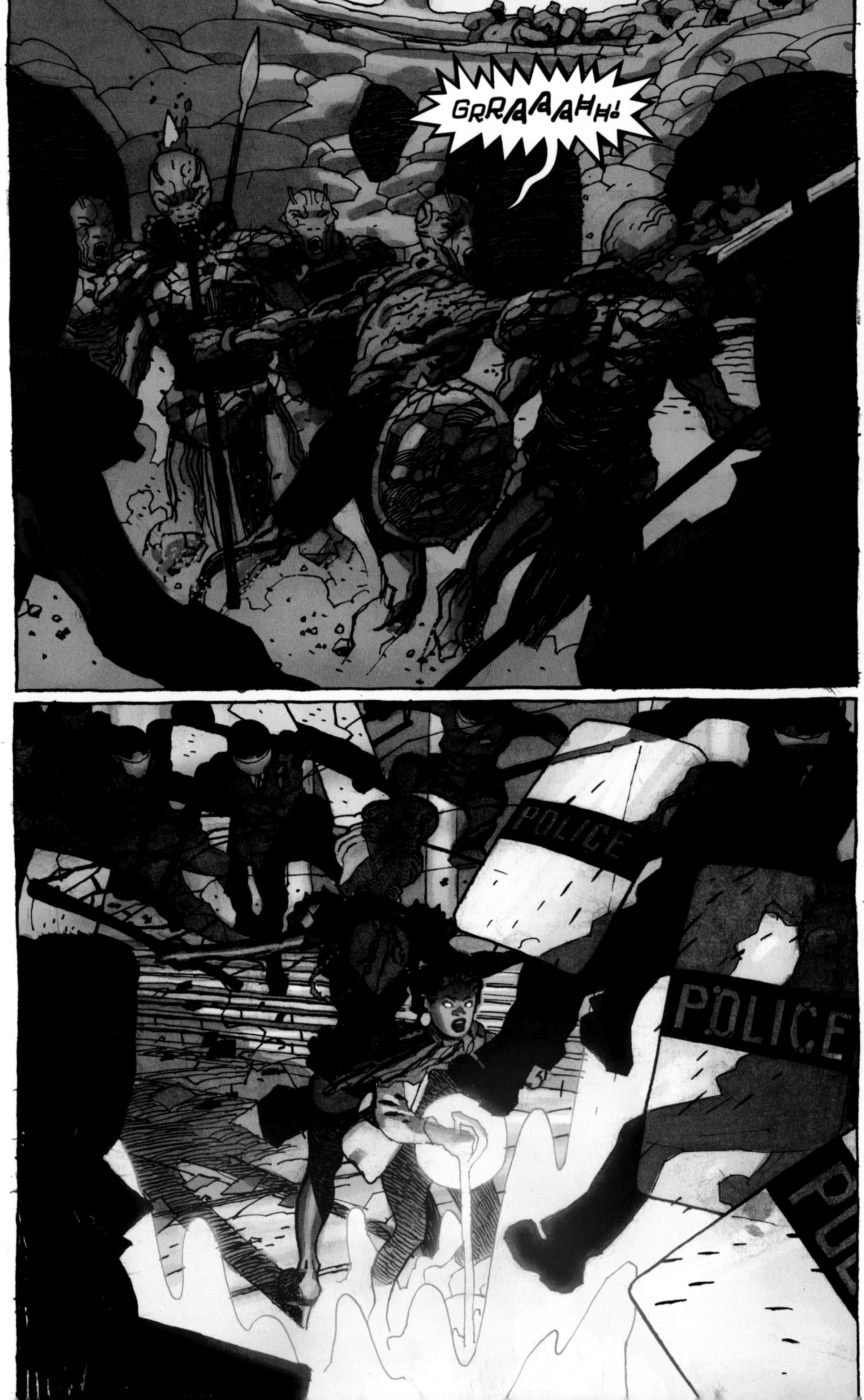
GRRAAAAHH!
POLICE
POLICE
POL

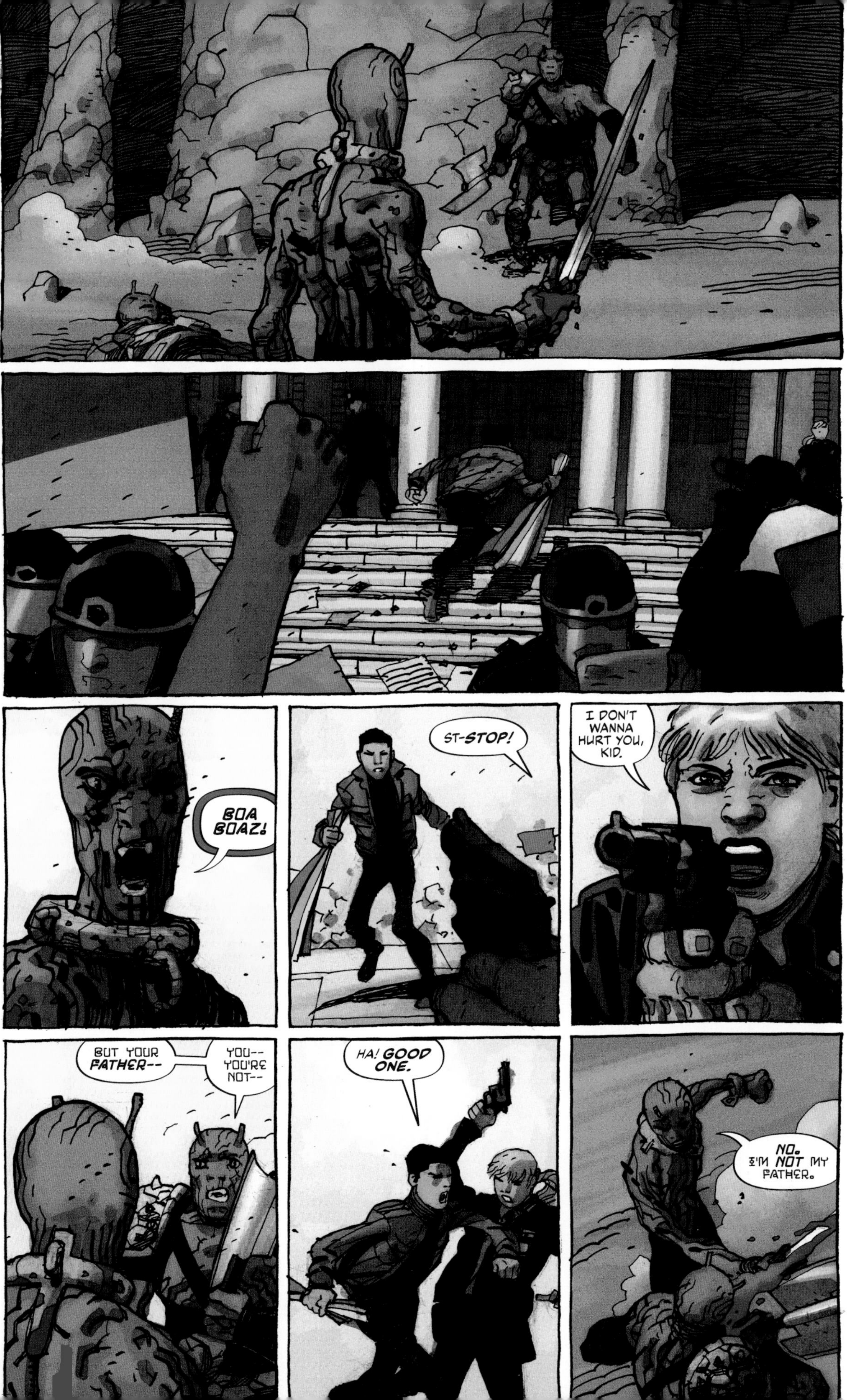
BOA BOAZ!
ST-STOP!
I DON'T WANNA HURT YOU, KID.
BUT YOUR FATHER--
YOU-- YOU'RE NOT--
HA! GOOD ONE.
NO. I'M NOT MY FATHER.

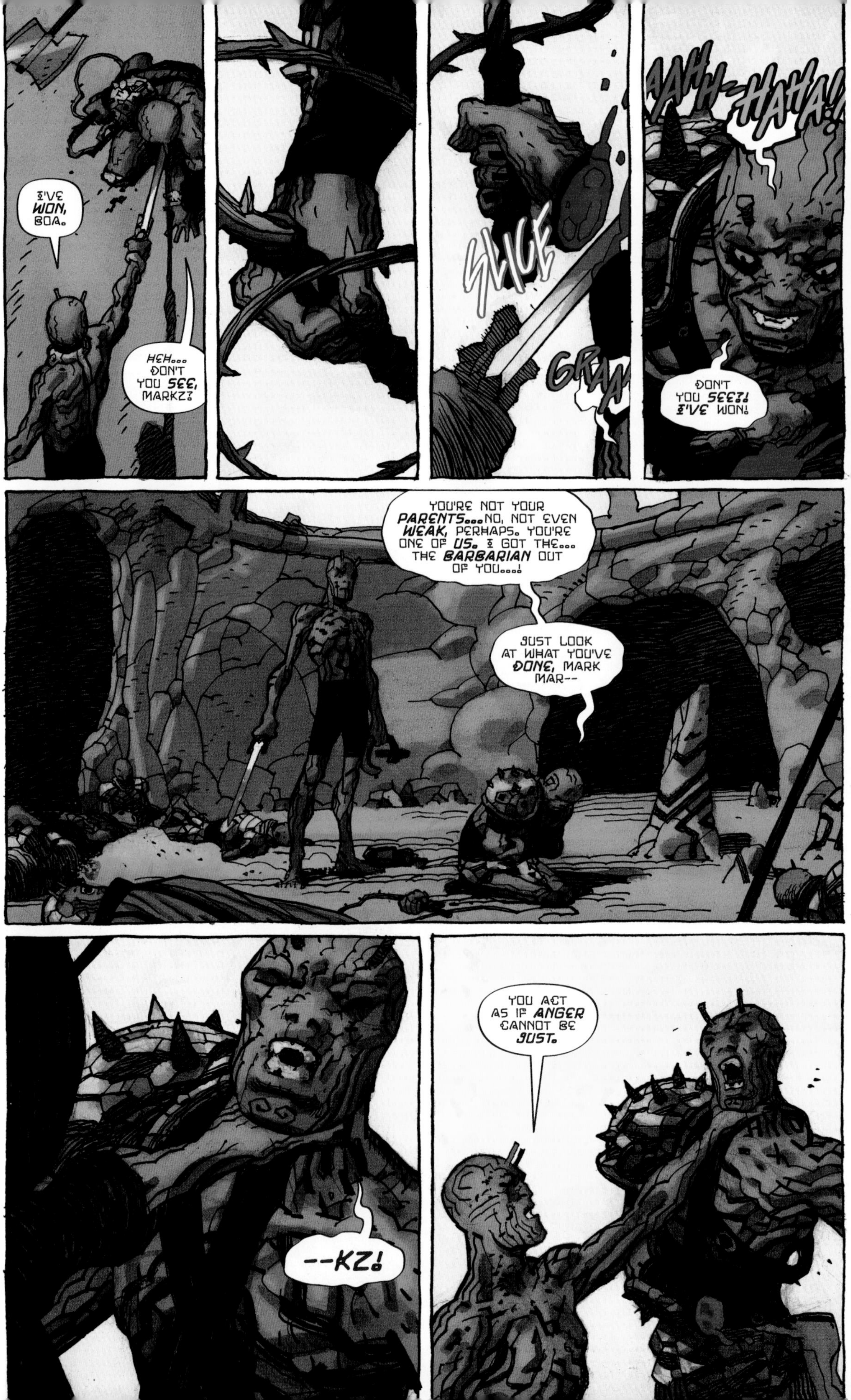
I'VE WON, BOA.
HEH... DON'T YOU SEE, MARKZ?
SLICE
GRAA
AAHH-HAHA!!
DON'T YOU SEE?! I'VE WON!
YOU'RE NOT YOUR PARENTS... NO, NOT EVEN WEAK, PERHAPS. YOU'RE ONE OF US. I GOT THE... THE BARBARIAN OUT OF YOU...!
JUST LOOK AT WHAT YOU'VE DONE, MARK MAR--
--KZ!
YOU ACT AS IF ANGER CANNOT BE JUST.

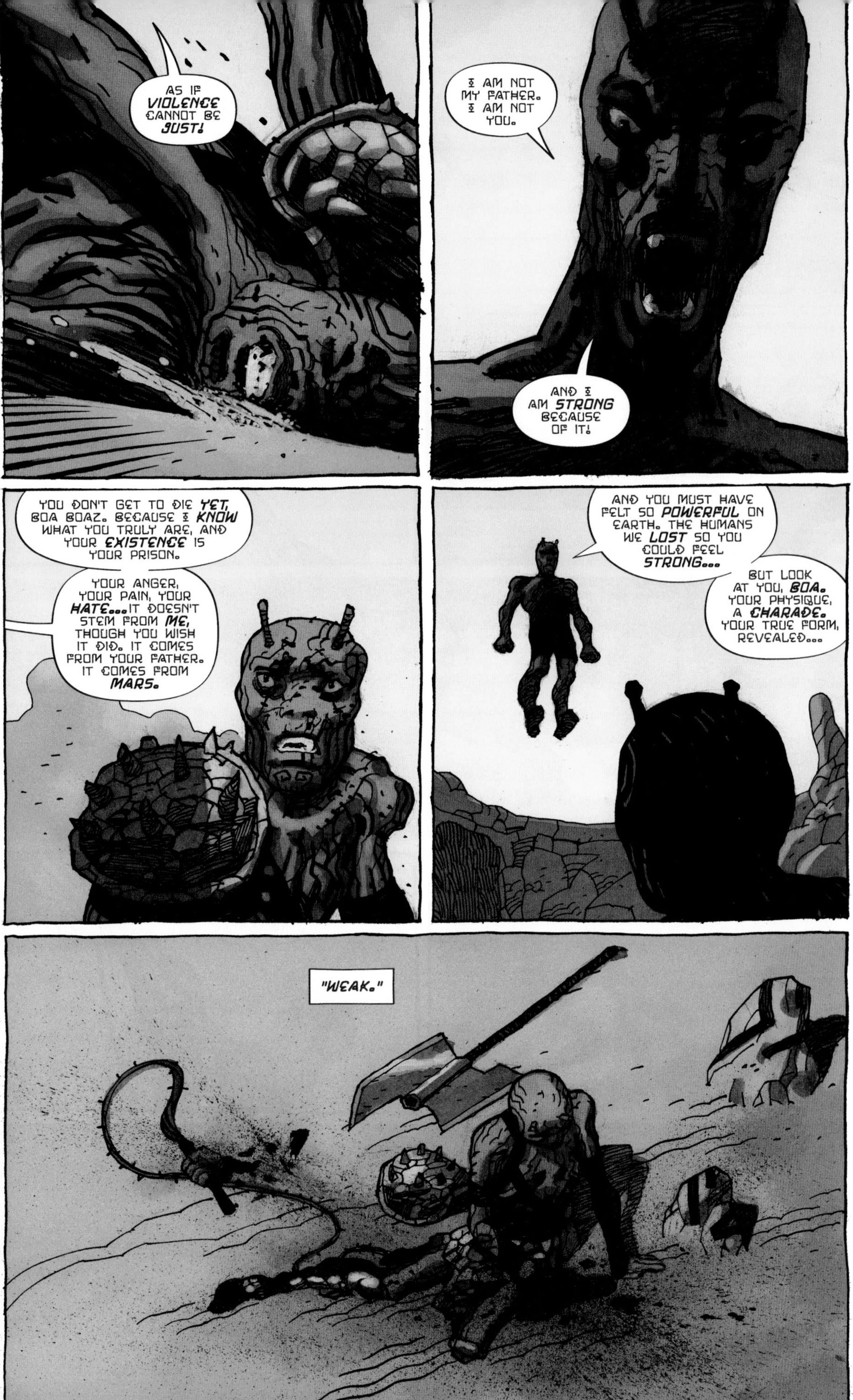
AS IF VIOLENCE CANNOT BE JUST!
I AM NOT MY FATHER. I AM NOT YOU.
AND I AM STRONG BECAUSE OF IT!
YOU DON'T GET TO DIE YET, BOA BOAZ. BECAUSE I KNOW WHAT YOU TRULY ARE, AND YOUR EXISTENCE IS YOUR PRISON.
YOUR ANGER, YOUR PAIN, YOUR HATE... IT DOESN'T STEM FROM ME, THOUGH YOU WISH IT DID. IT COMES FROM YOUR FATHER. IT COMES FROM MARS.
AND YOU MUST HAVE FELT SO POWERFUL ON EARTH. THE HUMANS WE LOST SO YOU COULD FEEL STRONG...
BUT LOOK AT YOU, BOA. YOUR PHYSIQUE, A CHARADE. YOUR TRUE FORM, REVEALED...
"WEAK."

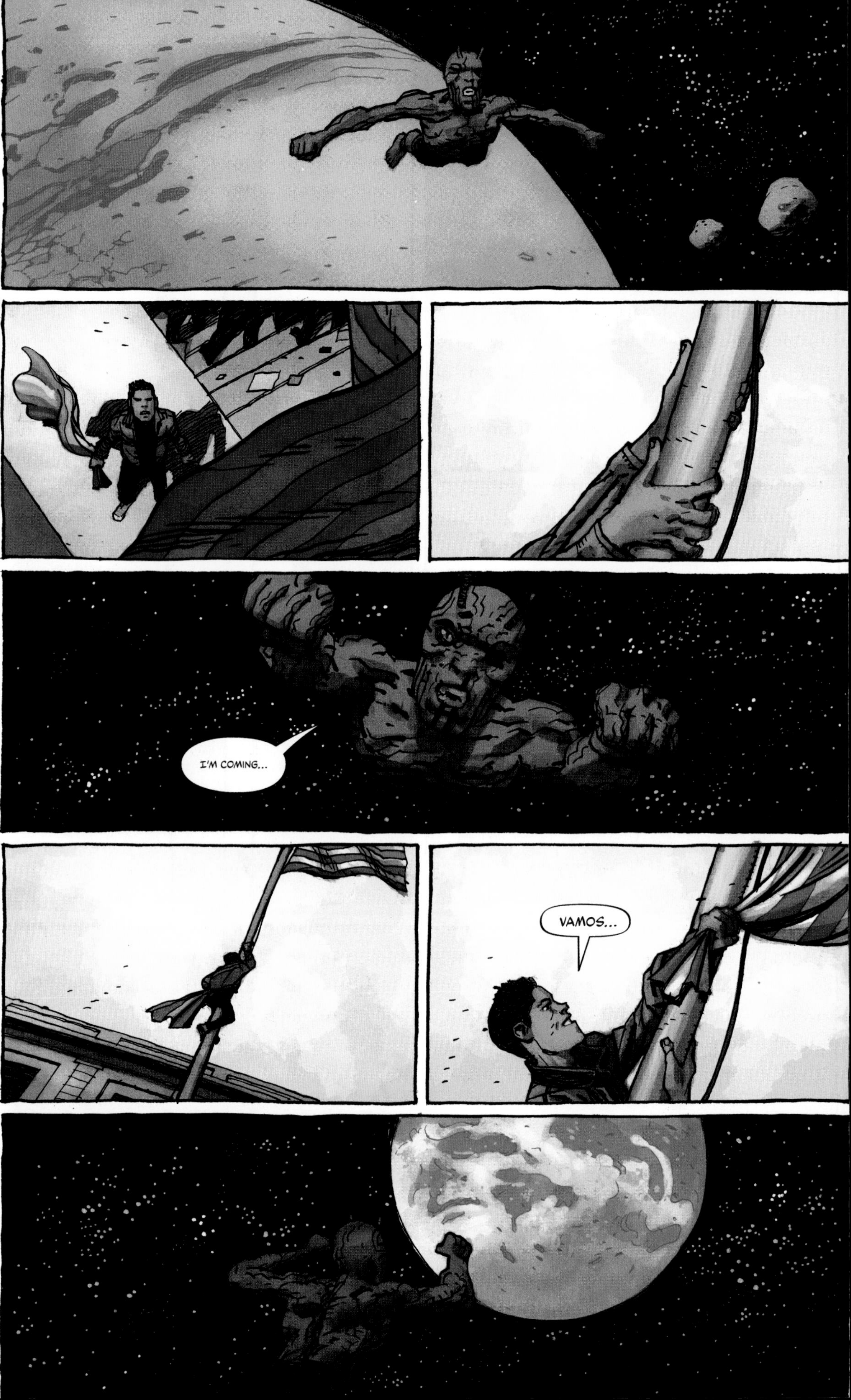
I'M COMING...
VAMOS...

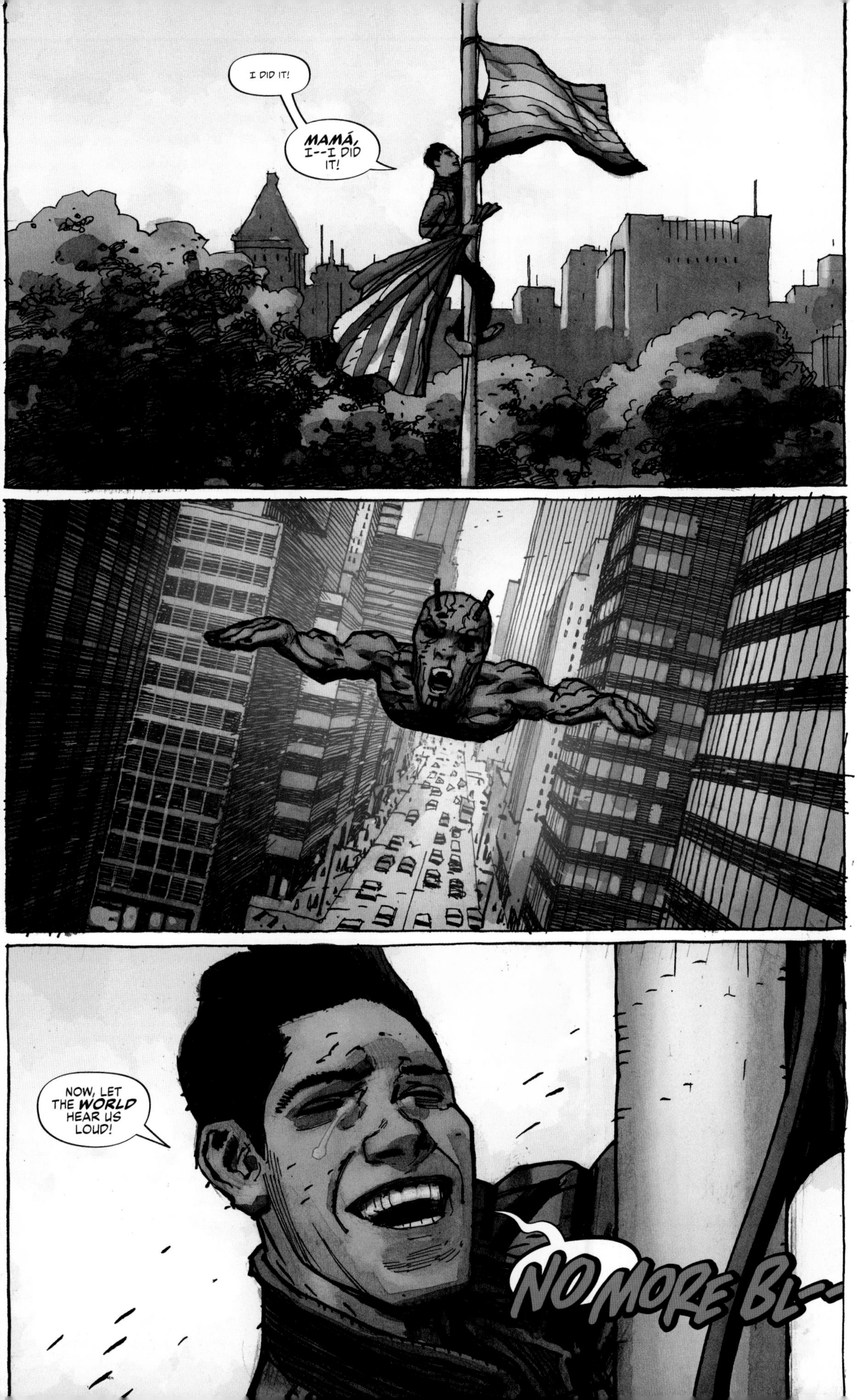
I DID IT!
MAMÁ, I--I DID IT!
NOW, LET THE WORLD HEAR US LOUD!
NO MORE BL--

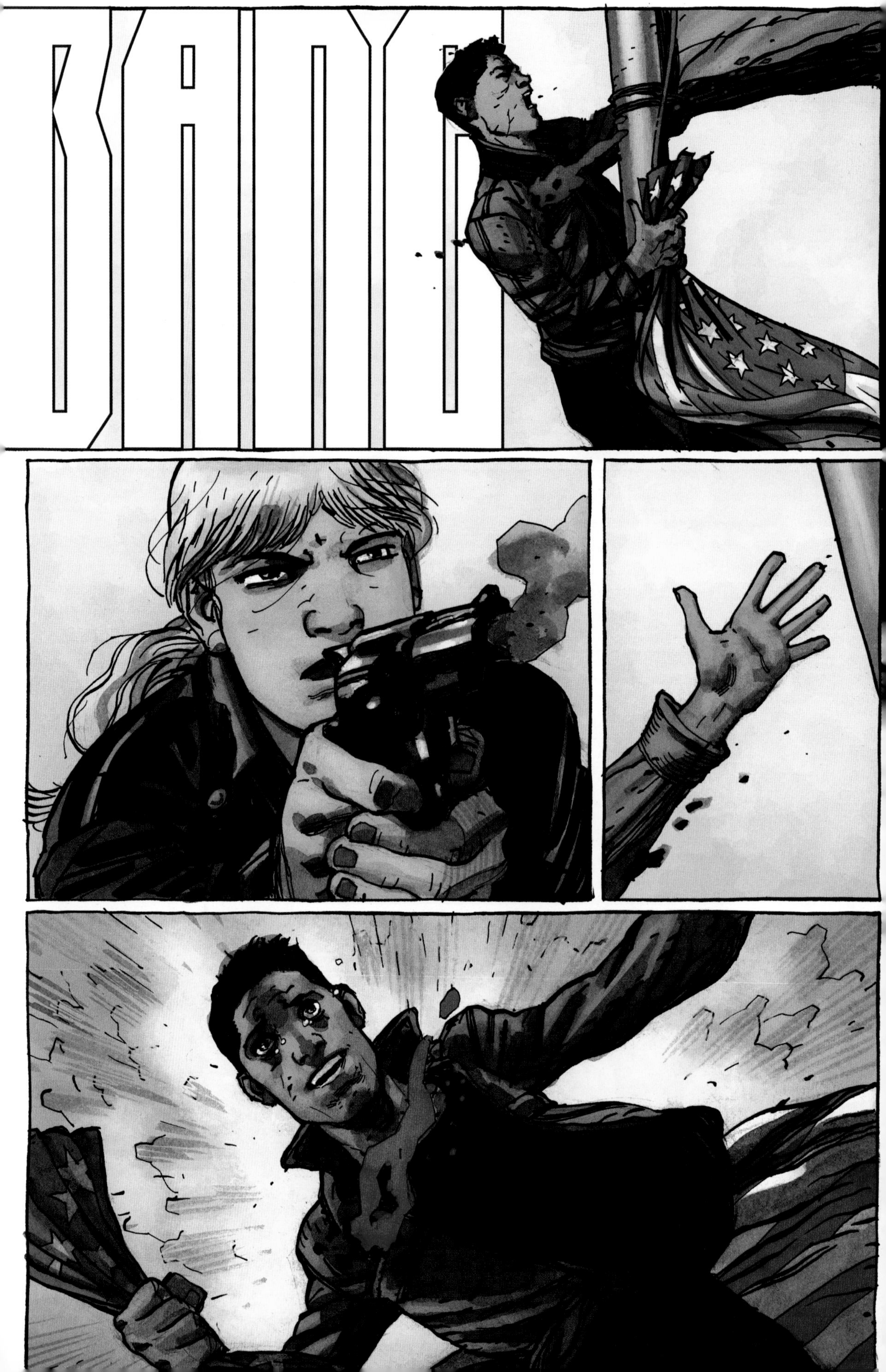
BANG

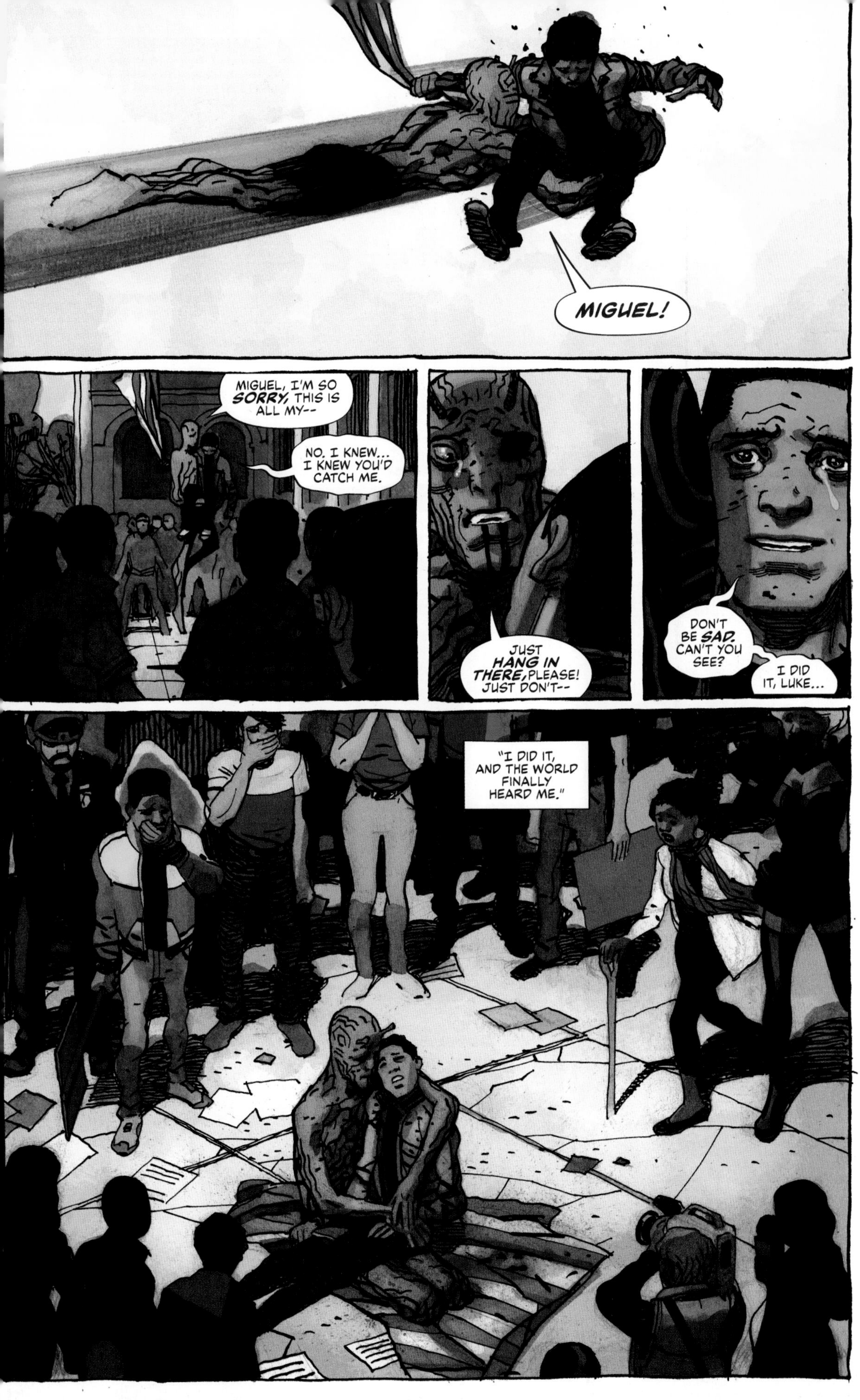
MIGUEL!
MIGUEL, I'M SO SORRY, THIS IS ALL MY--
NO. I KNEW... I KNEW YOU'D CATCH ME.
JUST HANG IN THERE, PLEASE! JUST DON'T--
DON'T BE SAD. CAN'T YOU SEE?
I DID IT, LUKE...
"I DID IT, AND THE WORLD FINALLY HEARD ME."

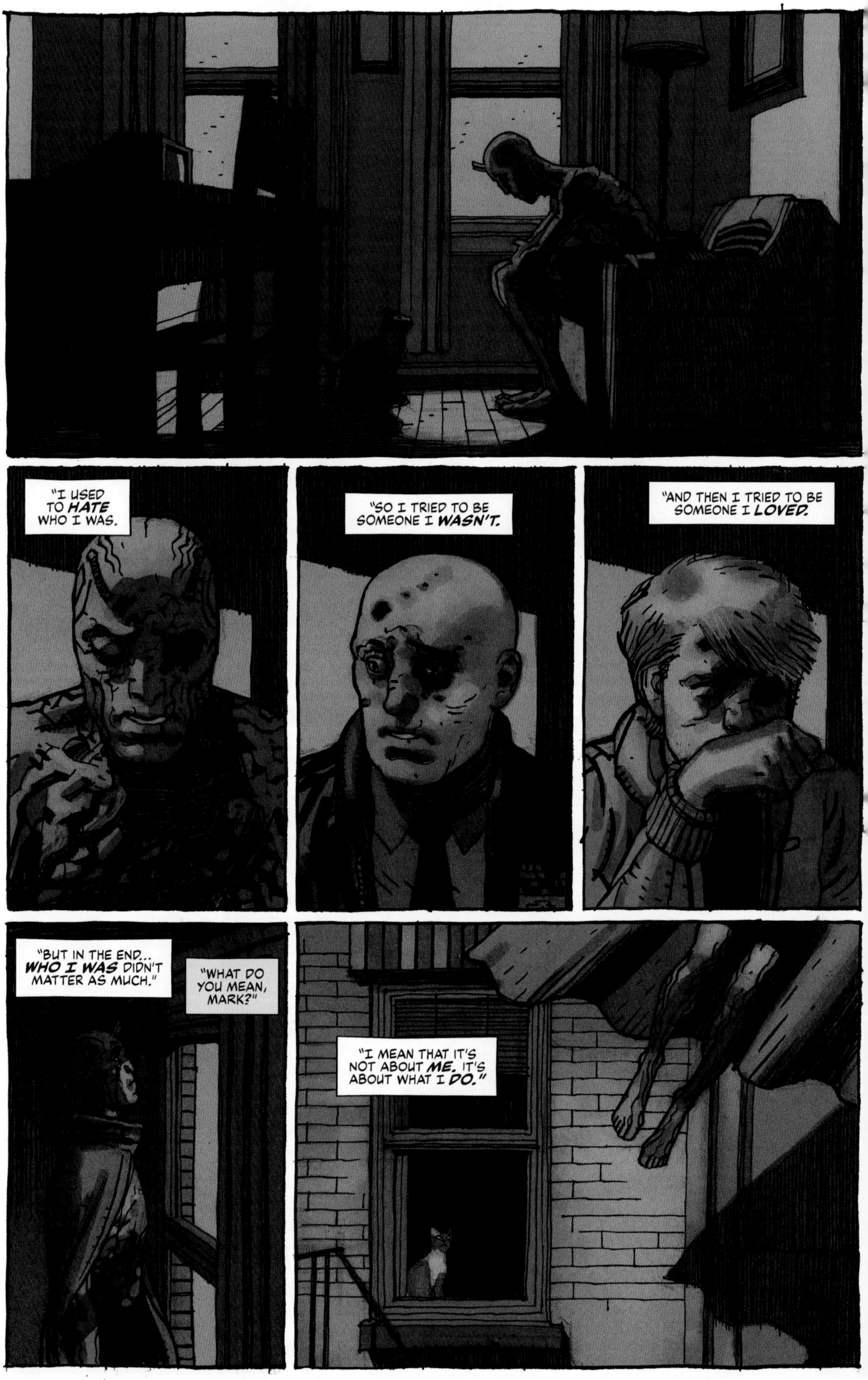
"I USED TO HATE WHO I WAS.
"SO I TRIED TO BE SOMEONE I WASN'T.
"AND THEN I TRIED TO BE SOMEONE I LOVED.
"BUT IN THE END... WHO I WAS DIDN'T MATTER AS MUCH."
"WHAT DO YOU MEAN, MARK?"
"I MEAN THAT IT'S NOT ABOUT ME. IT'S ABOUT WHAT I DO."

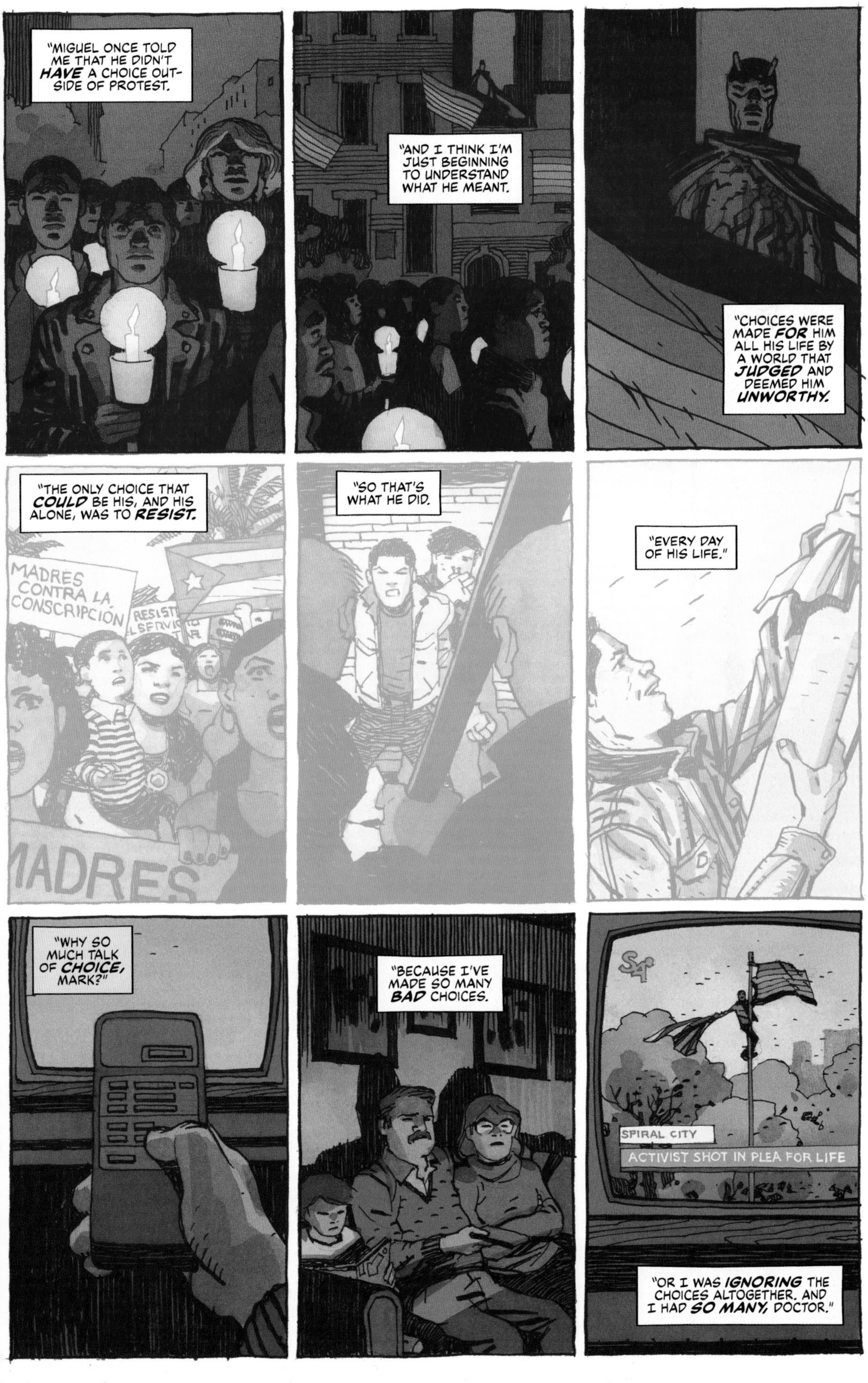
"MIGUEL ONCE TOLD ME THAT HE DIDN'T HAVE A CHOICE OUTSIDE OF PROTEST.
"AND I THINK I'M JUST BEGINNING TO UNDERSTAND WHAT HE MEANT.
"CHOICES WERE MADE FOR HIM ALL HIS LIFE BY A WORLD THAT JUDGED AND DEEMED HIM UNWORTHY.
"THE ONLY CHOICE THAT COULD BE HIS, AND HIS ALONE, WAS TO RESIST.
MADRES CONTRA LA CONSCRIPCIÓN
MADRES
"SO THAT'S WHAT HE DID.
"EVERY DAY OF HIS LIFE."
"WHY SO MUCH TALK OF CHOICE, MARK?"
"BECAUSE I'VE MADE SO MANY BAD CHOICES.
SPIRAL CITY
ACTIVIST SHOT IN PLEA FOR LIFE
"OR I WAS IGNORING THE CHOICES ALTOGETHER. AND I HAD SO MANY, DOCTOR."

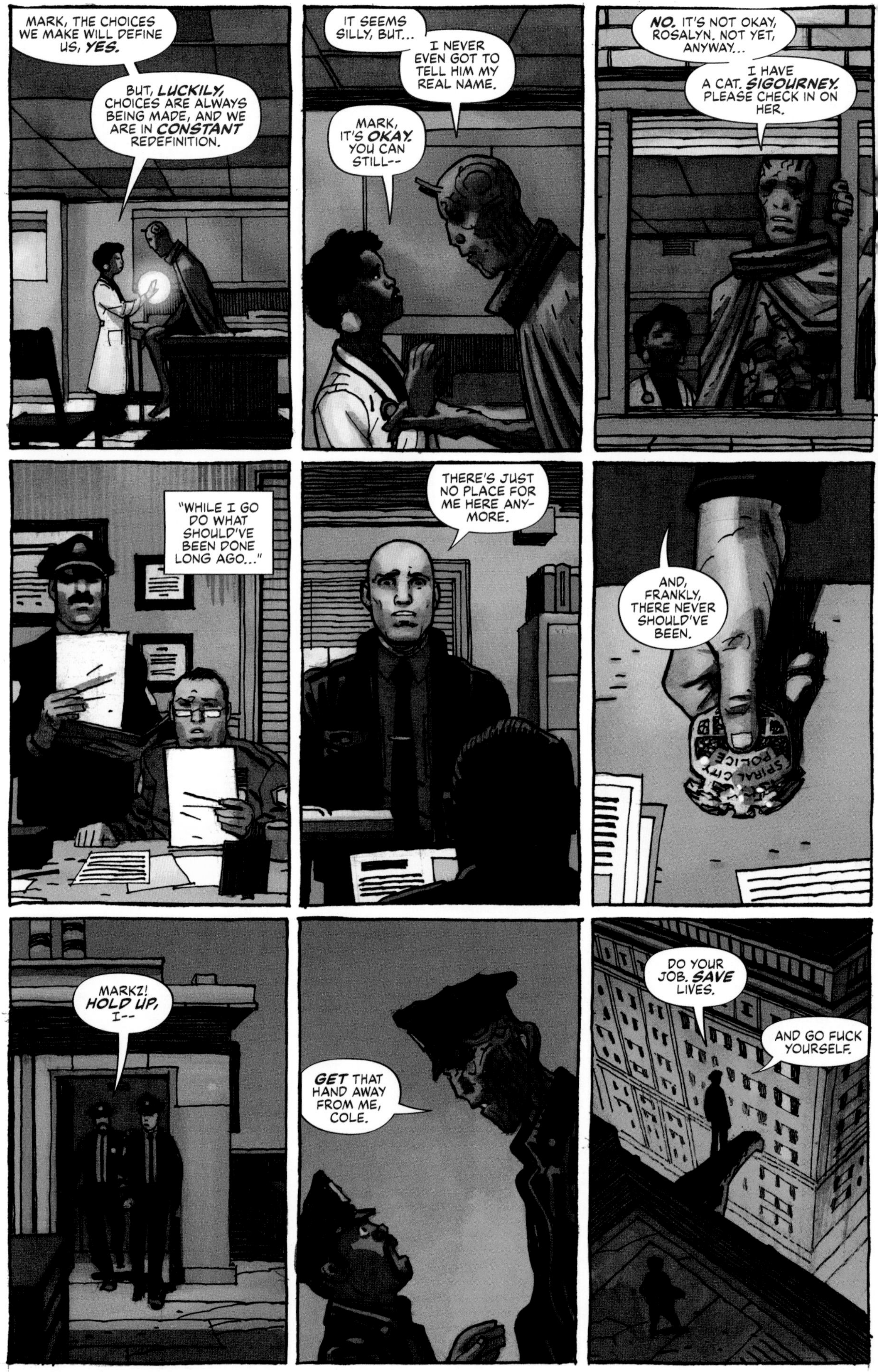
MARK, THE CHOICES WE MAKE WILL DEFINE US, YES.
BUT, LUCKILY, CHOICES ARE ALWAYS BEING MADE, AND WE ARE IN CONSTANT REDEFINITION.
IT SEEMS SILLY, BUT...
I NEVER EVEN GOT TO TELL HIM MY REAL NAME.
MARK, IT'S OKAY. YOU CAN STILL--
NO. IT'S NOT OKAY, ROSALYN. NOT YET, ANYWAY...
I HAVE A CAT. SIGOURNEY. PLEASE CHECK IN ON HER.
"WHILE I GO DO WHAT SHOULD'VE BEEN DONE LONG AGO..."
THERE'S JUST NO PLACE FOR ME HERE ANYMORE.
AND, FRANKLY, THERE NEVER SHOULD'VE BEEN.
MARKZ! HOLD UP, I--
GET THAT HAND AWAY FROM ME, COLE.
DO YOUR JOB. SAVE LIVES.
AND GO FUCK YOURSELF.

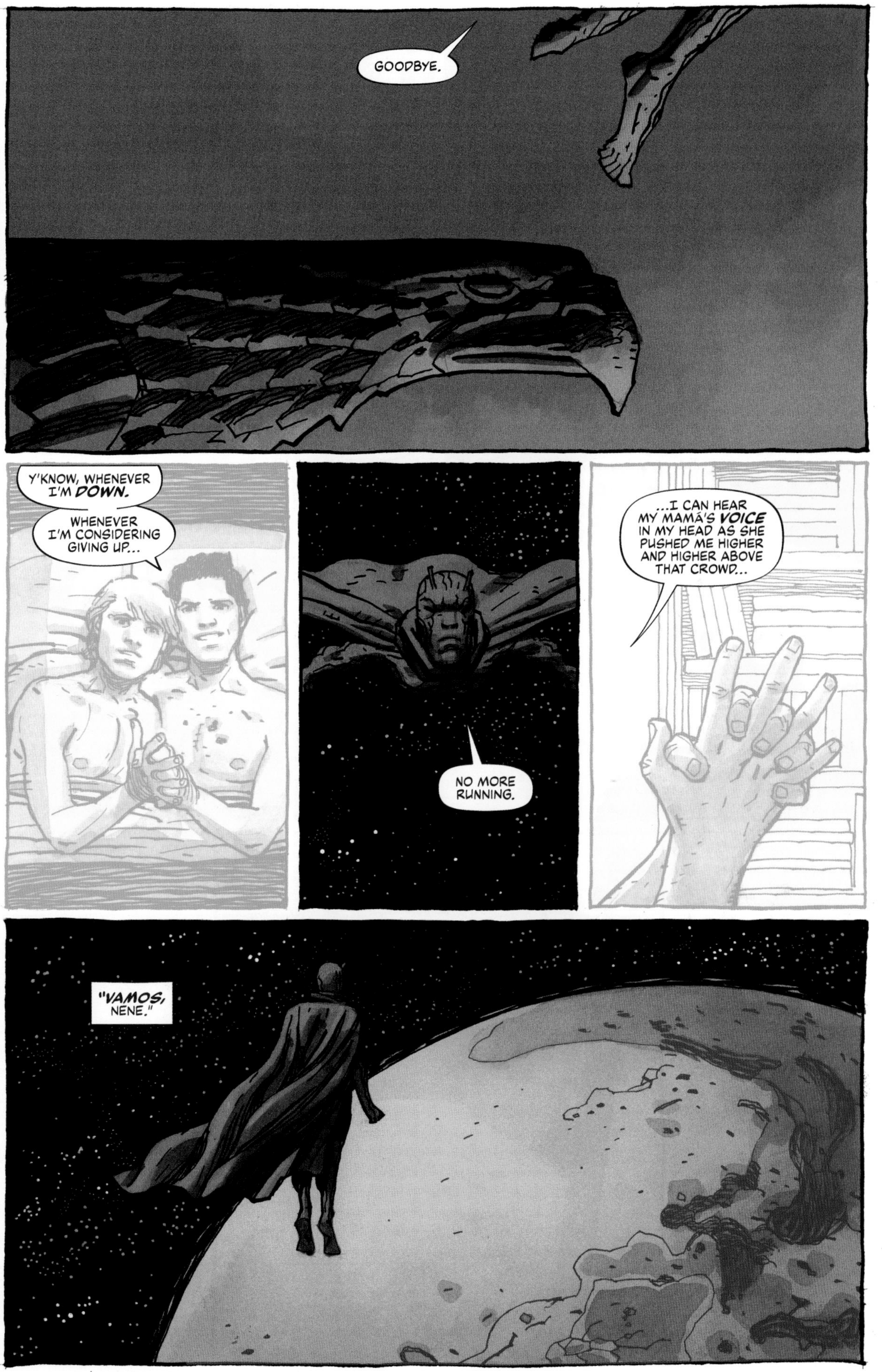
GOODBYE.
Y'KNOW, WHENEVER I'M DOWN.
WHENEVER I'M CONSIDERING GIVING UP...
NO MORE RUNNING.
...I CAN HEAR MY MAMÁ'S VOICE IN MY HEAD AS SHE PUSHED ME HIGHER AND HIGHER ABOVE THAT CROWD...
"VAMOS, NENE."

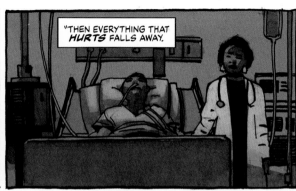

"THEN EVERYTHING THAT *HURTS* FALLS AWAY.

"AND EVERYTHING THAT *MATTERS* FALLS INTO PLACE."

SO, JUST SAY IT WITH ME...

"AND WE WILL NEVER STOP FIGHTING."

AFTERWORD

By Tate Brombal

The AIDS crisis never ended. As soon as a viable treatment became available for the White, affluent, cisgender world, HIV moved south. The disease continues to afflict sub-Saharan Africa, intravenous drug users, sex workers, and people of color at alarming rates—especially Black men who sleep with men. We have the antivirals, we understand that undetectable equals untransmittable, yet the AIDS crisis will not end until we've ended it *everywhere*. For *everyone*.

I just wanted to make that clear.

Now, the book you're holding was not easy to write. Though the more I wrote it, the more necessary it felt.

In fact, I never imagined it would ever even come to be. I pitched this book to Jeff off-hand—"*Wouldn't this be an exciting story?*" I never dreamed he'd consider it, then offer I write it myself. I still can't believe it's happened, that it was illustrated by masters Gabriel Walta and Jordie Bellaire, and that you're holding it in your hands, right now. *Why would I*? Queer writers don't often get to write queer stories for queer superheroes in mainstream comics—let alone one set during the AIDS crisis, a disease buried under metaphor or weaponized by supervillains. *Red Planet*, I knew, was a chance to right those wrongs.

But then I had to write the damn thing. And the more I read and the more I witnessed, the angrier, more frustrated I became. How could I capture the breadth of this crisis? The lives lost and fought for, the queer heroes that took my breath away? But just as Dr. Rosalyn Day needed to stop worrying about the shoes she could never fill, I too conceded that I'd never capture it all. However, I knew there was a chance that I could capture just a fragment of it; I could capture its undying spirit. I hope I was even a little bit successful in that.

Spiral City may be fictional, but it is filled with characters and events that are inspired by very real histories. This book is a love letter to them and all those we have lost—oftentimes far too soon. It is dedicated to Ray Navarro, Ryan White, Larry Kramer, Peter Stalely, Phill Wilson, Keith Haring, Cleve Jones, Kiyoshi Kuromiya, David Wojnarowicz, Dr. Kristen Ries and Maggie Snyder, Marsha P. Johnson, Sylvia Rivera, and all those I'm missing, and all those whose names were forgotten or erased from history. These names and legacies deserve further attention, research, and exploration.

I hope you've learned something from this book. I hope it inspired as much as it entertained. I hope it lit a fire in you, even if just a spark. Because the AIDS crisis never ended. Because our histories have been closeted for far too long. Because our stories will be read, and we will write them.

Because we will *never* stop fighting.

Tate Brombal,
October 2020

If you're intrigued and want to read more on the topic of the AIDS crisis, I've assembled some of the texts that impacted me and this book, below:

COMICS

- Pedro and Me *by Judd Winick*
- Taking Turns *by MK Czerwiec*

PROSE & POETRY

- AIDS and Its Metaphors *by Susan Sontag*
- And the Band Played On *by Randy Shilts*
- Christodora *by Tim Murphy*
- The Gifts of the Body *by Rebecca Brown*
- The Wisdom of Whores: Bureaucrats, Brothels, and the Business of AIDS *by Elizabeth Pisani*
- Don't Call Us Dead *by Danez Smith*

FILMS, TV, THEATER

- How to Survive a Plague *dir. by David France*
- We Were Here *dir. by David Weissmann*
- Paris Is Burning *dir. by Jennie Livingston*
- POSE *by Ryan Murphy, Brad Falchuk, Steven Canals, and Janet Mock*
- Angels in America *by Tony Kushner*
- The Normal Heart *by Larry Kramer*

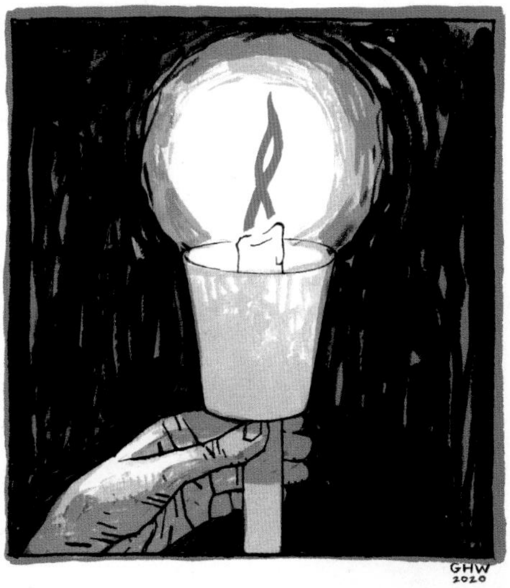
GHW
2020

BARBALIEN™

RED PLANET

SKETCHBOOK

NOTES BY GABRIEL HERNÁNDEZ WALTA

First Barbie and Mark Markz sketches. Here I was trying to find my own version of the characters while, of course, keeping true to the original designs by Dean and Jeff.

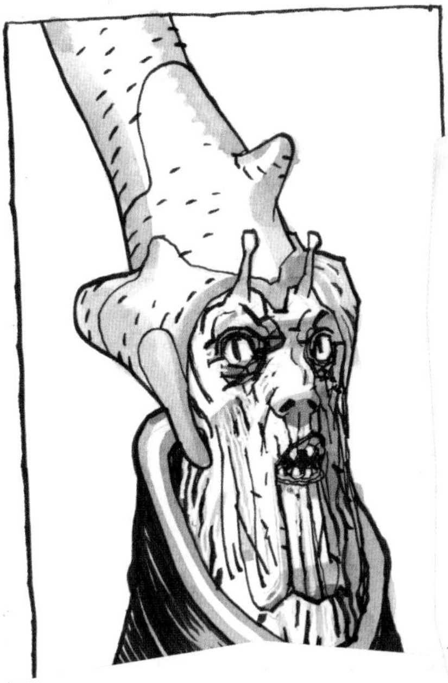

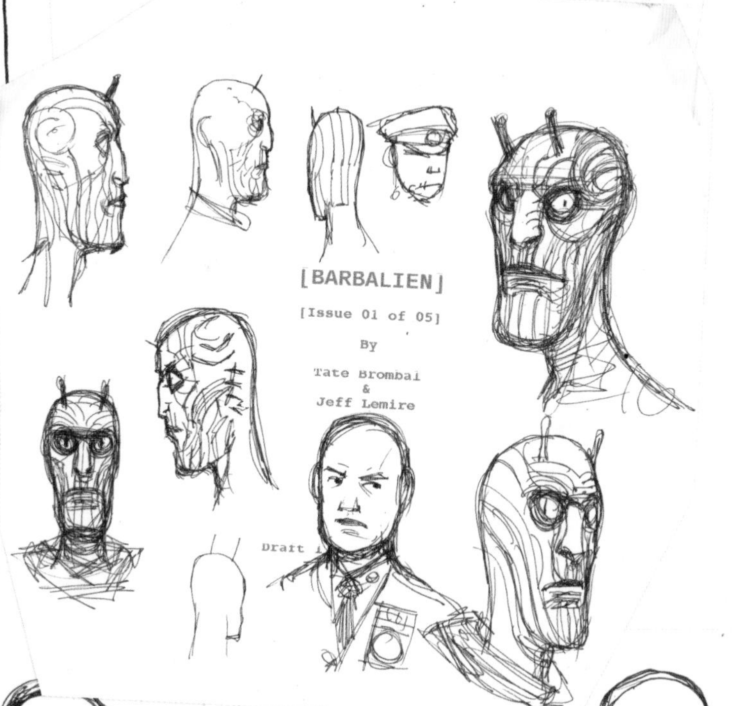
[BARBALIEN]
[Issue 01 of 05]
By
Tate Brombal
&
Jeff Lemire
Draft 1

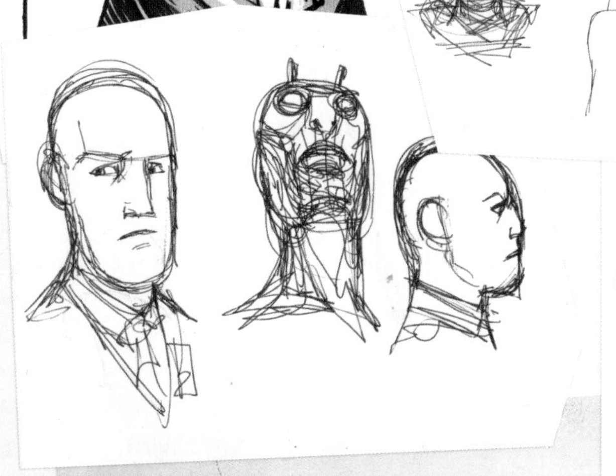

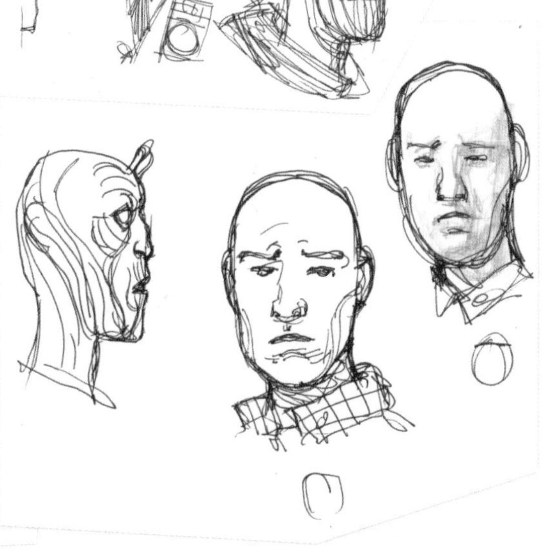

The Martian high chancellor. The martian characters were all *so* fun to design! I've always loved to draw those kind of ugly, fluid features.

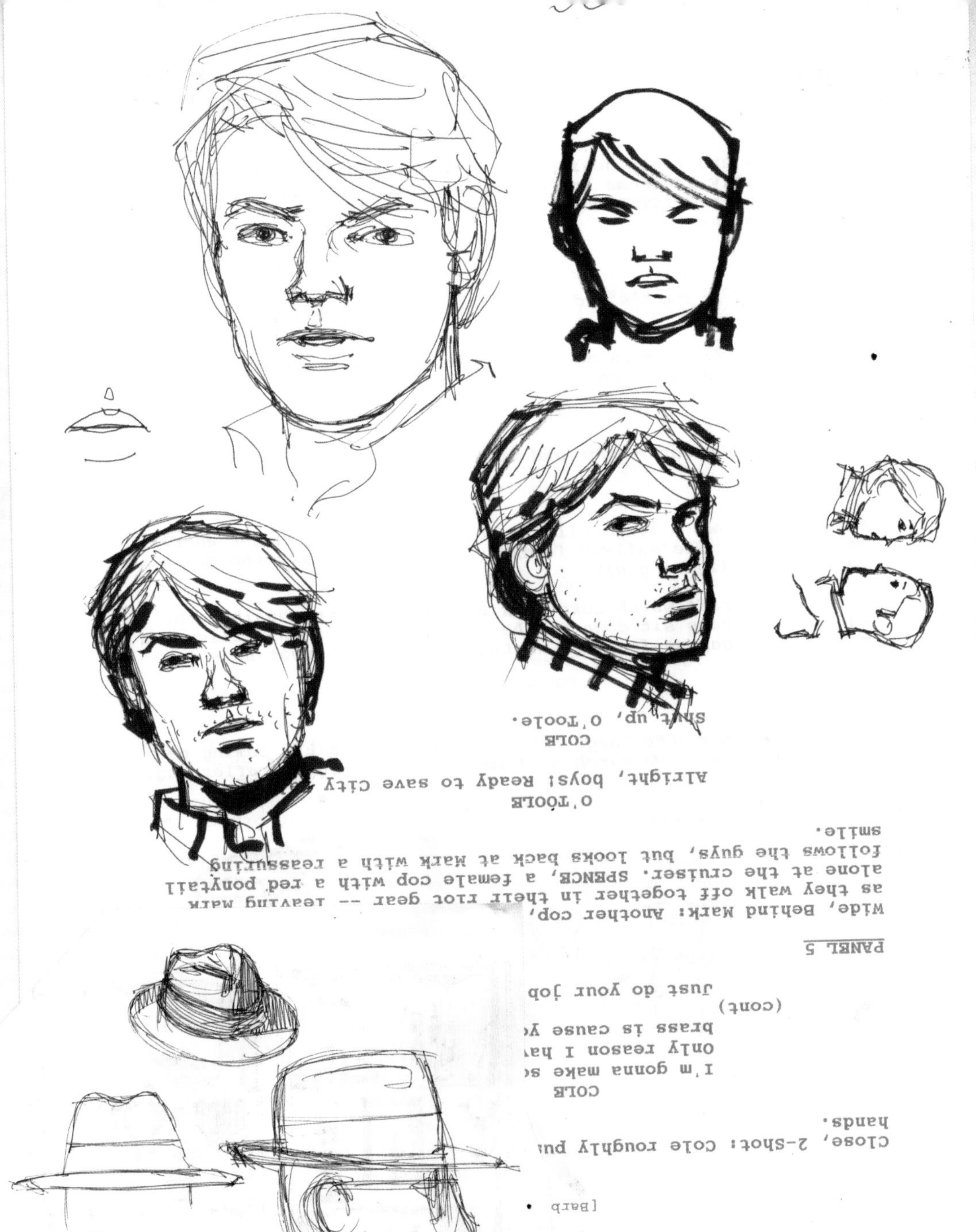
[Barb
Close, 2-Shot: Cole roughly pu
hands.
COLE
I'm gonna make s
only reason I hav
brass is cause y
(cont)
Just do your job
PANEL 5
Wide, Behind Mark: Another cop,
as they walk off together in their riot gear -- leaving Mark
alone at the cruiser. SPENCE, a female cop with a red ponytail
follows the guys, but looks back at Mark with a reassuring
smile.
O'TOOLE
Alright, boys! Ready to save City
COLE
Shut up, O'Toole.

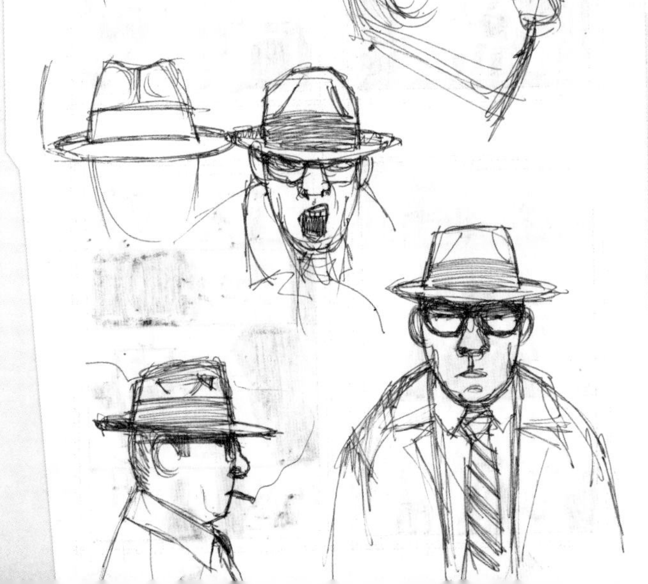

When designing "Luke" I was looking for an '80s handsome guy that didn't look like a dummy, so he was capable of being expressive. Also, I always tried to imagine that Barbalien was under Luke's "skin" and that they weren't different characters.

Fedora hats are *tough* to draw!!

HIGH CHANCELLOR
(cont) You had such a bright future, Mark Markz... A diplomat like your father.

But these choices of yours will cost you dearly.

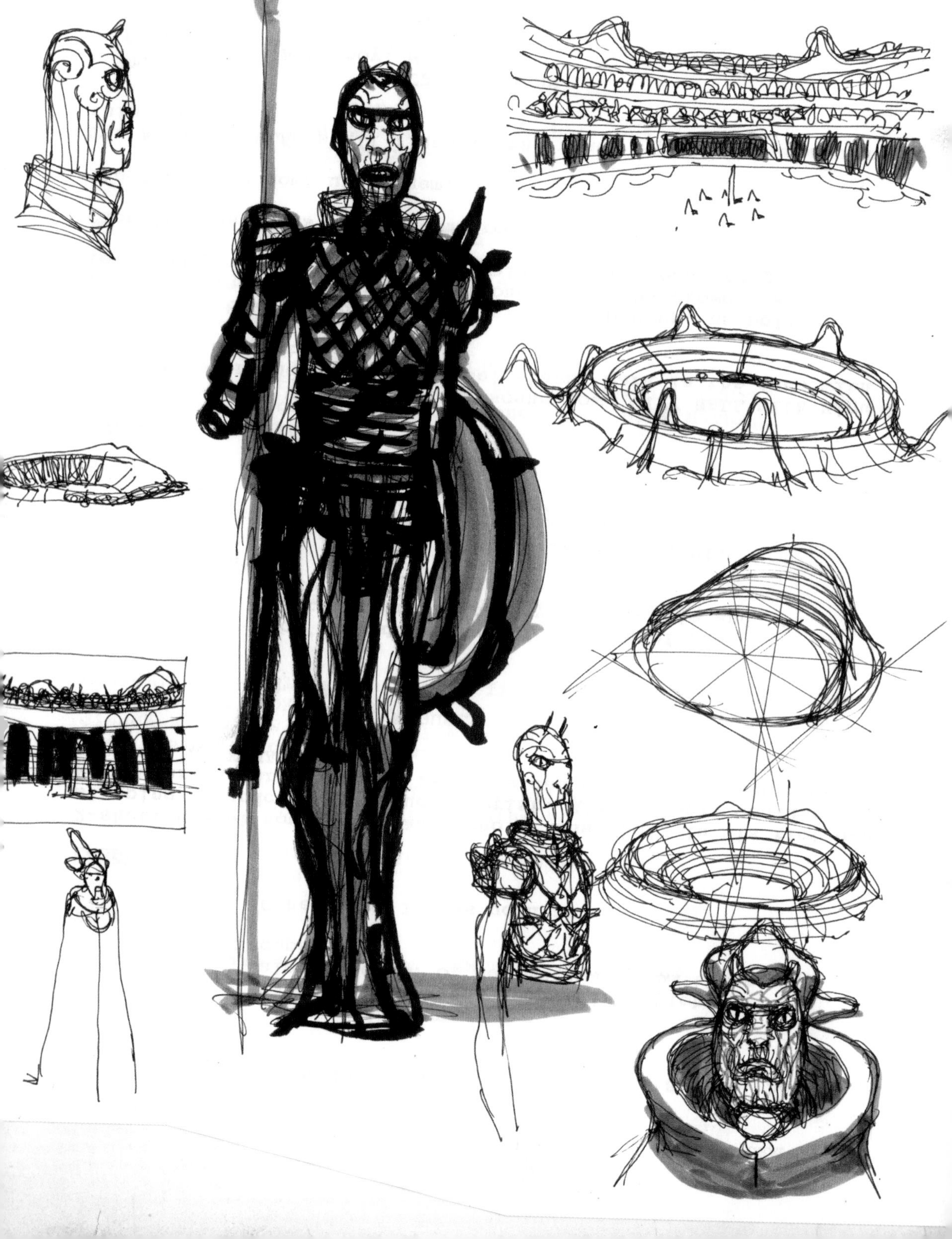

I really tried to get an authentic 1980s vibe in all the Spiral City scenes so I looked for a ton of references from photographs, movies, and videos of that decade.

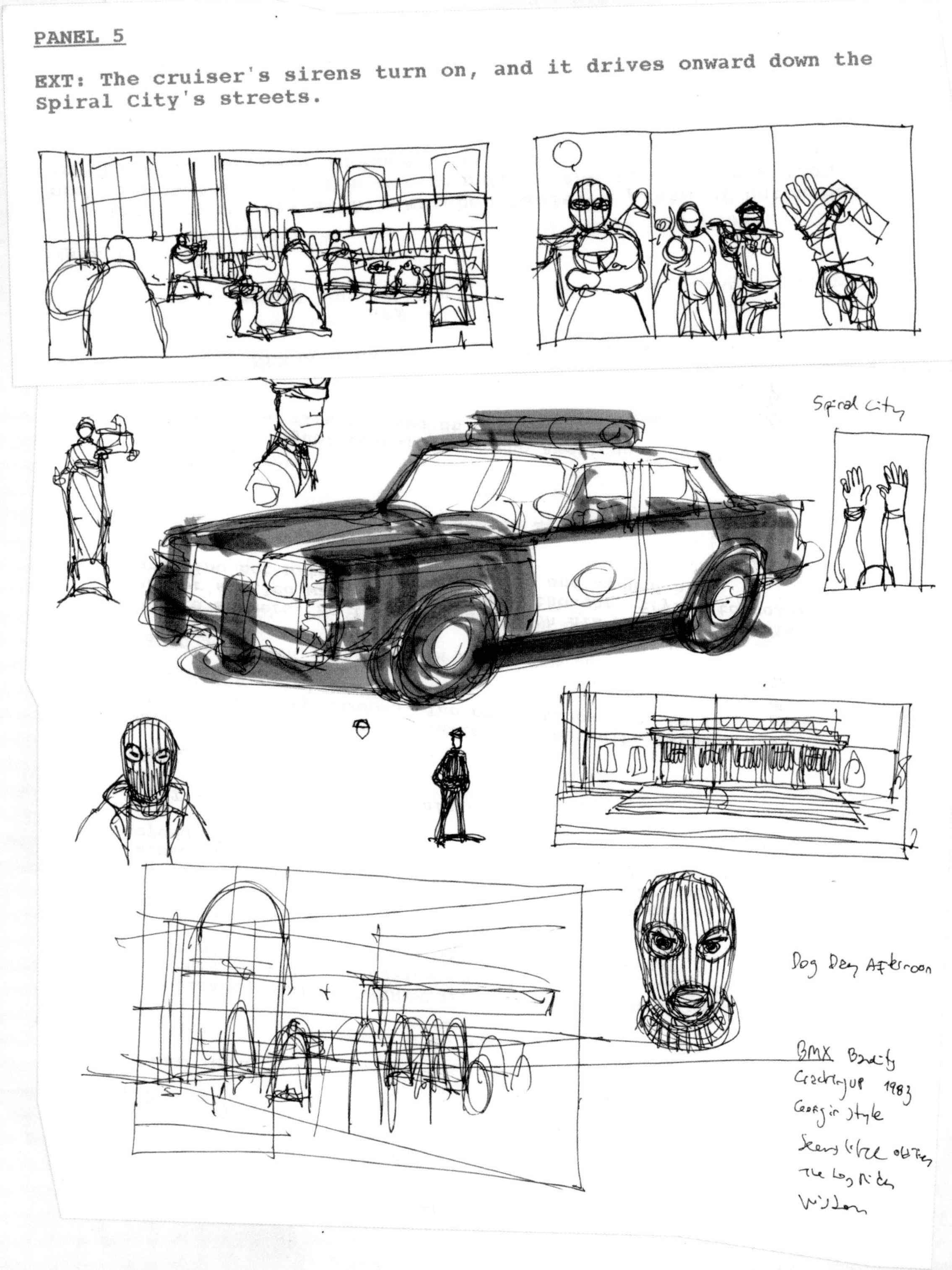
PANEL 5
EXT: The cruiser's sirens turn on, and it drives onward down the Spiral City's streets.
Spiral City
Dog Day Afternoon
BMX Bandits
1983

Boci is one of our three cats and she was the model for Sigourney. (There was a hard casting process to decide which one of them would get the role!)

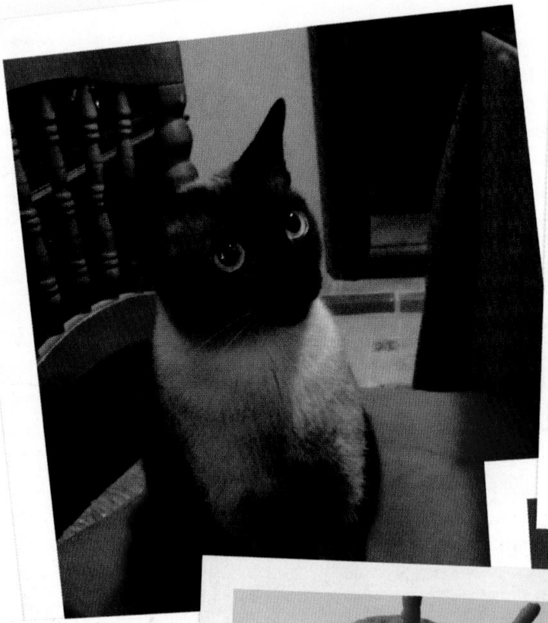

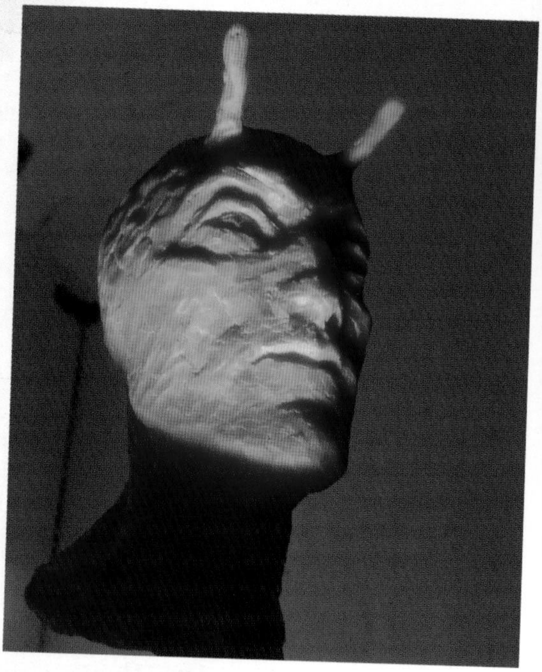

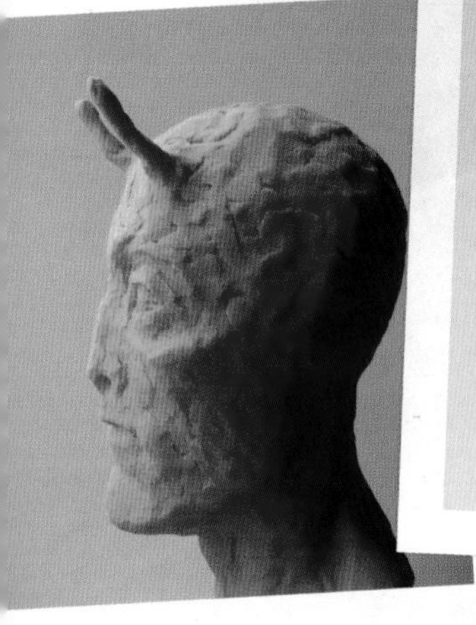

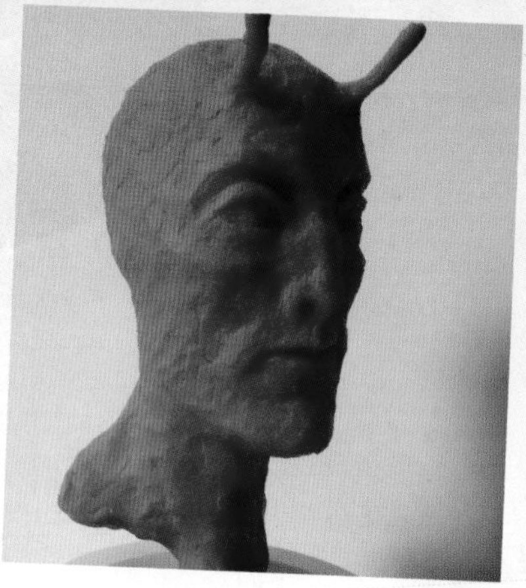

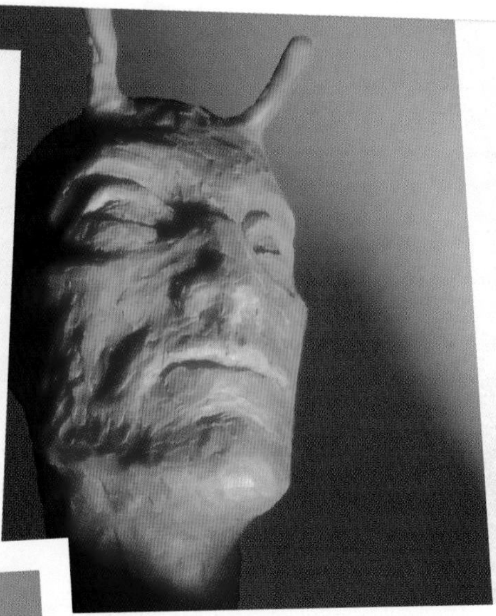

I made this Barbalien plasticine bust to better understand the character proportions and his non-human features. I also used it as a light reference for some panels.

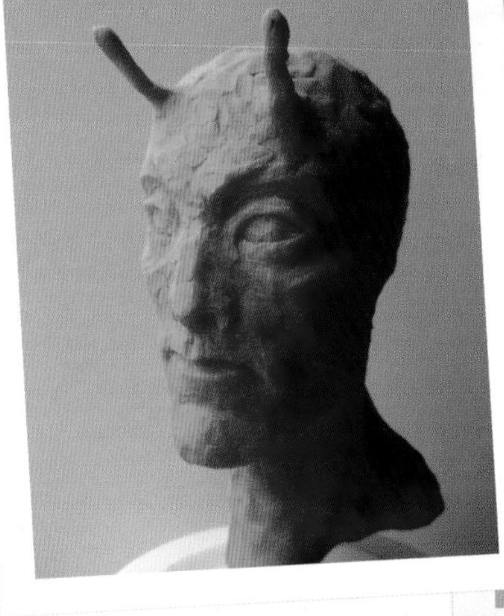

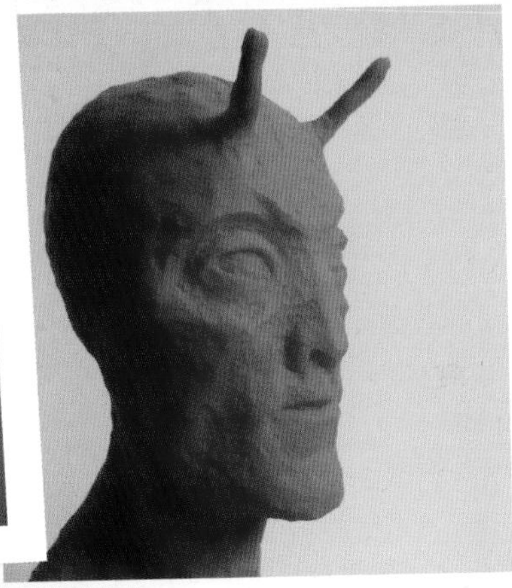

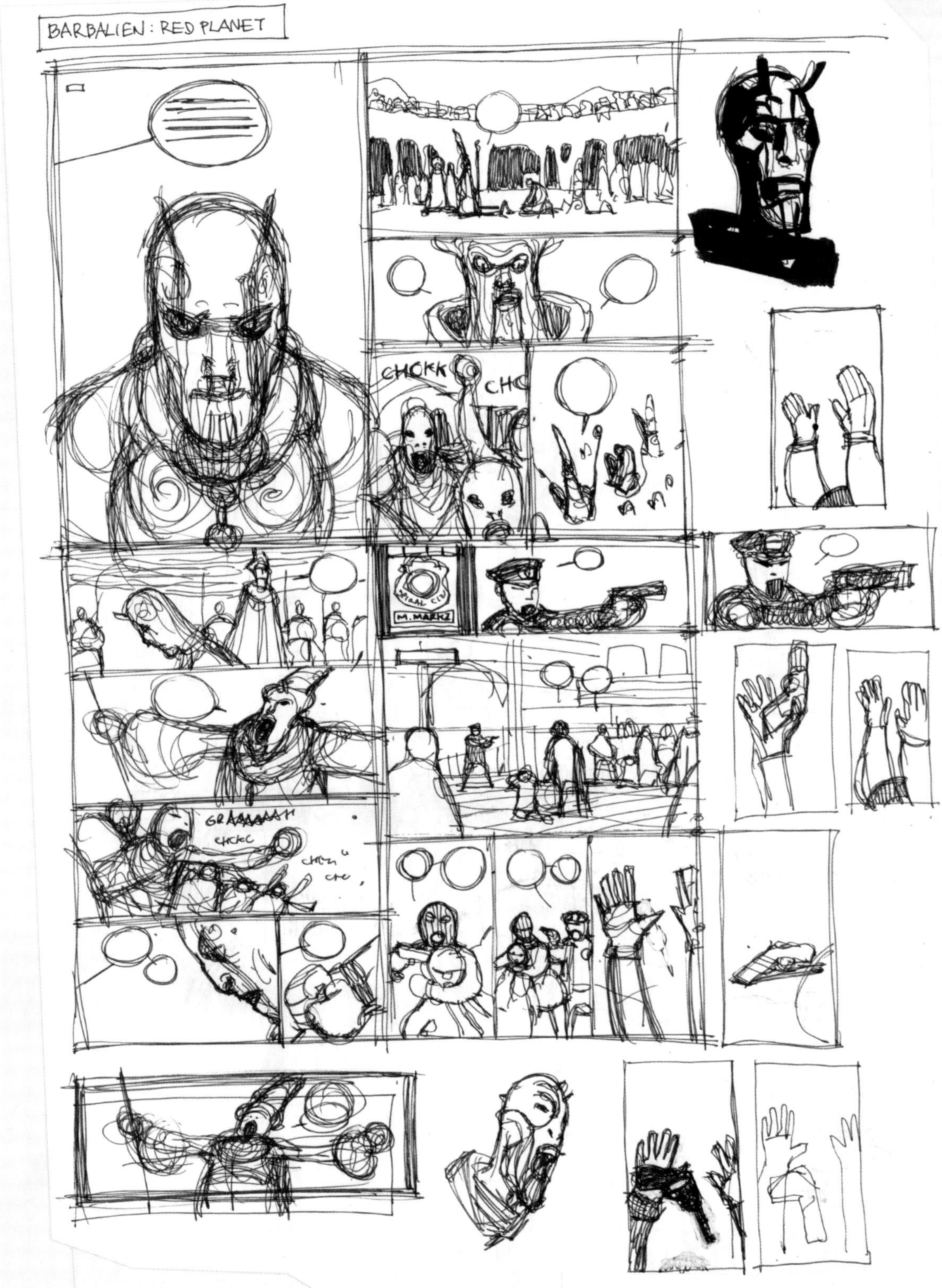
BARBALIEN : RED PLANET
CHOKK
M. MARKZ

When doing a cover sketch I always try to let myself go, brainstorming as many ideas and compositions as possible.

After three or four preliminary versions, I like to draw some definitive layouts so I can be sure that the story works visually and that it flows correctly.

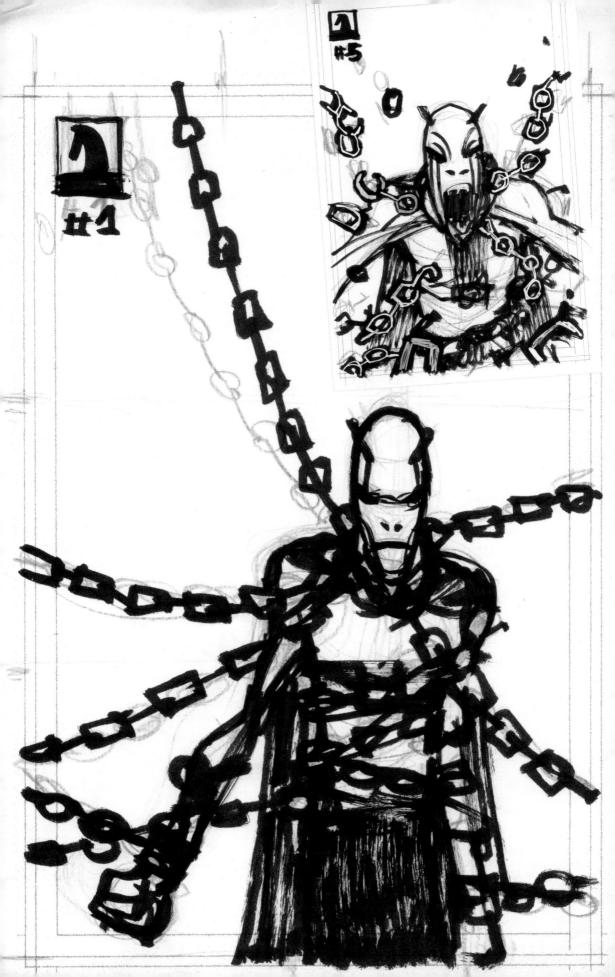

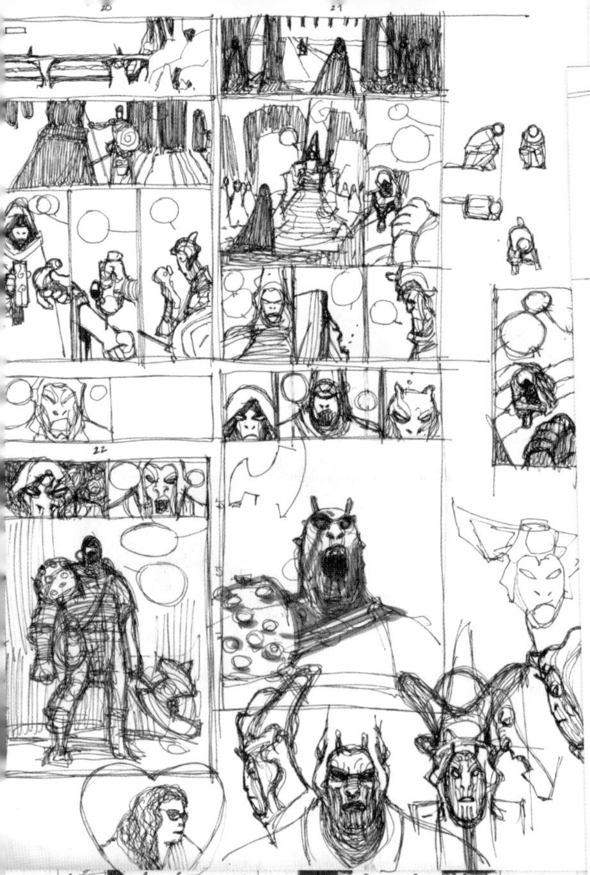

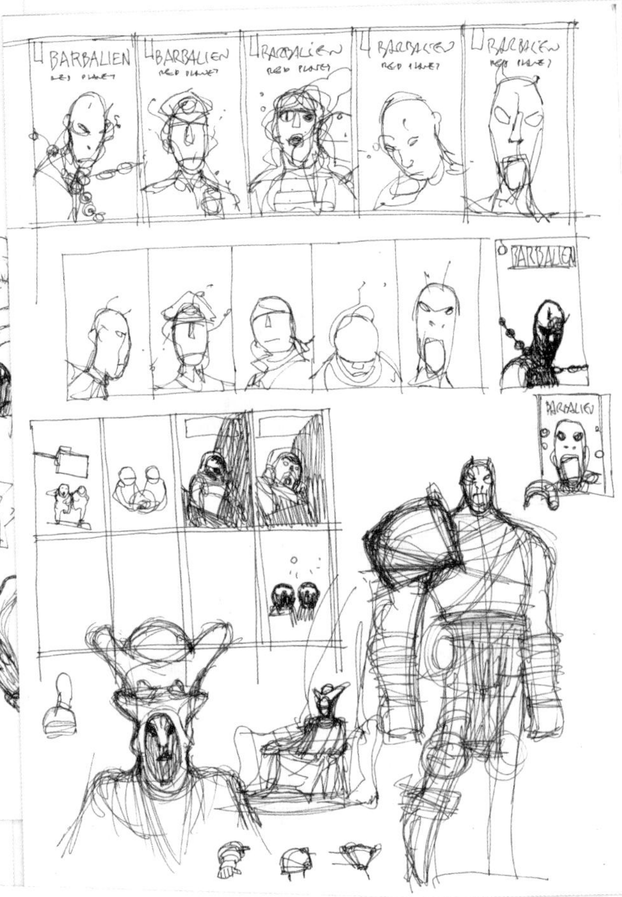
BARBALIEN
BARBALIEN
BARBALIEN

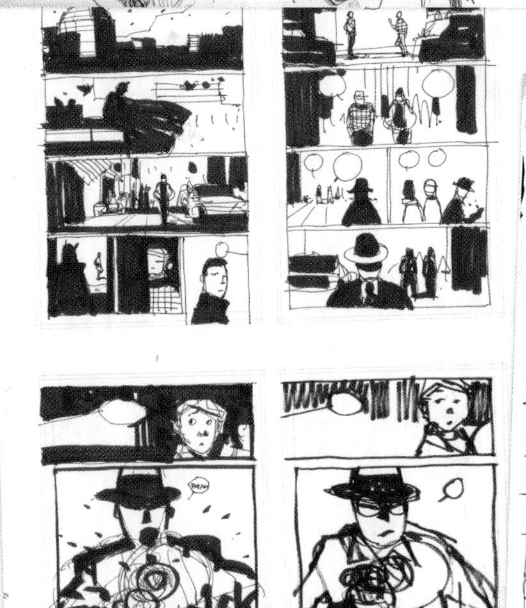
SHRACK

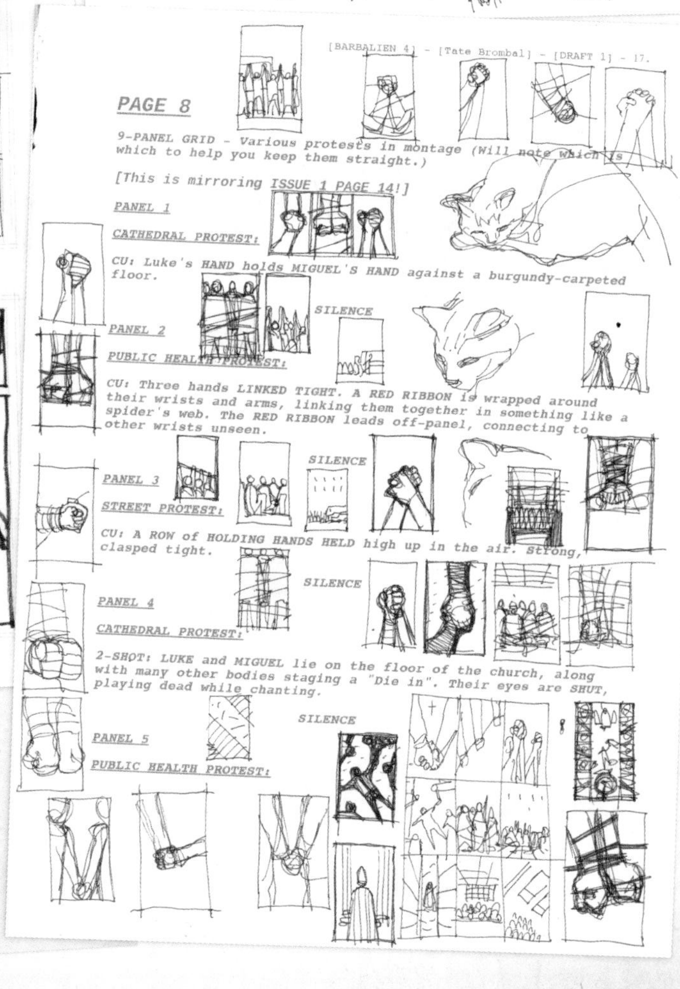
[BARBALIEN 4] - [Tate Brombal] - [DRAFT 1] - 17.

PAGE 8

9-PANEL GRID - Various protests in montage (Will note which is which to help you keep them straight.)

[This is mirroring ISSUE 1 PAGE 14!]

PANEL 1

CATHEDRAL PROTEST:

CU: Luke's HAND holds MIGUEL'S HAND against a burgundy-carpeted floor.

SILENCE

PANEL 2

PUBLIC HEALTH PROTEST:

CU: Three hands LINKED TIGHT. A RED RIBBON is wrapped around their wrists and arms, linking them together in something like a spider's web. The RED RIBBON leads off-panel, connecting to other wrists unseen.

SILENCE

PANEL 3

STREET PROTEST:

CU: A ROW of HOLDING HANDS HELD high up in the air. Strong, clasped tight.

SILENCE

PANEL 4

CATHEDRAL PROTEST:

2-SHOT: LUKE and MIGUEL lie on the floor of the church, along with many other bodies staging a "Die in". Their eyes are SHUT, playing dead while chanting.

SILENCE

PANEL 5

PUBLIC HEALTH PROTEST:

More preliminary and definitive layouts. I'm quite obsessed with achieving clear and attractive compositions in my pages. A few times I just go with the very first version, but usually I need to keep on trying until I come up with a good visual solution.

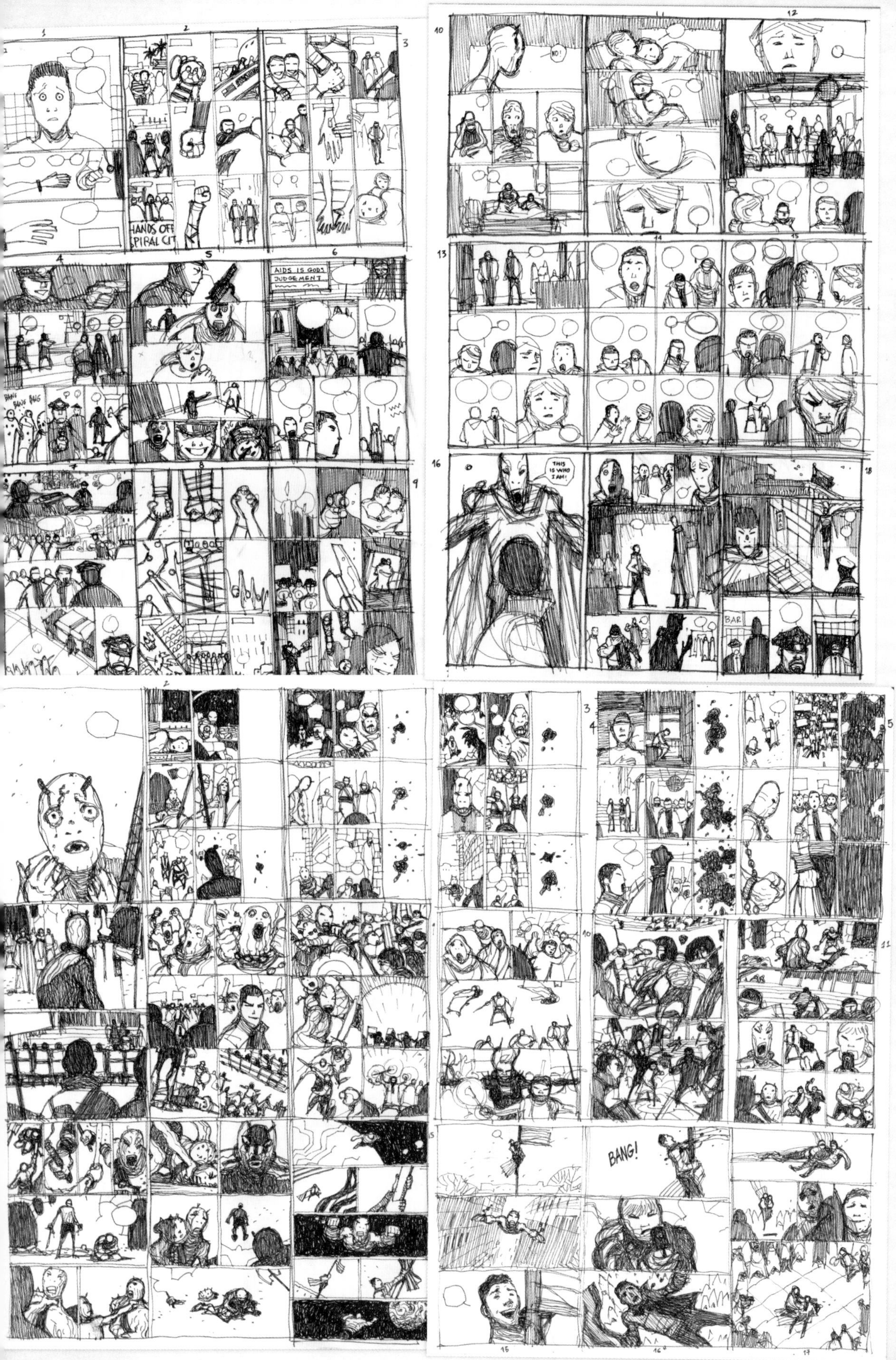
HANDS OFF SPIRAL CITY
AIDS IS GODS JUDGEMENT
BANG BANG BANG
NO!
THIS IS WHO I AM!
BAR
BAR
BANG!

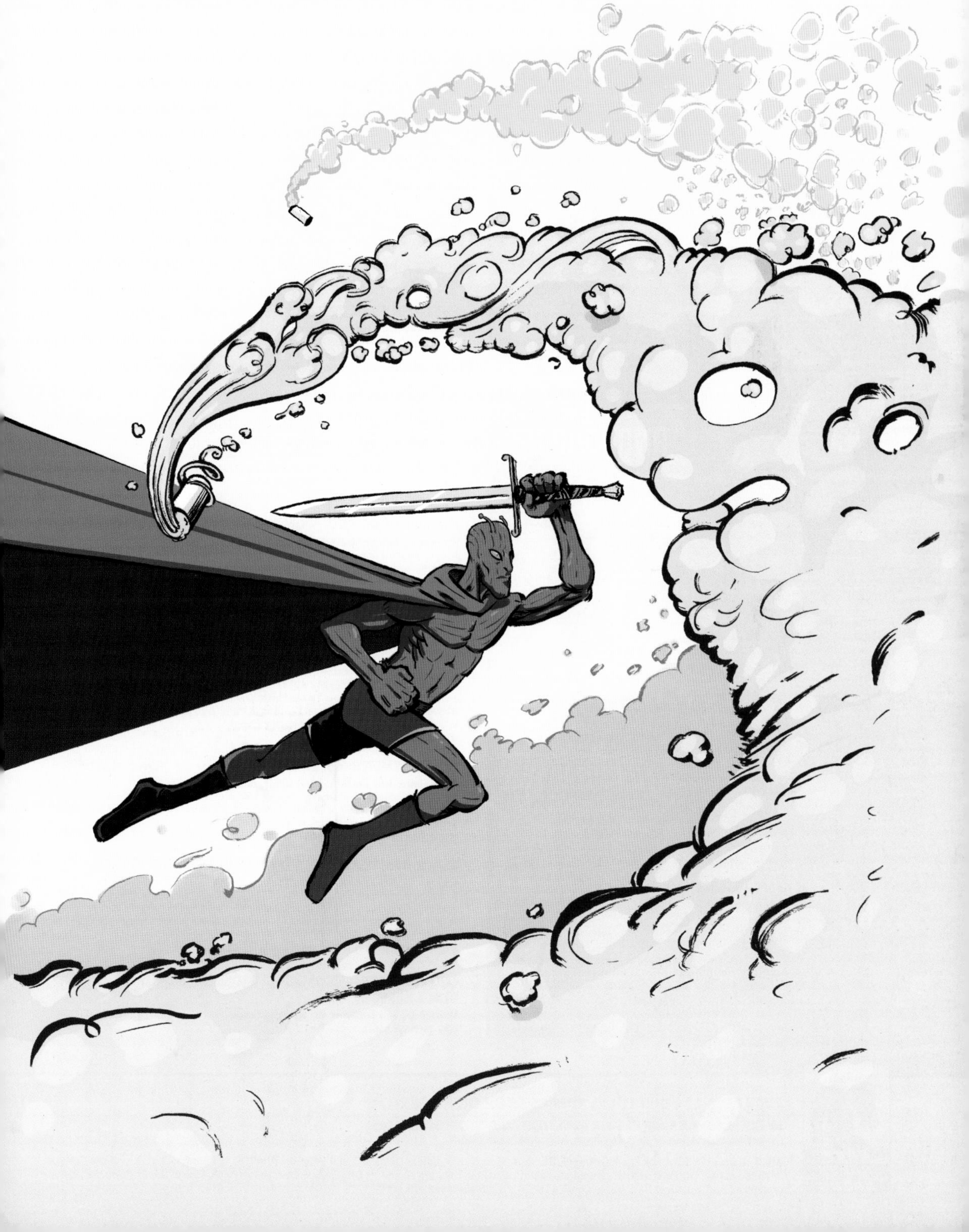

"If you think there's no room left in your life for another superhero comic, *Black Hammer* might just prove you wrong."—IGN

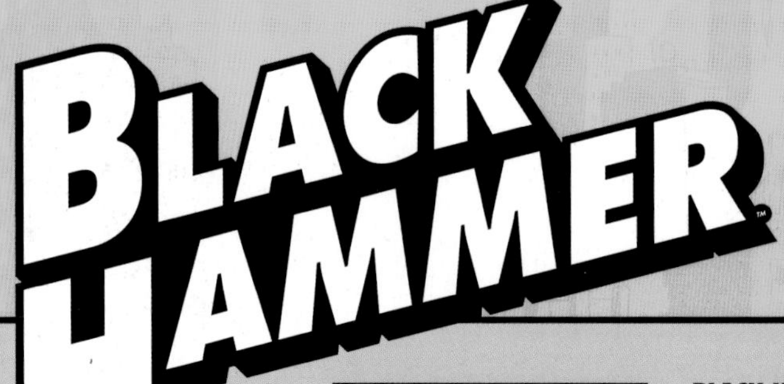
BLACK HAMMER

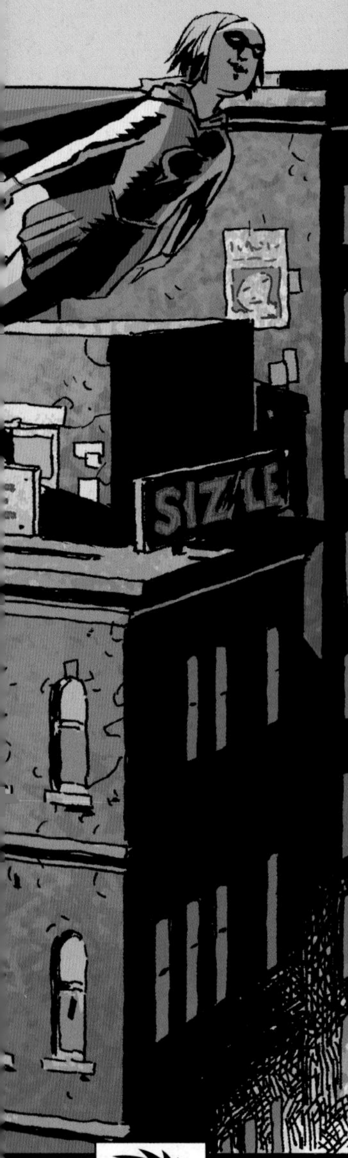

ONCE THEY WERE HEROES, but the age of heroes has long since passed. Banished from existence by a multiversal crisis, the old champions of Spiral City—Abraham Slam, Golden Gail, Colonel Weird, Madame Dragonfly, and Barbalien—now lead simple lives in an idyllic, timeless farming village from which there is no escape! And yet, the universe isn't done with them—it's time for one last grand adventure.

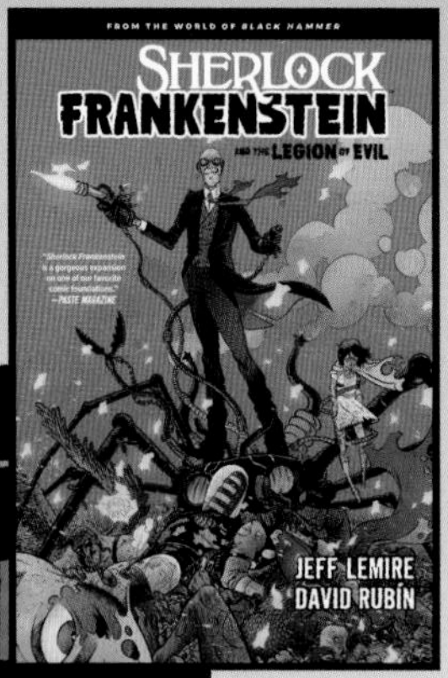
FROM THE WORLD OF BLACK HAMMER
SHERLOCK FRANKENSTEIN
AND THE LEGION OF EVIL
JEFF LEMIRE
DAVID RUBÍN

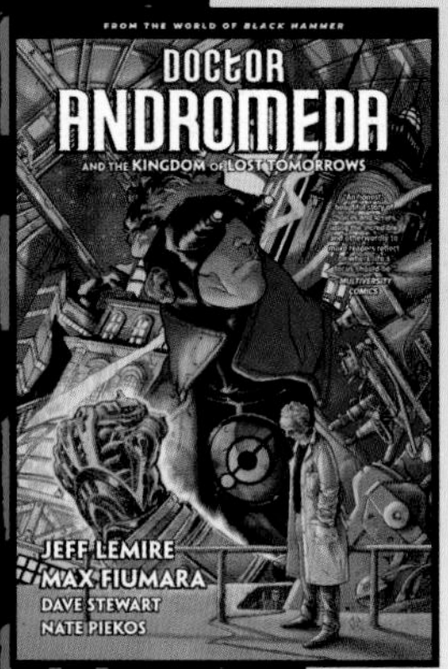
FROM THE WORLD OF BLACK HAMMER
DOCTOR ANDROMEDA
AND THE KINGDOM OF LOST TOMORROWS
JEFF LEMIRE
MAX FIUMARA
DAVE STEWART
NATE PIEKOS

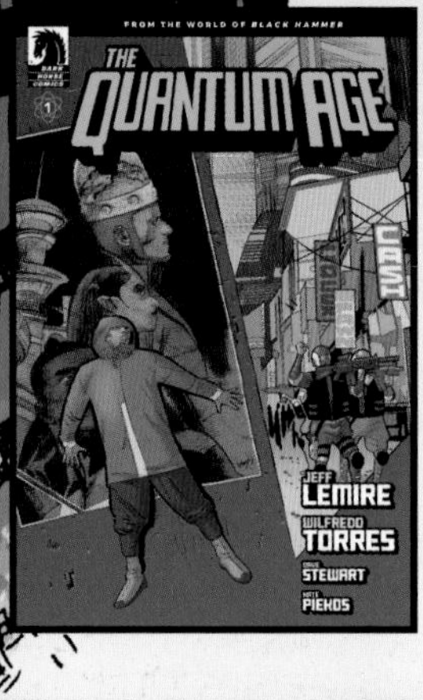
FROM THE WORLD OF BLACK HAMMER
THE QUANTUM AGE
JEFF LEMIRE
WILFREDO TORRES
DAVE STEWART
NATE PIEKOS

BLACK HAMMER
Written by Jeff Lemire
Art by Dean Ormston

THE WORLD OF BLACK HAMMER LIBRARY EDITION VOLUME 1
978-1-50671-995-5 • $49.99

THE WORLD OF BLACK HAMMER LIBRARY EDITION VOLUME 2
978-1-50671-996-2 • $49.99

VOLUME 1: SECRET ORIGINS
978-1-61655-786-7 • $14.99

VOLUME 2: THE EVENT
978-1-50670-198-1 • $19.99

VOLUME 3: AGE OF DOOM PART ONE
978-1-50670-389-3 • $19.99

VOLUME 4: AGE OF DOOM PART TWO
978-1-50670-816-4 • $19.99

BLACK HAMMER LIBRARY EDITION VOLUME 1
978-1-50671-073-0 • $49.99

BLACK HAMMER LIBRARY EDITION VOLUME 2
978-1-50671-185-0 • $49.99

SHERLOCK FRANKENSTEIN & THE LEGION OF EVIL
Written by Jeff Lemire • Art by David Rubín
This mystery follows a reporter determined to find out what happened to her father, the Black Hammer. All answers seem to lie in Spiral City's infamous insane asylum, where some dangerous supervillain tenants reside, including Black Hammer's greatest foe—Sherlock Frankenstein!
978-1-50670-526-2 • $19.99

DOCTOR ANDROMEDA & THE KINGDOM OF LOST TOMORROWS
Written by Jeff Lemire • Art by Max Fiumara
This dual-narrative story set in the world of *Black Hammer* chronicles the legacy of a Golden-Age superhero wishing to reconnect with his estranged son, whom he hoped would one day take the mantle of Doctor Andromeda.
978-1-50672-329-7 • $19.99

THE QUANTUM AGE: FROM THE WORLD OF BLACK HAMMER
Written by Jeff Lemire • Art by Wilfredo Torres
A thousand years in the future, a collection of superheroes, inspired by the legendary heroes of Black Hammer Farm, must band together to save the planet from an authoritarian regime, while a young Martian struggles to solve the riddle of what happened to the great heroes of the twentieth century.
VOLUME 1
978-1-50670-841-6 • $19.99

BLACK HAMMER: STREETS OF SPIRAL
Jeff Lemire, Dean Ormston, Emi Lenox, and others
A Lovecraftian teen decides she will do anything to make herself "normal," a bizarre witch guides her guests through her house of horrors, and an all-star slate of guest artists illustrate a bizarre adventure with Colonial Weird on the farm. Also features a complete world guide to the *Black Hammer* universe and its characters!
978-1-50670-941-3 • $19.99

BLACK HAMMER '45: FROM THE WORLD OF BLACK HAMMER
Jeff Lemire, Ray Fawkes, Matt Kindt, and Sharlene Kindt
During the Golden Age of superheroes, an elite Air Force crew called the Black Hammer Squadron bands together to combat the Nazis, a host of occult threats, and their ultimate aerial warrior the Ghost Hunter.
978-1-50670-850-8 • $17.99

BLACK HAMMER/JUSTICE LEAGUE: HAMMER OF JUSTICE!
Written by Jeff Lemire • Art by Michael Walsh
A strange man arrives simultaneously on Black Hammer Farm and in Metropolis, and both worlds are warped as Starro attacks! Batman, Green Lantern, Flash, Wonder Woman, Superman, and more crossover with Golden Gail, Colonel Weird, and the rest of the Black Hammer gang!
978-1-50671-099-0 • $29.99

COLONEL WEIRD—COSMAGOG: FROM THE WORLD OF BLACK HAMMER
Written by Jeff Lemire • Art by Tyler Crook
978-1-50671-516-2 • $19.99

DARK HORSE BOOKS

AVAILABLE AT YOUR LOCAL COMICS SHOP OR BOOKSTORE
TO FIND A COMICS SHOP IN YOUR AREA, VISIT COMICSHOPLOCATOR.COM.
For more information or to order direct, visit darkhorse.com.